Classical America IV

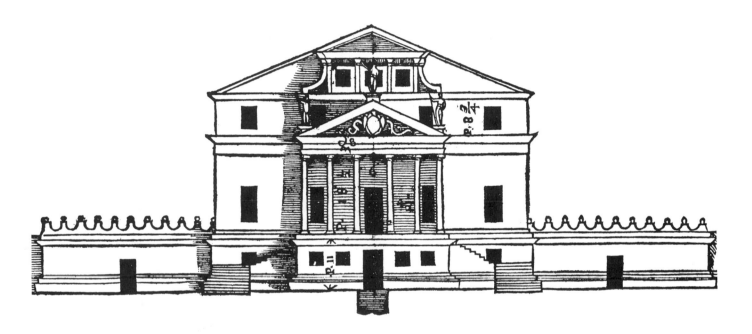

The Villa Foscari ("La Malcontenta") from Andrea Palladio's I Quatro Libri del Architettura *(p. 49). Classical America has sponsored an exhibition of Palladio models at New York's Cooper-Hewitt Museum.*

WILLIAM A. COLES, *Editor*

FIRST EDITION

Distributed to the trade by W. W. Norton & Company, Inc.

The publication of *Classical America IV* has been made possible in part through the generosity of the Atlanta Historical Society.

ISBN 0 393 04497 1

1 2 3 4 5 6 7 8 9 0

Contents

Introduction

THIS issue of *Classical America* is larger than any previous issue, and, like the last, is very varied in its coverage. We are especially pleased to join with the Atlanta Historical Society in documenting and paying homage to the remarkable work of Philip Shutze. That so fine an architect should be so little known outside Georgia testifies to the blindness of modernism. Not only does it expunge history from its own creation; it also edits history itself to delete silently what it cannot appreciate. Fortunately, however, there is abundant evidence that taste is changing. Not the least indication is the curiosity of the young—who have, after all, no vested interest in an aging modernism—about classical art and its traditions. Illustrations can be found in three articles written by students who find much to learn from classical architecture. Andrew Wallerstein, who writes on Horace Trumbauer, though now a student at Brown University, actually submitted his article while still at prep school. Thomas Elliott worked on Daniel Burnham for a doctoral dissertation at the University of Michigan, and Peter Federman, who is studying architecture at the University of Pennsylvania, is currently organizing a Cass Gilbert show for the Minnesota Museum of Art.

Especially important is the variety of recent classical work which we document in this issue. It includes both large and small jobs, interiors as well as exteriors, and runs the gamut from ecclesiastical to institutional, from domestic to commercial commissions. It is also surely noteworthy that two great museums have recently built in the classical style. The J. Paul Getty Museum we include in this issue. The new pavilion at the Frick Museum, designed by our President John Bayley, was completed too late for this issue, but, as the building itself is "not for any age but for all time," we can await the story of its design in that fullness which only time can allow and which its achievement surely merits. It is also immensely valuable and instructive for us to be able to include in this issue a retrospective showing of the works of Raymond Erith, the English classical architect, and his surviving pupil and partner Mr. Quinlan Terry. The fortuitous comparisons that are here occasioned between the work of Shutze, Bayley, Erith, Blatteau, and others bear abundant witness to the variety and richness of the classical tradition and its idioms, which are at once paradoxically international and national. Our own classical tradition has drawn on many sources to make its unique style. In its triumphant achievements during the American Renaissance it has also sent its influence abroad. It is to be hoped that, in the future rebirth of classicism, this cross-fertilization will continue to the mutual advantage of both Europe and America.

Those of us who have labored so long in the cold to restore the classical tradition, might be excused for a certain measure of optimism when we look at the contemporary condition of the arts. The day of dogmatic modernism is over. The Museum of Modern Art can exhibit Beaux-Arts architects, and traditional schools of painting are once again in vogue and commanding strong prices in sale rooms and galleries. Critics can openly lament the impact of modernism in city planning and the architectural environment. Preservation and restoration are now the biggest news in architecture. And yet it would be easy to be deceived as to the depth of today's tolerance for and understanding of the classical. A moderately attentive listener to a recent series of lectures given by the New York *Times* architecture critic, Ada Louise Huxtable, on the topic, "The Death and Rebirth of Modern Architecture," could be forgiven for not perceiving any real distinction between what had died and what was being reborn. *Plus ça change!* Modernists can only embrace the past up to yesterday. Today is still a special dispensation. The old modernist fallacies of originality and progress seem as powerful and confining as ever.

WILLIAM A. COLES

4

America's Greatest Living Classical Architect: Philip Trammell Shutze of Atlanta, Georgia

by

HENRY HOPE REED

To an age which has too often assumed that the Classical period passed out of existence over a generation ago, it is always a surprise to learn that the tradition is still very much with us. Nowhere is this more true in the Western world than in the United States. Here certain men have continued to design in the Classical, thanks to a sympathetic patronage. Such an architect is Philip Trammell Shutze whose work has been confined, with some few exceptions, to the state of Georgia, with a concentration in Atlanta. A glance at the pictures of his buildings which illustrate this article is sufficient to discover the range of the man, a range which includes a synagogue as well as a church, college buildings along with banks, and a broad spectrum of residences.

Philip Trammell Shutze was born in 1890 in Columbus, Georgia, 110 miles southwest of Atlanta on the Alabama border. His father was a prosperous businessman. Mr. Shutze has fond memories of a house covered with a climbing Maréchal Niel rose and morning glory. Tragedy came to what was a cloudless childhood in the form of his father's death in 1900. His mother, left with three children and a small income, moved to Atlanta, then to West Point, Georgia, and back again to Atlanta.

In 1908, on obtaining a scholarship, the young Shutze entered the Department of Architecture of the Georgia Institute of Technology, the famous "Georgia Tech." There he soon had the attention of the department head, Francis Palmer Smith, who, in later life, was to remark that he had never met with a student who had such a wonderful grasp of proportion as the young Shutze. His training was Beaux Arts, as was that of all American architectural schools in those days. Shutze was able to put his skills to the test while at school because, in his free time, he worked for the new firm of Hentz & Reid, soon to become recognized as Atlanta's best. In his junior year the routine was interrupted by a voyage to Europe, at a cost of a dollar a day for twenty-two days from Savannah to Rotterdam. He and a friend spent most of their time exploring France.

On graduation in 1912, he was urged by Hal F. Hentz, Neel Reid, and members of his family to complete his training by going to the Columbia School of Architecture, the country's best at the time. This he did, again with the help of a scholarship. In the course of his two-year study at Columbia he saw an exhibition of work by men who had come back from the American Academy in Rome, among them Edgar Williams, Paul Manship, and Ezra Winter. So impressed was he that he decided to try for the Rome Prize. On the basis of a required esquisse (sketch)—Beaux Arts cant was in vogue— he was one of four accepted to compete in designing a monument for an island. Turning to the resources of Avery Library, still the finest of its kind in the nation, he produced the design which won the prize for 1915.

The Academy, by then on the Janiculum, was, as it still is, a most restful spot. Fellows were encouraged to explore the imperial city and its environs at their ease before turning to the drafting board, canvas, or clay, although the latter were by no means neglected. Shutze, in his first year, had to draft a restoration of a pavilion at Hadrian's Villa at Tivoli. In his second year he studied the works of the Renaissance, selecting in particular the Villa Turini-Lante and the Villa Spada, both on the Janiculum. These studies he supplemented with drawings of Pietro da Cortona's Santa Maria della Pace, the well-known Fontana delle Tartarughe or Turtle Fountain (a copy of which exists on San Francisco's Nob Hill), several doorways, loggias, and vaults. For his third year, by now completely free of the Beaux Arts influence and having become wholly Italian, he did "a villa to house the American ambassador at Rome," a splendid conceit. It was a collaborative project on which he was joined by the sculptor Tom Jones, who was to execute the reliefs on the Tomb of the Unknown Soldier, and the landscape architect Edward Lawson. Looking at the plan, elevations, and the model, this last being the work of Tom Jones, the beholder cannot help but be in awe of the ambition, let alone the skill, represented here. (Where are the drawings and the models?)

Plan for the Decoration of an Island Commemorating Its Purchase, Mr. Shutze's winning scheme for the Rome Prize in 1915. Photo: courtesy of Philip Trammell Shutze.

World War I, at least in the first years, did not interfere with work. If anything it added to life in Rome because of persons drawn there for war work. One was Geoffrey Scott, author of *The Architecture of Humanism*, who was working at the British Embassy. Shutze also had a family connection with the American-born Princess di San Faustino, maternal grandmother of the present head of Fiat and of Suni Agnelli, author of *We Always Wore Sailor Suits*.

This country's entry into the war in 1917 ended what, at this distance in time, appears a charmed life. At least the change for the Rome Prize men was eased by their finding themselves commissioned first lieutenants serving with the Italian Red Cross under Chester Aldrich of the firm of Delano & Aldrich.

Mr. Shutze was still in uniform in early 1919 when his mother died and he returned to Atlanta. Most of that year he spent with his former employers, now become Hentz, Reid & Adler. One of the buildings he did at the time was the Howard Theatre, the façade of which was inspired by Palladio's Palazzo Chiericati in Vicenza (*see* illustration in *Classical America* II). Another was the Andrew Calhoun house. Neil Reed had proposed a wood house but the client asked for an Italian villa. As Reid was already sick from the illness which led to his death, Mr. Shutze was given the job by the firm.

THE DECORATION OF AN ISLAND COMMEMORATING ITS PVRCHASE

Elevation of Mr. Shutze's prize winning scheme. Photo: courtesy of Philip Trammell Shutze.

These and other projects were interrupted when he had to return to Rome to complete his work at the Academy. Rome Prize men in those days had serious obligations. Among the work he finished was his "Villa for an American Ambassador at Rome." At the same time he, Tom Jones, and the painter Allyn Cox did a scheme for "A Monument to a Great General." The association with Cox, who had come to the Academy in 1916, was to be a lasting one; the painter was to decorate a number of Atlanta houses, including two of Shutze's.

On returning to America in 1920 Mr. Shutze paused in New York with the object of gaining a broader professional experience. He was offered a job as instructor at the Columbia School of Architecture which he turned down in favor of working for F. Burrall Hoffman, Jr., architect of the Villa Vizcaya in Miami (*see Classical America* III), and Mott Schmidt, best known for his houses on Manhattan's Sutton Place. The New York stay did not last. Neel Reid was by then very ill, and the firm needed a designer. Mr. Shutze abandoned New York for Atlanta in 1923 to work for his old firm. On Neel Reid's death in 1926 he was admitted as full partner in Hentz, Adler & Shutze.

Hentz, Adler & Shutze continued to 1944 when it became Shutze, Armistead & Adler. A year later it was Shutze & Armistead until 1950 when Mr. Armis-

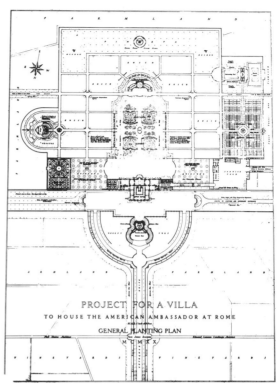

Plan for "Project for a Villa to House the American Ambassador at Rome." This was executed in 1920 by Mr. Shutze in collaboration with the sculptor Tom Jones and the landscape architect Edward Lawson. Photo: courtesy of Philip Trammell Shutze.

Model of the Villa. Photo: courtesy of Philip Trammell Shutze.

Elevation of the entrance front of the villa. Photo: courtesy of Philip Trammell Shutze.

Elevation of the garden front of the villa. Photo: courtesy of Philip Trammell Shutze.

Cross-section of the villa from the entrance to the end of the garden. Photo: courtesy of Philip Trammell Shutze.

tead retired. The firm had a substantial practice, even in the 1930s, numbering among its clients such firms as the Southern Bell Telephone company, Sears, Roebuck & Company, and the Citizens and Southern National Bank, and several federal agencies, including the United States Army. The work for these big clients is best described as "well-mannered." There is always an indication of a superior touch, as in a columned entrance or the handling of the fenestration, as, for instance, in the Southern Bell building in Charleston, South Carolina.

As might be expected, Mr. Shutze had freer rein with the special, as distinguished from the large corporate, client. One exception to this was in 1927 when he remodeled the main office building of the Citizens and Southern National Bank in downtown Atlanta. (His later work for the bank is in the category of "good manners,"—not to be dismissed, but less interesting.) The project has all the vigor and distinction found in the earlier Calhoun house and Howard Theatre. It consisted in transforming the first three floors into a great hall and in remodeling the same height on the outside. For the exterior he looked to Michele Sanmichele, best remembered for the bold rustication of his fortress work, notably the Porta Palio in Verona. In the deep relief of the coigning and the voussoirs, Mr. Shutze attained the scale which is one of the wonders of Italian architecture. For the hall he obviously found inspiration in the interior of the Pantheon. Although still magnificent, the banking room has been shorn of some of its original glory due to subsequent changes.

His finest work in this first decade was unquestionably the Swan House, now owned by the Atlanta Historical Society. Built in 1926 for Mr. and Mrs. Edward H. Inman, it is one of America's more splendid houses. In this instance he turned to the English Classical, strongly influenced by the Italian. Mr. Shutze had no single model in mind. If, indeed, he took a device or a partie from one or another old building, he would so transform whatever he borrowed that he made the design wholly his own.

Mr. and Mrs. Inman took great pride in their house. Ample evidence of that is the opulence of the furnishings which they assembled over the years (*see* the accompanying article by Nancy K. Lester).

The same opulence on a modest scale occurs at the Horgan Curtis house in Macon done in the early 1930s. Here Mr. Shutze turned again to the Roman model. To come on this villa just outside the grounds of Wesleyan College is to be taken utterly by surprise. The beholder, once over his astonishment, can only wish that it had been imitated elsewhere in the South. The Baroque outline of the gabled roof, the burnt

sienna of the walls, the raw sienna of the trim and detail combine to make a truly exotic wonder for this part of the world.

When Mr. Shutze turned away from the Italian Classical it was most often to the English of the eighteenth century, even to the Classical vernacular derived from it as found in his native Georgia. Such a building is the Temple of the Hebrew Benevolent Congregation constructed in 1931-32. It must rank with the finer synagogues of the country along with the Touro in Newport and the Temple Emanu-El in New York. A decade later he did the Academy of Medicine for the Fulton County Medical Society. Here he had a model, the Medical Society building in Augusta, Georgia.

After 1930, he confined himself largely to the vernacular, at least with his residences. His clients no doubt had some influence in this. One of them, built for Mr. and Mrs. Harry English in 1929 and now belonging to Mr. and Mrs. Robert W. Chambers, is of white-painted brick with an Ionic porch. A much later one is the handsome residence built for Mr. and Mrs. Julian Hightower in Thomaston, Georgia, in 1947-48.

Others include two in Albany and one in Savannah. Those for Mr. and Mrs. Francis Wetherbee and Mr. and Mrs. William C. Potter are in Albany and the one for Mr. and Mrs. Raymond Demere is in Savannah. They have that particular charm which stamps them as Deep South. The last of the vernacular houses was built for Mr. and Mrs. Charles Daniel in Greenville, South Carolina, in 1954.

Mr. Shutze moved from one manner of the Classical to another with ease. At Emory University there is a mixture. An early campus work is the Glenn Memorial Church, 1929-30, to which was added a Sunday School and Chapel in 1940. The latter looks to the Italian while the former leans to eighteenth-century England. When he did the Whitehead Memorial addition to the university hospital in 1945, he turned to the Italian. Once again there is the bold rustication, the treatment in depth which he first exploited in the Citizens and Southern National Bank. Nor should the handling of the fenestration of the wing's side be overlooked.

A note here. The curious will be surprised to learn that Mr. Shutze's alma mater, Georgia Tech, never called on him for even one building. All the more credit goes to Emory University for having done so; he well repaid its initiative.

For those interested in the Classical tradition it may seem a great loss that Mr. Shutze did not obtain recognition beyond the environs of Atlanta. One cannot help wondering if his *Romanità* would not have found converts.

Still, it is never too late to learn from the work of a master. Mr. Shutze has given a fresh dimension to the Classical in America. And no less important, his success has underscored the lesson of the pilgrimage to Italy. Despite the vandalism and the destruction of Modern Art, Rome remains the *urbs*, the city above all others. We can only follow in the footsteps of Mr. Shutze to that never-ending source of inspiration.

Office building, 1938, for the Southern Bell Telephone Company in Charleston, South Carolina. Photo: courtesy of Southern Bell Telephone Company.

The interior of a monument to a great general, a collaborative problem by Philip Trammell Shutze, the sculptor Tom Jones, and the painter Allyn Cox. Photo: courtesy of Philip Trammell Shutze.

The Calhoun-Thornwell House, 1919-1922, Atlanta

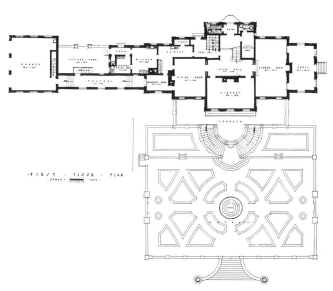

Plan of the first floor and garden. Photo: courtesy of Philip Trammell Shutze.

THE Calhoun-Thornwell house was Mr. Shutze's first building in his Roman manner. It is a long narrow structure set on the top of a rise. The drive leads to a graveled court. The principal rooms open on a terrace above a garden. The stucco of the exterior is burnt sienna with the trim in raw sienna. Mr. Shutze took special pains to give the stucco a slightly sandy surface.

Other than the style, the house's distinction is the presence of mural decoration by Allyn Cox, best known for his work at the William A. Clark Library in Los Angeles and for completing the Brumidi frieze in the National Capitol Rotunda. One of his murals is still to be found in the house.

Nor must the plaster ornament of the main rooms, especially the drawing room, be overlooked. When asked how he was able to obtain such work, Mr. Shutze said that there was a lot of plaster work being done in the 1920s, even the gas stations were stuccoed.

Calhoun-Thornwell House entrance Front. The roof decoration, in this instance flaming urns, is as much a Shutze signature as the style. Photo: H.H. Reed.

Entrance hall with the mural by Allyn Cox. Photo: courtesy of Philip Trammell Shutze.

The drawing room as it was originally. Photo: courtesy of Philip Trammell Shutze.

"Philemon and Baucis," the entrance hall mural by Allyn Cox. Photo: courtesy of Allyn Cox.

Italian scene executed by Allyn Cox for the drawing room. Present location unknown. Photo: courtesy of Allyn Cox.

The dining room as it was originally. Photo: courtesy of Philip Trammell Shutze.

The overmantel is an example of the beautiful plasterwork to be found in the house. The floor is terrazzo. Photo: H.H. Reed

Door of the drawing room leading to the porch. The molding of the door frame and the entablature with the broken round pediment are triumphs of their kind. Photo: H.H. Reed

The garden and garden front in 1924 when the house was finished. Photo: courtesy of Allyn Cox.

The same with later improvements consisting of wine jars and statues. Photo: courtesy of Philip Trammell Shutze.

The garden and garden façade today. Wisely left alone, both have attained that special quality which only time can give. Photo: H.H. Reed.

Detail of the garden terrace. A coral grotto with an elaborate scallop shell is set in the terrace wall. Photo: H.H. Reed.

The parterre of the garden in 1924. Photo: courtesy of Allyn Cox.

Main Office of the Citizens and Southern National Bank, 1929, Broad Street, Atlanta

Main office of the Citizens and Southern National Bank, façade on Broad Street. Photo: courtesy of Citizens and Southern National Bank.

A portion of the façade showing the fenestration. Photo: H.H. Reed.

B ANK architecture of the American Renaissance has not been surpassed anywhere. Mr. Shutze's contribution is among the best. He certainly learned the lesson of Sanmichele by giving the stonework deep relief. The bold quoining and voluted keystones of the round-arched bays and the use of rustication and quoining inside the entrance bay result in a masterly play of light and shade and convey an imperial sense of scale.

There is also his way of bringing together the different parts of the façade. A course with a Vitruvian scroll serves both as a cornice to the windows and a springing to the round-arched bays.

The imperial treatment extends to the banking hall. The inspiration of the Pantheon is seen in the pedimented niches. The Corinthian pilasters are Mr. Shutze's. The marble floor, molded on that of the Pantheon, should be noticed. Unfortunately the bank has removed the beautiful bronze fixtures, which once adorned the hall.

The upper portion of the entrance bay showing rustication and quoining inside the arch. Photo: H.H. Reed.

The banking hall, a triumph of the American Renaissance. Photo: courtesy of Citizens and Southern National Bank.

Swan House, 1926-1928, now part of the Atlanta Historical Society, Atlanta

SWAN House is *primus inter pares* of Mr. Shutze's work. Mr. Shutze has remarked that the inspiration is Queen Anne. Certainly the entrance façade leans to the English, although, to the untutored eye, the garden façade is Italianate. Whatever the influences, the result is most successful.

The Tuscan entrance porch is a wonder in the height, width, and entasis of its columns. The doorway is equally noble with its rusticated sides and square-headed arch supporting a round pediment. To either side are pedimented niches sheltering large elaborate urns. Even the window moldings have their distinctive touch in the crossettes and keystones.

Both wings are fronted by round-arched bays set in rustication. The south one faces a small garden with a fountain with a beautiful basin. At the end of this garden are two pairs of columns with broken pediment.

On the garden façade a horseshoe flight of steps rises to a central doorway with a round pediment. The attic gable with its two pairs of giant volutes to either side of an *oeil-de-boeuf* is very fine. The most distinctive feature of the terrace is the cascade of five basins built between two flights of steps. Each flight is framed by a retaining wall with vases encrusted with imitation sponge stone. From the terrace a green carpet of lawn spreads down the hill, now flat, now sloping.

When asked about flowers, Mr. Shutze explained that here he had a "green garden." Flowers in urns and pots, he explained, should be placed in the Italian fashion to either side of the cascade, on the steps, on the retaining wall, and on the terrace proper.

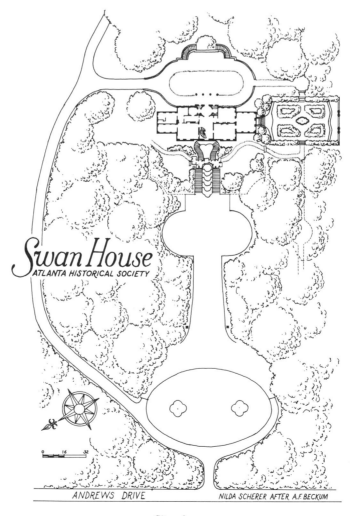

Site plan.

Swan House, a view of the porch showing the doorway and niches. Photo: H.H. Reed

Another view of the porch. Photo: H.H. Reed

The doorway with its rusticated sides and square-headed arch. Photo: H.H. Reed

Keystone of a bay of the south wing. Photo: H.H. Reed

The south wing overlooking the south garden, now overgrown with box. Photo: H.H. Reed

South garden as seen from the south porch. Photo: H.H. Reed

Pedimented attic of the garden façade with the two statues. Photo: H.H. Reed

The fountain at the top of the cascade of the garden terrace. Photo: H.H. Reed

A detail of the terrace wall with the encrusted urns. Photo: H.H. Reed

A second-floor view of the terrace, the cascade and the sweep of lawn. Photo: H.H. Reed

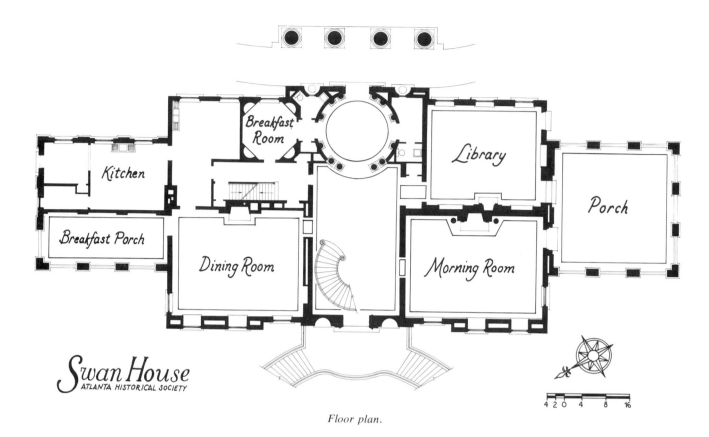

Floor plan.

The Interiors of Swan House

"CHOSEN with impeccable taste" — so the architect described the clients' furnishing of his masterpiece, the Swan House. His praise is testimony to a happy rapport between the clients, Emily and Edward Inman, and their architect, Philip T. Shutze. Shutze's mastery of Italian and English classicism enabled him to design a house in which, as he explained, "there was no attempt to adhere slavishly to any predetermined style or period." Rather, in this house he was successful in catering to the owners' admiration for architecture of the first half of the eighteenth-century—in the interior details was well as the exterior—and to their need for twentieth-century comforts and conveniences, and he was able to accommodate their taste for currently fashionable decorations.

For the Swan House, Shutze designed a series of rooms based on a succession of eighteenth-century styles. In these rooms, comfortable furnishings provided harmonious settings for the real masterpieces of antique furniture in the Inmans' collection. They purchased some of the English, European, and American antiques shortly before the house was built. Other important pieces were family heirlooms. Much of the furniture was brought to the Swan House from the Inmans' earlier Atlanta home—a Tudor-style house built in 1913.

Although each room conveys the aura of a distinct eighteenth-century style, in each there is free adaptation of that style in architectural detail, and in the imposition of twentieth-century decorations. Mr. Shutze related that Mr. Inman's eclectic and personal tastes determined the furnishing of the interior. No impulse toward the scholarly "correctness" which guided some American collectors who furnished now-famous houses, like Harry duPont at Winterthur and Ima Hogg at Bayou Bend, dictated Mrs. Inman's choices. She was creating an elegant, stylish, and comfortable home, not a museum. Handsome reproductions and adaptations of early forms provided comfortable and sturdy surroundings, particularly in the seating pieces.

A swan, centered in the fanlight over the entry door leading from porte cochère to round entrance hall, announces the decorative theme for the house. According to Philip Shutze, Mrs. Inman chose the name "Swan House." She liked the swan motif in decoration and loved birds in general. The fact that she had purchased the magnificent Swan tables four years before the house was completed, doubtless influenced her choice of the name.

In the halls, classical architectural details—columns and broken pediments, elements borrowed

Entrance Hall, Swan House. Photo: courtesy of the Atlanta Historical Society.

from the exteriors of classical buildings—have been brought indoors, as is typical of eighteenth-century English houses designed by admirers of Palladio. The visitor enters a round entrance hall, surrounded by paired columns with Ionic capitals. These are designed to lead the eye through to the main hall. On the floor, a rounded, concentric adaptation of a checkerboard pattern of black and white marble accentuates the shape of the round hall. The pieces are so neatly joined that the grouting is hardly visible. The architect's attention to detail extended to the design of the registers for the heating system: the registers are set into the marble pattern in such a way as to be barely noticeable.

The round entrance hall is a prelude to a stair hall which is the most spectacular interior space in the house, with a fifteen-foot high ceiling open to the second floor over its curving staircase. The stair hall has been compared to a great courtyard which, in Italy, would have been open to the sky. Philip Shutze has

lent grandeur to his design by allowing the fine spiral staircase to sweep up from the black and white marble floor in an elegant curve. The treads and railing are black-stained walnut. The bronze balustrade was made by W.A. McCormack of Rome, Georgia. Elegant plaster panels adorn the staircase walls. Handsome and intricately detailed woodwork frames the windows and doors. It was carved by Herbert J. Millard, a native of Bath, England, who was working in Cincinnati during the time he, with the assistance of four or five artisans, executed all of Shutze's designs for woodcarving in the house.

A pair of carved pine console tables in the stair hall correctly follow eighteenth-century English precedent for furniture in such surroundings. They have been stripped of their original finish since they were made in England in the very architectural style of William Kent about 1725-1750. They are now topped by marble slabs of about 1820. A pair of carved and

Stair Hall. Photo: R. Cotton Alston, Jr.

Stair Hall. Photo: courtesy of the Atlanta Historical Society.

painted side chairs with gros-and-petit-point needle-work covers bear the stamped brass plates of a fashionable West End London firm of the second quarter of the nineteenth century: Trollope and Sons of Belgrave Square.

Other hall furnishings reflect the personal, eclectic taste of Mrs. Inman. A nineteenth-century Chinese screen with Coromandel lacquer work is divided in two parts providing an eye-catching and colorful decorative accent. A portrait of an unknown man attributed to John Zoffany (1733-1810), and a painting of an imaginative scene, probably showing defeated ships of the Spanish Armada in a storm off the coast of Ireland, add to the antique effect. That effect was further enhanced in the evenings when the rooms were lighted by sconces, electrically wired to simulate candlelight. These were used in other principal rooms, as well as in the hall.

The library evokes the mood of the great English interiors of the late seventeenth century in its architectural detailing. Mr. Shutze designed this room around the antique overmantle carving which the Inmans had used once before in their earlier house. The splendid and intricately carved swags of fruit and flowers now over the mantlepiece are naturalistically carved in limewood, in a style frequently associated with the name of the late seventeenth-century English carver and sculptor Grinling Gibbons. There were, however, many excellent carvers in England; and this particular overmantle, made about 1690, is by an unidentified craftsman. The English mantlepiece below was carved about 1750. Shutze's designs for the white pine panelling and for the linden wood pediments and door surrounds are based on late seventeenth-century models.

The room is furnished as a comfortable sitting room with many of the accessories of an eighteenth-century English library. Fine antique pieces are focal points of interest, including the mid-eighteenth-century Dutch tall-case clock which was made by C. Van der Hey of Amsterdam. Mr. Inman inherited this walnut clock from his parents. The woven Axminster carpet, made early in the nineteenth-century, adds lightness and gaiety with its red flowers on a white ground.

The Green Room or Morning Room is quite different from the library. A beautifully proportioned room with carved cornice, simple classical moldings,

Library. Photo: courtesy of the Atlanta Historical Society.

Library. Photo: courtesy of the Atlanta Historical Society.

Green Room or Morning Room. Photo: courtesy of the Atlanta Historical Society.

gadrooned trim around the windows, and tall fluted columns flanking the fireplace, it recalls the well-defined clarity of an early eighteenth-century Palladian interior. Mr. Shutze has described the room as "life-enhancing." Reflections of the personal tastes of owners and architect are apparent, particularly in the carving of the capitals on either side of the overmantle: each boasts neatly-executed lilies and delicate little swans, as well as asymmetrical cartouches borrowed from the vocabulary of rococo ornament. Bits of Mrs. Inman's collections of small objects—fans, ceramics, glass, and silver salt cellars are visible in the photograph. A fine pair of seventeenth-century Venetian console tables and an early-nineteenth-century English secretary bookcase are among the outstanding antiques in this room.

The presence of a large (8'8" long) chintz-covered sofa clearly marks the morning room as a decorative product of the twentieth century. A taste popularized in Elsie de Wolfe's influential book of 1913 *The House in Good Taste* is apparent in the choice of its bright, gay chintz, and in its very presence in the room. Miss de Wolfe, writing specifically to women, as those who make a house a home, had advised "when you have set your dropsical sofas where you want them for talk, warmth, and reading . . . this . . . sense of your rights is acknowledged, . . . your rooms will always have meaning in the end." Amidst beautiful, rare, and delicate antiques, the meaning of comfort and practicality in the success of a home was well understood by Mrs. Inman.

In the dining room, although architectural detailing in the style of William Kent is ponderous and formal, the wallpaper sets a tone of gaiety and lightness. Colorful flowering trees bedecked with exotic birds were painted over a ground of a light peach color in the style of the eighteenth-century Chinese wallpapers which adorned the finest English and American houses. A handsome ceiling is ornamented with oval moldings in high relief.

This room is the setting for the prizes of the Inman collection: a pair of marble-topped console tables, with picturesque bases realistically carved, painted and gilded in the form of swans on rocks amidst water plants. The Inmans bought them in Bath, England, in 1924. These fantastic products of eighteenth-century London have recently been attributed by Helena Hayward to the carver Thomas Johnson, active between 1734 and 1775. Another console table, with a base in the form of a gilded crane with outstretched wings stands in this room. It was made in England during the 1750s.

The oriental theme for the room, set by the wallpaper, is echoed in the chinoiserie decoration of a Dutch commode on stand dating from the second quarter of the eighteenth century. Properly a bedroom piece, it is used here as a sideboard. The piece is a good example of eighteenth-century Japanning—black and red paint have been used with gilt to imitate oriental lacquer. Chinoiserie figures and floral motifs deco-

Dining Room. Photo: courtesy of the Atlanta Historical Society.

Dining Room. Photo: courtesy of the Atlanta Historical Society.

Console table with carved swan decorations. Photo: R. Cotton Alston, Jr.

rate the drawers, cupboard doors, and apron. A large mahogany breakfront bookcase, made for an English library during the second quarter of the nineteenth-century, was used by Mrs. Inman in her dining room for the display of Derby porcelain in a "Japan" pattern of 1800-1825. A large Aubusson carpet of the early nineteenth-century covers the floor in this room.

A loggia, or screened porch, opens off the dining room. With its stone floor and high ceiling supported by arched openings, it provided a cool and charming place for dining in an era predating air-conditioning. A larger porch with vaulted ceiling at the opposite end of the house, opening to the library and morning rooms, offered another cool haven with a delightful view of the formal gardens.

In addition to the principal rooms pictured on these pages, there is on the ground floor a charming octagonal breakfast room with beautiful plaster ceiling decoration incorporating sea-shells in relief. Nor are kitchen, pantry, powder rooms, mens' toilet, and closets, which provided twentieth-century conveniences, pictured in this article.

On the second floor, four large bedrooms, each with bath, open onto the large oblong stair hall. At the north end of this hall, a smaller hall gives access to a sewing room and to a service stair which rises to a third floor. On this top floor are two servants' rooms, a bath, a cedar closet, and a large attic.

The house was completed in 1928. Sadly, Mr. Inman was to live but three years to enjoy Atlanta's most exquisite architectural expression of the early twentieth-century local preference for classicism. Mrs. Inman lived in Swan House until her death in 1965. When the Atlanta Historical Society purchased Swan House from Mrs. Inman's heirs in 1966, it was able to purchase most of the furniture from the first floor. Several of the more important antique pieces reserved by the estate have subsequently been purchased and presented to the Society by generous individuals and groups. The heirs of the estate gave the window hangings, all of which are original to the 1928 building date of the house, or are restorations made for Mrs. Inman during her lifetime, following the original patterns and using fabrics woven to duplicate the originals. Although the heirs removed a few major pieces shortly after Mrs. Inman's death—a grand piano in the morning room, and a sofa in the library—and many small decorations like fans, boxes, and small pieces of silver, the Historical Society is now able to show the principal rooms on the ground floor, and Mrs. Inman's bedroom on the second floor, much as they appeared during her lifetime.

Philip Shutze, Mrs. Inman, and her decorators achieved an effect of graciousness and beauty at Swan House, a background for life in an era that has all but disappeared from Atlanta. The Atlanta Historical Society preserves this house as an outstanding example of the best of early twentieth-century architecture in Atlanta, as a rare document of luxurious living during an important era in the history of the city, and as a fascinating revelation of taste in interior decorating during that era.

NANCY K. LESTER—*Coordinator, Swan House*

Detail of console table. Photo: R. Cotton Alston, Jr.

The Horgan-Curtis House, Macon, Georgia, early 1930s

The Horgan-Curtis House, entrance façade, showing the perron with its two flights of steps, the richly decorated gable, and the porches at the north and south ends. Photo: Helga Photo Studio.

MR. Shutze designed this small villa in the early thirties for Dan Horgan, a florist. A central hall, with a dining room to the left and a salon to the right, leads to a second hall running at right angles, beyond which steps go down to a library facing an enclosed garden. The façade with its gable and perron steps, as well as the ornament, shows that Mr. Shutze had absorbed all the vocabulary of the Italian Classical.

The grounds consist of a lawn and drive at the front, enclosed terraces at the back, and a small formal garden off the north end.

Portion of the entrance front below the gable. Cream-coffee ochre detail against a wall of burnt sienna. Mr. Horgan's business is evoked in the flower basket and garlands. Photo: H.H. Reed.

An extension of the gable. The elaborate molding is typical of Mr. Shutze's work. The crossed flowers, of course, help identify the florist-client. Photo: H.H. Reed.

Detail of the window pediment. Photo: H.H. Reed.

The formal garden as seen from the north porch. A central pool is flanked by beds raised and retained by low walls. At the far end a bust in the ancient manner is set in a round-arched niche. Photo: H.H. Reed.

The English-Chambers House, 1929, Atlanta

English-Chambers House: the Ionic porch showing the urns in the niches. Photo: H.H. Reed.

THIS substantial residence stands across from the Governor's Mansion. The ornament of the entrance front is the Ionic porch. Inside the porch to either side of the door are niches with urns, a device Mr. Shutze adopted at Swan House.

The most sumptuous interior is in the dining room, done in the manner of Claydon House, with Chinoiserie details and Chinese wallpaper.

English-Chambers house: the dining room with its Chinese wallpaper. Courtesy: Philip Trammell Shutze.

The Temple, 1931-32, 1589 Peachtree Street, Atlanta

THE Temple of the Hebrew Benevolent Congregation is a wing of a larger building which includes a school and office quarters. Only the Temple can be seen from the street. In plan it is a square crowned by a dome resting on a drum with a Doric colonnade. The façade is particularly handsome. An entablature and pediment are upheld by four engaged Ionic columns. From the central bay extends a small semicircular porch of two Tuscan columns above which is an elaborate curved entablature, the frieze of which depicts various emblems associated with the Jewish religion. Above the entablature is a cartouche framing the Tablets of the Law.

The auditorium is a square with a saucer dome resting on four widespread pendentives. In its center is an ocular opening into the drum of the outer dome. The saucer dome is broken into bays of ornament, each with a banner with a symbol and a tondo with the name of one of the Twelve Tribes in Hebrew. The ornament of the pendentives is dedicated to the four seasons.

The Inner Sanctuary is set in a semicircular apse with four black marble Ionic columns. The Ark is set on a platform reached by two flights of steps. (The Ark is of carved gilt wood.) Behind it are the two Menorah and, above, is the Ner Tomid or Perpetual Light. The impression of the whole is one of subdued richness.

The façade of The Temple behind which rise a drum and dome. Photo: H.H. Reed.

The saucer dome of the auditorium, showing the twelve bays with the banner and Hebrew name of the Twelve Tribes. Photo: H.H. Reed.

View of the Inner Sanctuary or Holy of Holies, showing the Ark. Photo: courtesy of The Temple.

A pendentive with a stand of fruit, symbolizing autumn. Photo: H.H. Reed.

The Academy of Medicine, 1940, Atlanta, Georgia

WHEN the author told Mr. Shutze that he thought the Academy of Medicine was Russian-inspired, the architect said "not at all. It looks back to the Academy of Medicine, with wings added, which stands in Augusta, Georgia."

This is a very handsome building. It shows Mr. Shutze's mastery once again, this time in a relatively simple structure. Its most distinctive feature, other than the Doric porch, is the low rectangular tower with its large lunette windows. As with so many of his buildings, it is reveted in stucco, in color a café-au-lait ochre.

The Academy of Medicine: built in 1940 for the Fulton County Medical Society. Photo: H.H. Reed.

The Julian Hightower Residence, 1947-1948, Thomaston, Georgia

THE Hightower house is approached by a drive around a large meadow. The style is Georgian of the early part of the last century. The interior leans to the English Classical. H. J. Millard, who did the wood carving in Swan House, also worked on the doorway entablatures and the pedimented chimneypieces. A lawn with brick walks and encrusted urns takes the place of a garden. From it another lawn slopes to an 80-acre lake created especially for the grounds. It is a sheet of water which reflects wooded shores and passing clouds.

Julian Hightower Residence: the entrance front with its Tuscan porch. Photo: H.H. Reed.

Julian Hightower Residence: doorway in the dining room with carving by H.J. Millard. Photo: Helga Photo Studio.

Julian Hightower Residence: view of the lake from the lawn-terrace. Photo: H.H. Reed.

Julian Hightower Residence: the living room. The carving of the chimneypiece is by H.J. Millard. Photo: Helga Photo Studio.

Three Houses in Albany, Georgia, and One in Savannah

THESE houses with double porches (porches superimposed) are in the Classical vernacular of Georgia.

The William C. Potter House in Albany, Georgia, ca. 1930. Photo: Helga Photo Studio.

The Raymond Demere House in Savannah, ca. 1930. Photo: Helga Photo Studio.

The Francis Wetherbee House in Albany, Georga, ca. 1930. Photo: Helga Photo Studio.

The Charles Daniel House, 1954, Greenville, South Carolina

THE Charles Daniel house consists of a massive central wing with two flanking extensions. Several devices make the house outstanding. One is having high ceilings on two floors. Another is the high steep roof, and a third is the cupola surrounded by a balustrade.

Ornament is abundant on the interior but it is always judiciously handled. Perhaps the finest room is the dining room with its splendid chimneypiece.

Charles Daniel House: the house viewed from the garden. Photo: H.H. Reed.

Charles Daniel House: the dining room. Note the beautiful chandelier. Photo: Henry Elrod.

Glenn Memorial Church, 1929-1930, and Sunday School and Chapel, 1940, at Emory University, Atlanta

GLENN Memorial Church gave Mr. Shutze an opportunity to use the column. As at the Temple he adopted an Ionic Order for the three-sided porch at the base of the church tower. Behind the columns can be seen a rusticated wall going from floor to ceiling. The middle portion of the tower is plain but for a round window in each of the four sides. This plain middle sets off the two top divisions, the lower one with open bays and the upper one a round tempietto with a circular arcade where the bays are divided by paired Corinthian columns. Added detail comes in the form of balustrades and urns.

The Sunday School and Chapel show Mr. Shutze, as always, a master of Classical detail and of proportion. Here the Ionic Order is backed by deep quoining. At the window over the entrance, moldings end in graceful volutes and the niches at the second floor have scallop shell inserts.

Entrance to the Sunday School and Chapel. Photo: H.H. Reed.

The porch and tower of the Glenn Memorial Church. Photo: H.H. Reed.

Whitehead Memorial Annex to the University Hospital at Emory University, Atlanta, 1945

MR. Shutze is always in command of the Roman style. Here, at the main entrance to a hospital, he has a round-arched bay framed by two Tuscan columns and a broken pediment. A voluted keystone links the arch and the cornice. Above, a window is set in the broken pediment and is topped by a triangular pediment.

To either side of the entrance are windows framed with massive quoining which might serve as Mr. Shutze's signature. Below each window are balusters.

A view of the side of the annex shows how he treated the fenestration. The first-story windows have the quoining seen at the entrance; the second-story are framed with plain molding; the third-story are bare save for the extending lintels. A bold coursing divides the first three window rows from the upper two. Of the upper two rows, the first has alternate segmental and triangular pediments; the second has only lintels. A cornice and a balustrade provide the silhouette. Altogether, the treatment is stunning.

The beholder has one complaint. As so often in this country, trees, in this instance elms, were planted too close to the building. Loud protests, no doubt, would come at the suggestion that they be removed; it is sufficient that they be severely cut back on the building side.

The entrance of the Whitehead Memorial Annex at the hospital of Emory University. Photo: H.H. Reed

View of the flank of the Whitehead Memorial Annex. Photo: H.H. Reed

A Masterpiece Dishonored

by

R.H. IVES GAMMELL

The Frieze of the Prophets.

DURING the first third of our century reproductions of John Singer Sargent's *Frieze of the Prophets* adorned the wall of countless schoolrooms, courthouses, and private homes. The widespread popularity of this fragment of a great decorative unit was thoroughly justified, especially wherever the Old Testament was familiar reading, because its expressively gesticulating figures symbolize, in terms compatible with modern Bible study, the sorrows, hopes, and ecstasies associated with the Hebrew visionaries better than any other representation in the visual arts. But today the extraordinary agglomeration of mural paintings, bas reliefs, and ornament of which the Frieze is but one feature collects dust, forgotten, unnoticed and seriously disfigured, deteriorating day by day in a dimlit hall of the Boston Public Library. Few people, even among educated Bostonians, now realize that John Sargent, the most famous portrait painter in the world during his lifetime, devoted a substantial part of his energies to painting murals for the Library and the Boston Museum of Fine Arts, where they are currently treated with similar disrespect although they have not as yet been damaged. Even fewer know that these murals, especially those in the Library, were once greatly admired by very knowledgeable persons. What brought about the eclipse of a major work of art

by an artist of such indubitable stature? Can anything be done to correct the damage and to arrest the persisting disintegration which threatens to efface important areas of the painted surface?

The first question could easily be answered since the record is available and fully documented. But publicizing the details at this late date would create bitterness without serving any useful purpose. Those chiefly responsible for the inexcusable decisions which had such disastrous consequences are dead. An outline of the episode, however, should be made available to future painters, scholars, and art lovers so that they may interpret what remains of the Sargent Hall and regain some idea of a decorative ensemble which, for inventiveness, originality, and intellectual scope, has no parallel in the art of the last hundred years.

When the Library trustees selected the thirty-four-year-old John Sargent to decorate a large, rather gloomy hallway of the edifice still under construction the painter had given no indication that he was equipped for mural painting. That was in 1890 and Sargent had already exhibited some of his most memorable canvases: *El Jaleo, The Boit Children, Madame Gautreau, Carnation, Lily, Lily, Rose,* pictures which in their kind he never surpassed. He had been exclusively concerned with painting directly from nature,

Side-wall panel of the Frieze of the Prophets.

with rendering his impressions of visual aspects which he interpreted with exceptional brilliance. Nothing in his already large output suggested a gift for architectonic design, for decorative pattern, or for visualizing imagined subjects. The trustees were taking a wild and seemingly unwarranted chance. But they gambled and they won.

The opportunity aroused unsuspected aptitudes in this reserved and inarticulate young man, and the Sargent Hall, which he did not complete until 1922, records play by play the transformation of an extraordinarily gifted impressionist painter into a full-fledged mural decorator of genuine distinction. The Hall would justify its existence regarded solely as a demonstration of how such a feat is accomplished by a superior creative intelligence. It is, of course, a notable work of art into the bargain. But it also provides a fascinating opportunity to follow the evolution of Sargent's decorative esthetic over the thirty-two years he was preoccupied with the task. His continually changing viewpoint undeniably militated against the unity desirable in the adornment of a single architectural setting and the discrepancies between the style adopted for the earliest panels and those used in the successive additions detract somewhat from the total effect. But each portion, considered by itself, has a beauty of its own while the superlative passages, the *Frieze of the Prophets* together with the superb archivolt which spans it, the *Dogma of the Redemption* and several of the smaller lunettes were profoundly moving works of art until much of the paint and gilding was scrubbed off by bungling hands in 1953 and the lighting system was inexcusably tampered with.

The lighting of these decorations is of critical importance. The Public Library was built just when electric lighting came into general use. Prior to that mural

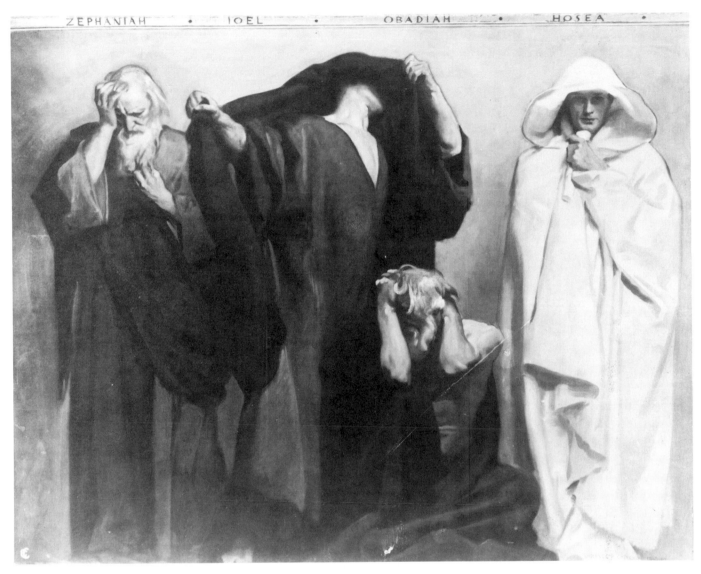

ZEPHANIAH · IOEL · OBADIAH · HOSEA ·

Side-wall panel of the Frieze of the Prophets.

paintings were intended to be looked at in the daytime and to contribute background richness after the candles were lit. Sargent's were probably the first important decorations ever carefully planned with the new illumination in mind. Although the now blocked skylights admitted daylight until a few years after Sargent's death they were really effective only on brilliant days, and it was obvious from the start that the Hall would most often be seen by artificial light. Sargent quickly realized how much judiciously placed electric bulbs of predetermined wattage might enhance the impact of his decoration, enabling him to use bas-relief and gold in previously untried ways to increase the atmosphere of mystery and awe called for by the rituals and symbols he intended to depict. He proceeded to exploit the new possibilities with great ingenuity and when he had completed his work and all the bulbs were still in place the impression made on perceptive visitors by the combined media was nothing less than overwhelming.

But in 1953, while the disastrous cleaning was under way, the architect in charge of the Boston Public Library decided to alter the lighting arrangements installed under John Sargent's supervision, substituting fixtures of an entirely different character located in positions which cast light on the relief work from angles other than those planned by the artist. How this amiable and in many respects intelligent man could have committed such an act of artistic vandalism, after the role played by the placement of the lights in John Sargent's decorative and dramatic scheme had been painstakingly pointed out to him on the spot, baffles the mind. He had assured his advisers that he would adhere strictly to the original system and then adjust the bulbs empirically in consultation with them. He did not reveal his new project until the work was well

The Dogma of the Redemption.

along and then he blandly informed his bewildered auditors that he intended to make the decorations appear to better advantage than Sargent had believed possible. When the scaffolding was removed the full measure of the disaster was immediately apparent to every knowledgeable person who had studied the masterpiece when it was first unveiled, and the protests slowly brought the perpetrators to some realization of what they had done. Areas keyed for a penumbra were glaringly exposed, contours intended to be just perceptible told as dark outlines, and unforeseen cast shadows obliterated significant details. The subtle accentuation of the relief work was effaced or exaggerated by the glare, and the calculated glint of the gilded surfaces, as well as the powerful modeling of the figures in high relief, were thrown out of kilter. Finally, even the Library officials appreciated their error and all the lights were dimmed, leaving John Sargent's

decorations in the discreet twilight which has enshrouded them ever since. The episode passed almost unnoticed and scandal was averted.

The original lighting can be restored with a little intelligent effort but the havoc wrought by the reckless cleaning is beyond repair. Fortunately, a happy accident has kept the first segment to be completed relatively unscathed. This less impaired area comprises the *Frieze of the Prophets* and the paintings above it, for which the still inexperienced young mural painter used a technique not very different from that of his portraits. The Prophets in particular are quite realistically rendered with considerable impasto. Although Sargent soon had second thoughts about the suitability of that technique for mural decoration he continued to use it in modified form throughout the first group of pictures to be installed.

But, with the *Dogma of the Redemption*, unveiled

eight years later in 1903, Sargent emerges as an experienced muralist in full command of his resources and prepared to experiment in directions both original and startling. To create the effect called for by his conception he centered his composition around a crucifixion executed in high relief, although he had no training in sculpture. He further emphasized this central feature on the axis of the hall by decorative devices of his own inventing. The massive gilded base of the cross, adorned by an impressively patterned bas-relief representing the traditional pelican nourishing her brood with her own body, symbol of the Church, is supported by two winged figures clad in Byzantine magnificence. Their brocaded stoles and the embroidered hems of their robes are fashioned out of tin on which Sargent's ornamental patterns of vine leaves, grapes, and ears of wheat were embossed and flecked with gold that glittered in the electric light. The metal sheets were affixed to the painted wall surface but the stoles curve over the modeled forearms of the angels holding the crucifix whose hands, protruding in considerable relief, effect a transition between the wall level and the varied levels of the carving. The beautifully contrived interplay of these contrasting planes and significant symbols is no longer apparent to the eye in the tarnished wreckage on the wall. Originally the patterns of this gleaming centerpiece were counterpointed by subsidiary details such as the curving wingtips which project over the cornice in two places, the "Instruments of the Passion" held by attendant angels and the toe-caps of their footgear, while passages brightened with gold leaf distributed their glitter throughout the decoration. This is true decorative inventiveness which meets the demands of an exceptional subject matter triumphantly. Although many of these features have been obliterated by incompetent custodians the sense of mystery and splendor formerly communicated by Sargent's creation may be recaptured to some extent with the help of photographs taken before the damage was done.

These photographs give a fair idea of how the resplendent vision conjured up on the south wall of the Sargent Hall once looked. The over-all design is a pictorial realization of one of the most abstruse metaphysical concepts ever formulated by man in his endless attempts to define the nature of God and solve the enigma of human suffering. Most of the painters who have grappled with such themes have foundered, overwhelmed by the sheer weight of their intellectual content. They were unable to create visual patterns adequate for their purpose, which is precisely what John Sargent did do successfully when depicting the Dogma of the Redemption. Felicities comparable to those which I have pointed out in the lower frieze also abound in the upper section where the cloaked figures

Our Lady of Sorrows.

The Law.

Hell.

The Messianic Era.

representing the Trinity formerly towered in a penumbra. The viewer first grew aware of the parts raised in low relief, the haloes, the tiaras, the stylized contours of the group and the intricate arabesque of the orphrey which borders the great mantle enfolding the Three in One. Gradually details became comprehensible; the embroidered word *Sanctus* repeated throughout the length of the orphrey, the subtle differentiation of the three tiaras, the similar but not identical gestures of the hands uplifted in perpetual benediction, the scarcely discernible faces; all of them traditional forms hallowed by long usage but chosen with unerring taste from the repertory of Christian iconography and, in each case, artfully amended by the painter and given fresh significance through their unwonted juxtaposition. The impact of the ensemble awakened associations dormant in the hinterland of the mind such as are evoked by the chant of ancient liturgies whose words we only partially catch or by the majestically obscure phrasing of the Nicene Creed. Even in its present impaired state the nobility of the concept still captures the imagination of an attentive observer.

Space does not permit further enumeration of the praiseworthy constituents which make up this impressive complex of interrelating decorative elements. The Sargent Hall still stands, although approximately one third of its decoration has been irreparably defaced. Given expert care, however, a good part of what remains could be restored to a semblance of its former appearance which would facilitate at least a mental reconstitution of Sargent's masterpiece with the aid of pictures taken soon after the first unveiling. So I will conclude by answering the second question raised in my opening paragraph. What must be done to minimize the damage and arrest further deterioration?

Two things, one of which must be done promptly. The more urgent measure consists of putting up a scaffolding so that the entire decorated surface can be examined and the minimum indispensable restorations be made, after which a mat varnish must be applied to the painted areas. When they removed the accumulated dirt together with, alas! a substantial amount of paint and gold leaf, the "cleaners" apparently neglected to apply this protective coat of varnish after their ministrations were concluded. Consequently, the pigment continues to powder off and more and more of the decoration is disappearing. It is important that all future work on the Sargent Hall be done under the watchful eye of an experienced mural painter who understands and respects Mr. Sargent's idiom. "Experts" on the staffs of art museums do not necessarily qualify under this definition. Above all, no general repainting should ever be attempted. A damaged masterpiece is better than a repainted one.

The second step will be to restore the original lighting system from photographs of the Hall as it looked in 1922. This operation should not present any difficulty. It is imperative that both these measures be taken, the first immediately and the second as soon as practicable.

All photographs are through the courtesy of the Trustees of the Boston Public Library.

Building the J. Paul Getty Museum—A Personal Account

by

NORMAN NEUERBURG

THE construction of the new J. Paul Getty Museum in Malibu, California, in the form of an ancient Roman villa, is possibly the most encouraging piece of news that the members of Classical America have had in more than three decades. It is yet too early to say whether it marks a new direction in architecture, but, quite apart from that, it is remarkable proof that the classical tradition is still alive and that it is still possible to find skillful craftsmen if one is ready to insist on quality and is able to pay for it.

After leaving California in the early 1950s Mr. Getty had opened a portion of his home, with his art collection, to the public on a rather limited basis. This arrangement prevailed until the late 1960s when he decided to send back to California many of those pieces which he had kept in his residence in England. About this same time he also began to enlarge his collection which had remained static for a number of years. His first thought was to add a wing onto the existing building, a structure of a vaguely "Mediterranean" style, and the architects duly drew up a plan and had a rendering made. He soon decided against that, however, feeling that he did not wish to have large numbers of the public so close to the home to which he had always intended to return. The next design was on another site on his extensive property and was a rather larger structure in a Beaux-Arts Roman style to be totally faced in white marble. In both of these schemes the interior arrangements were to have been done subsequently, perhaps even by another architectural firm. It had also been Mr. Getty's desire to install replicas of certain rooms of his Tudor country house, Sutton Place, within the shell. This second design appears not particularly to have pleased Mr. Getty and work remained at a standstill in the spring of 1970 when Mr. Getty finally decided what he really wanted to be the design of his museum. Once that was decided there was to be no stopping or even slowing down until the inauguration of the museum in January 1974.

As early as 1912 he had visited the Naples Museum, Pompeii, and Herculaneum (of which only a tiny part could be visited at that time) and he became fascinated with the story of the Villa of the Papyri. This villa, which may have belonged to Lucius Calpurnius Piso, the father-in-law of Julius Caesar, had been covered by the eruption of Vesuvius in A.D. 79 and was discovered by chance in 1750; during the next fourteen years excavations were carried on by means of wells and tunnels. While the remarkable treasure of sculpture and other objects and the unique library on the rolls of papyrus which gave the name to the villa were removed and became part of the collection of the Bourbonic king, the building remained hidden to view permanently after the site was abandoned, due to poisonous gases which filled the tunnels. Fortunately, though, an accurate plan had been made by Karl Weber, the Swiss engineer in charge of the excavation. The story of this undertaking has long fascinated archaeologists and scholars as well as the educated public, and the villa formed the setting for a chapter in Mr. Getty's book *Collector's Choice*, published in 1955; in 1970 he decided that a recreation of this villa was to be the setting for his art collection. Although the logical approach might have seemed to do a new excavation of the villa according to modern criteria, the length of time for such an undertaking and the cost of it (Mr. Getty remarked that "it would be like digging the Suez Canal"!) caused this suggestion to be rejected at the outset. Instead, he opted for a re-creation that would be an educated guess of what it might have been.

The architectural firm of Langdon and Wilson in Los Angeles had been chosen for the project from the beginning as they had done other work for the client. They had no particular experience in working in the classical tradition, however, (nor did any other local firm for that matter) and it appeared advisable to appoint a historical consultant to guide the archeological aspects of the design; it was the author's good fortune to be chosen for this position. Although it was at first assumed that the consultations would be few and rather routine, eventually practically the whole design, where archaeological advice was necessary, became my responsibility, and throughout the project I suggested and approved thousands of details and followed through in the execution of the work. Robert

Bird's-eye view of the new J. Paul Getty Museum, Langdon and Wilson Architects. Rendering by David Wilkins.

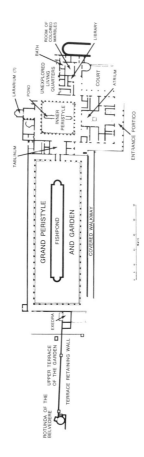

Schematic plan of the Villa of the Papyri, Herculaneum.

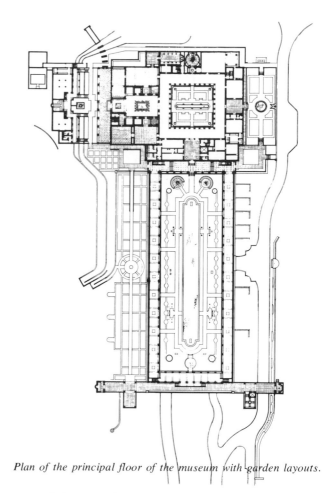

Plan of the principal floor of the museum with garden layouts.

Langdon graciously relinquished much of his normal authority in the design, while Edward Genter, the project architect, and I worked hand and glove in a most harmonious association. A perfectionist, he had also been trained during the years when period architecture was the norm, and thus he was in total sympathy with the spirit of the project. We were joined by an extensive crew of consultants – structural, civil, mechanical, and electrical engineers as well as others—who contributed their essential parts to the design. Emmet Wemple and Denis Kurutz were responsible for the superb gardens in the Roman style and while I acted as their "conscience," as they put it, the work of research and design was theirs. The general contractor, the Dinwiddie Construction Co., brought together a remarkable group of the finest craftsmen available. The workers, in turn, contributed their best to this most unusual project, and each one considered this "his" museum!

Since Mr. Getty had remained in England he engaged an English architect, Stephen Garrett (now Deputy Director of the Museum), as liaison. Mr. Garrett made periodic trips to Los Angeles to check on the progress of the design and construction and then wrote up lengthy reports on his findings for Mr. Getty. Photographs of the construction progress as well as most of the drawings were sent to Mr. Getty along with daily job reports, and I kept Mr. Garrett informed, in a less formal fashion, on the progress and discussed endless problems by letter. Thus Mr. Getty, although he was never to visit his Museum, was kept apprised of the state of the project, and all but minor details of design were presented for his approval, especially when they had an effect on the cost of the building. On five separate trips to Italy for various problems I stopped in England to meet with Mr. Getty to report on the progress of the work and to present various proposals to him for aspects of the design. The whole project is extensively documented both by Mr. Garrett's reports and by our correspondence.

Even under the best of circumstances the project would have been a difficult and demanding one as nothing of this nature had been built for many decades. The reconciliation of the concept of re-creating an ancient Roman villa with the needs of a twentieth-century museum, combined with the requirements of a very stiff building code, presented a challenge of formidable proportions. Ideally one would have hoped for an extended period of research and planning, perhaps two or three years, as is common with many contemporary museums. Mr. Getty's orders, however, were to proceed at once with both design and construction, and the first ground was broken less than six months after the go-ahead on the concept of the design had been given. Over a period of three years drawings and construction were being carried on at the same time, concrete pouring often being held up till a pertinent drawing could be completed, and the final drawing having arrived on the job a week before the inauguration of the facilities. Considering the breathless pace of the whole production it is miraculous that major mistakes were not made in construction, though the concrete mixer was a familiar sight on the job due to changes and refinements in the mechanical facilities of the building. That it should have come out so well is to be credited to the exceptional cooperation and good will of the designers and the construction crews. No visitor to the building today can imagine the number of *ad hoc* decisions made and the crises faced up to and resolved in every aspect of the project.

The basic preliminary adaptation of Weber's plan of the ancient villa at Herculaneum had already been made by Mr. Garrett with modifications to fit the site when I first entered the picture. The site in Herculaneum sloped gently to the sea with the length of the building parallel to it, possibly supported by substructures on the side toward the bay of Naples. The chosen site in Malibu was a narrow canyon descending rather less gently to the sea. The plan consists principally of a huge rectangular peristyle and a smaller square one surrounded by the house proper which was to be used as the museum. In a first version the main peristyle had been stepped down three levels, but this was not a Roman solution and I suggested placing it on a single level on a hollow terrace and pointed out that the substructure could be used as a parking area, a solution the Romans would have approved of! The problem of the significant difference in elevation from one end to the other was partly resolved by raising the level of the wing of the peristyle colonnade next to the museum proper. This created a "Rhodian peristyle" with column heights and order changed at this one side. Examples of this arrangement can be found in houses in Pompeii, though the invention appears to have been first used in Greece. The change from simple Doric to more elaborate Corinthian columns permitted making this end the principal façade of the museum and the peristyle became a magnificent forecourt.

Since the Weber plan says nothing about building materials (only once in the records was there a reference to columns made of brick and plastered) and otherwise only occasionally refers to types of floors (i.e. whether mosaic or marble) decisions had to be made as to what surfaces walls would have and what details would be used. Other contemporary structures in Pompeii, Herculaneum, and Stabiae were turned to

as sources, though in more than a few cases it became necessary to make a decision first and find the source afterward. In effect one had to think in terms of Roman forms, textures, and colors.

Mr. Getty's first instructions were that the exterior of the building was to be in red brick, even the inner walls of the peristyles. Quite apart from aesthetic objections felt by us, however, brick would have been totally incorrect from a historical point of view as the Romans did not make extensive use of brick until the second half of the first century A.D. while the Villa of the Papyri had been constructed in the second and first century B.C. Fortunately Mr. Getty yielded to this argument and the whole of the museum building and the walls of the large peristyle were executed in smooth finish concrete simulating plaster. But for contrast, and to emphasize its function as a supporting element, the walls of the substructures were treated more rustically with a veneer of stone simulating the Roman "opus reticulatum." This type of facing with squared stones set on a diagonal was originally designed to be plastered over, but in many cases simply never was gotten around to, and eventually the Romans came to appreciate its aesthetic value (a fourth century A.D. room in Ostia was veneered with fine colored marbles imitating just such masonry, even to representing the grout). Unplastered "opus reticulatum" is especially common at Herculaneum. The arches are surrounded by a combination of Roman brick and stone in alternating schemes. In two panels on the front a checkerboard pattern is formed by using buff and grey stones. The buff stone, a sort of tufa, was imported precut from Gallipoli in Southern Italy while the grey is a lava from the Naples area. Inlaid disks with geometric patterns in colored stone enhance the importance of the entrance façade and are based on examples in Pompeii.

This façade has undergone a variety of transformations. The open walk-way at the garden level in front of the outer colonnade was extended to the two hillsides, thus forming a sort of bridge. Since the building could not be centered within the valley at this point the original composition was asymmetrical with three arches, one over the road to the east and an open stair tower to the west projecting outward. The fine stand of native sycamores here also indicated the desirability of such an informal approach. Mr. Getty wished instead, however, that this be treated in a purely symmetrical manner "like Piazza San Pietro" in spite of the difficulty of actually perceiving it on the symmetrical axis. Although the architects were opposed to this, Mr. Getty stood firm, and the final solution—one of many suggested—consisted of adding two projecting tower-like structures to flank the upper colonnade. The actual access most used to reach the main peristyle is

Original façade design. Rendering by Denis Kurutz.

through one of these which contains both an open stair and the modern convenience of an elevator.

The cast-stone grilles in the garage level were required by a desire for adequate natural ventilation, but the final design was due to a request of Mr. Getty's. At first the design was a rather simple diamond pattern, but he had seen a photograph showing the forms—with spokes—for the pouring of the arches and requested something of that sort. The best (and practically only) solution which I could find was a pair of inlay lunette designs in dark and light stone on a tomb in Ostia. They were modified by piercing the dark parts and are equally effective from the interior of the structure. These fill the arches while the lower rectangular sections are pierced by rows of small arched openings in a Pompeian design.

The Weber plan would seem to indicate that the large peristyle was almost totally enclosed, but from the beginning it had been decided to open the south end with a colonnade to the sea. This has Corinthian columns cast in drums in a material to simulate the tufa used on the lower level. Flat walls closing the side porticoes have windows with a molded frame and pediment and above each is a "corona civica," the sort of wreath placed above the door to the residences of

citizens who had performed noteworthy services for the community. These seemed particularly appropriate in view of Mr. Getty's magnificent gesture in conceiving and financing this unique structure. The exterior side walls are articulated by pilasters to break up their great length (over 300 feet). These walls are further articulated by windows in every other bay; although there is no evidence for them in the Weber drawing they seemed wise both to facilitate ventilation and to permit views into the adjoining landscaped areas. They are filled with grilles, cast in white cement, to avoid accidents. Three different types are used and they add a picturesque note to the sobriety of the exterior.

As they were rather simpler in their construction and function the garage and large peristyle above were built first, thus permitting a longer period of planning for the museum proper. The decision to use the Roman Doric order for the colonnades of the porticoes was fairly simple and logical. The originals probably would have been of brick and plastered, but here the columns were cast in place in reinforced concrete in waste molds. An open-beamed ceiling (concrete simulating wood) was rejected for a coffered ceiling cast in plaster and painted. The design with moldings and large roset-

Façade as completed. A second tower is behind the trees at right.

tes derives from the impressions left in the ashes of a fine ceiling in the portico of a villa at Boscoreale near Pompeii and appears in its full richness in the Corinthian portico next to the museum and in a simpler version in the Doric porticoes. Plaster beams divide the ceiling into bays which are echoed in both the floor and wall designs.

It is quite possible that this floor in the original villa may have been mosaic, but practical considerations, particularly of time of execution, dictated a substitution of terrazzo, the Roman "opus signinum," and mosaic was limited to meander strips connecting the columns and the walls to the columns and defining bays similar to those on the ceiling. Alternating bays of the terracotta-colored floor have inset designs in white based on motifs from terrazzo floors in Pompeii and Herculaneum; three different geometric compositions are used. In the original floors the white is mosaic, but since mosaic and terrazzo represent two separate trades today we had to substitute white terrazzo in specially made frames in a sort of cloisonne technique for the mosaic. The designs are placed opposite solid portions of the wall while the plain bays are next to the windows and at certain hours of the day the grilles cast patterns alternating with the inset designs in the floor.

The decorated walls of the peristyle are one of the most characteristically Roman aspects of the whole building and perhaps one of the most misunderstood. Such an expanse of inner wall (the roof defines the porticoes as interior space) would not have intentionally been left undecorated in even a relatively modest house, and in a villa of this size it would have been a very important element. The decoration took its point of departure from the same villa at Boscoreale as the ceiling coffers and is typical of the first century B.C., the supposed period of the building of this peristyle. In my first sketch an extensive use of red proved a bit too strong for Mr. Getty's taste, and instead, we chose a more subdued, if less typical, color scheme. Mr. Getty then approved the basic design: painted columns corresponding to the real columns in front of a wainscote and paneled wall, about two-thirds of the total height, with a garland hanging between the capitals in front of an open sky; in the window bays the openings were simply to break into the design in a typical but rather unfortunate Roman manner. The design was put out to bid and the three competitors were to make color renderings based on my design. The winner, Garth Benton, not only made the best sketch and had the lowest estimate but also clearly was the one best

Main peristyle looking toward the sea.

Main peristyle looking toward the museum.

Detail of main façade, balcony level.

Portico of museum at end of main peristyle.

Corner in portico of main peristyle.

Interior of portico across front of museum.

suited to follow instructions in what was essentially a problem of executing designs not his own. He did not in any way disappoint us. After his approval of the original design, Mr. Getty made the felicitous suggestion that not all bays be identical and we introduced a rather complex scheme of alternation, permutations, and combinations which add variety without denying the unity of the all-over wall design. The paneled wall behind the columns carries through unchanged, but the wainscoting has three slight variations while the columns occur in pairs, flanking the garlands, in four variations. The window bays dispense with the garlands and instead contain the illusion of a recess in painted stonework. Each window is topped by a pediment and is flanked by metal urns, again both elements of four different types. The garlands alternate between ones laden with fruit and ones with flowers and each of these has two variations. Four different theatrical masks appear above the garlands, while birds, lizards, and grasshoppers are placed "ad libitum." These variations on the walls, combined with those on the floor and in the window grilles, mean that for the length of the portico no two bays are identical in every detail.

Throughout the job every new element completed tended to change everything else in relation to it. Be-

fore the installation of the grilles the window bays had a certain inconsistency, with great gaping holes in the center of an illusionistically painted three dimensional space; but as soon as the grilles were installed they reestablished the integrity of the wall.

As the north wing of the portico was at a different level and had a different order its decoration did not follow the same scheme. The transition is formed by corner pavilions separated by arches in both directions. In each an architectural scene on a flat wall is framed by one arch as seen down the length of the side portico, while bronze doors framed by *trompe l'oeil* architecture open in the contiguous exterior walls. The wall in between the pavilions has illusionistic paintings of Corinthian columns with square bosses on smooth shafts in front of a simple paneled wall. Only a minimum of spatial depth is delineated. A patterned floor of five types of marble and the richly coffered ceiling unify the three interconnecting areas.

The upper façade is enclosed by projecting rooms above the corner pavilions. The section in between is richly articulated with panels, alternating segmental and triangular pediments, pilasters and Corinthian capitals, and is highlighted with color. The central element consists of an arcuated lintel within a triangular pedi-

Detail of ceiling and lantern in portico of museum.

Detail of wall painting in main peristyle. Still life reproduces a fragment from the original villa.

ment and there are smaller pediments above the projecting corner rooms. The main part of the façade was done in a single pour of concrete with about half of it being formed with plaster-waste molds; only the capitals were precast and added later. Both the arcaded cast-stone railing here and that on the bridge above the garage entrance repeat a typical, if unfamiliar, Roman solution; the bronze railing between the columns of the portico below more closely fits usual concepts of Roman design. The view from this upper terrace into the garden below and with the sea beyond is especially delightful.

The formal garden in the peristyle is dominated by the great reflecting pool which was one of the principal features of the original building. Although the pool in Herculaneum appears to have been about 14 feet deep, the depth here had to be reduced to 18 inches because there was a garage below and also because, for code reasons, anything deeper would require a six-foot fence around it and a full-time lifeguard.

Although a huge amount of sculpture was found in the garden there was no really clear organization of it that could easily be followed. Mr. Getty approved our having reproductions of the large bronze pieces made in Naples to decorate this and other gardens. In ap-

proving the suggestion he perceptively remarked that the ancient pieces were probably copies anyway! We were fortunate enough to find that the firm of Chiurazzi in Naples still had molds taken from the originals and Professor Sgobbo of the Naples Museum graciously offered to supervise the execution. Two fauns, one sleeping and the other drunken, are placed on rustic blocks of travertine at the ends of the pool, near where they had been found, while the Resting Hermes and the Wrestlers are placed to the sides in the center of the peristyle. Two graceful deer greet visitors at the south end and twenty bronze busts on marble posts have been placed in the garden and porticoes. At the north end of the peristyle are two large semicircular benches in cast stone based on examples in Pompeii. They are paved with striking black and white limestone and slate floors in the design of a spinning wheel. We had hoped to carve the seats in tufa in Italy but the material proved too friable and had to be abandoned. Two simple grape arbors and two lattice-work structures complete the architectural features.

The planting, however, is the most important aspect. At the very beginning it was decided that the gardens should not only be laid out in what we assumed to be the Roman fashion, but also that the plant

Bench with inlaid floor in main peristyle garden.

material would be authentic for the time and area. Our authorities were the ancient authors such as the Plinys and Varro, painted representations in Pompeii, Herculaneum, and Rome, and the somewhat enigmatic results of excavated ancient gardens. Much of this is unsure and there are those who might not accept all of the choices, and, in truth, occasionally substitutions of certain species had to be made when the right ones were simply unavailable. Mature plant material was brought in when practical, even such things as century-old Mediterranean fan palms and good sized laurel and pomegranate trees. Box is used in abundance—the whole complex of gardens has about a mile of box hedges—as is myrtle, acanthus, ivy (mounded in the Roman fashion), roses of fragrant old-fashioned varieties, campanula, dianthus, anemones, candytuft, santolina, calendula, chamomile, iris, crocus, violas, narcissus, grape hyacinth, and oleander. At certain times of the day and in certain seasons the garden is filled with delightful perfumes. With California's mild climate it has become one of the most popular spots in the museum for visitors.

Occasional evening events required some sort of outdoor lighting and the solution here was to adapt a type of lantern carried through the unlighted streets of ancient Roman towns. It was made in two sizes: a larger version to be hung between the columns and a smaller one to light the walkways around the pool. The level of light is low, though adequate for safety, and is decisively nontheatrical; the effect rather is more dreamy and evocative.

The terracotta tile on the portico and museum roofs constitutes an important element in the total impression of the building. Made according to Roman specifications which are considerably larger than current types, they also represent the items which took the longest to procure. Initially no American company was willing to undertake producing them. Then an Italian factory near Salerno was found which produced them for restoration work at Pompeii and Herculaneum, but as their technique was of the simplest imaginable they proved incapable of supplying them within the limits of our construction schedule. Then attempts were made to find a supplier in Mexico but with disastrous results; one sample arrived broken into small pieces and a second came glazed purple. Suggestions that the tiles be made of colored cement were successfully rejected when it was shown that the color would fade, and anyway no one could be found to manufacture them. Finally, Interpace, one of the firms which had declined originally, agreed to manufacture them and turned out a very creditable product, even if it has a little less of the romance of the handmade Italian tiles. Besides the characteristic flat pan tiles and semicircular covers, the roofs were completed with rows of antefixes to close the ends of the cover tiles in order to keep birds from nesting there, and these enliven the outlines of the roofs against the sky.

The planning and construction of the museum building proved to be much more complicated and had more modifications throughout the course of the work. The concept of an empty shell to be filled later seemed to make even less sense here and was never seriously entertained. Mr. Getty, however, did at times request moveable partitions for greater future flexibility, but they proved to be impractical within the concept of the project and there were numerous practical objections to them. I, personally, was strongly opposed to the idea as I felt that Roman architecture was perhaps even more concerned with interiors than exteriors, and not to make the interiors Roman would eviscerate the building. There were those who felt that Roman interiors might fight too much with the objects to be displayed, but, after all, they had been created for just such settings. Mr. Getty himself had often expressed a preference for "environmental" museums and I think, in the end, he was pleased with the result. The problem of the aggressiveness of the setting has remained, however, and some visitors, not totally in jest, have suggested that the objects get in the way of the enjoyment of the architecture of the rooms! Nonetheless, the objects in the collection can be seen without any difficulty and in many cases are considerably enhanced by the setting, especially in those rooms which have been created for a particular object.

A lower floor, a sort of basement entered from the garage, was largely nonhistorical in its design as it was to contain mechanical services, storage, conservation laboratories, a library, a photographic collection, offices, and a lecture hall. Only an entrance lobby next to this latter was to have a Roman feeling. This was limited to a series of groin vaults in a rather simple architectural space. No groin vault, however, had been made in a building in Los Angeles in thirty or forty years, it would seem, and the drawings proved unintelligible to the workmen. This was the first of a number of challenges that the lathers and plasterers had to face as they got into even more complicated ceilings. It was decided that the lecture hall would have a modern appearance and that was designed totally in the architects' office, though I had been the one initially to insist on the necessity of a truly efficient and functional lecture hall; I had both given and attended lectures in hopelessly inefficient halls (includ-

ing the one that served the purpose in the old museum!) and know how lecturers felt about the problem. Since the opening of the museum the lecture hall has proved to be most useful and, apart from the usual "bugs" in a new facility, has worked extremely well.

The main floor was the most complex and interesting to design, and in spite of certain changes in the first version the most important parts of the final layout were established quite early, even including certain of the more complicated finishes. Thinking ahead here proved most wise as the rather significant additional cost of such items as marble could be included in the budget before restrictions began to be placed on it. We did not design with a specific budget figure in mind but as the costs increased Mr. Getty did attempt to put a limit on what he wished to spend. The final figure given by him, $17 million, is about three times the original estimate, which, however, was based on the square footage cost of a typical office building. Although the various finishes instigated by me certainly entered the picture, much of the additional cost came from mechanical features which proved to be much more complicated or had not been included in the original design. No aspect of the project turned out to be as simple as first thought!

Apart from the square peristyle, the only elements preserved in this part of the Weber plan were the atrium complex and a vestibule between the two peristyles. The latter was somewhat reduced in size for reasons of space economy. This floor was to contain the galleries for the antiquities collection, a bookstore, and the principal offices as well as a trustees room. The non-display areas again were worked out by the architects alone, while I was responsible for the galleries and in certain cases even made the initial drawings to be shown Mr. Getty. The first room to be designed was the atrium, and it was to be decorated in the fashion of the second century B.C., with false ashlar on the lower section and an engaged colonnade on the upper section, both typical of the so-called first style as found in Pompeii and Herculaneum. The ceiling was to be wooden with coffers with gold-leafed rosettes and moldings and the floor a black and white mosaic as the original was recorded to have been. Although among the first to be designed, it was one of the last to be completed because of the varied trades involved.

The piece that Mr. Getty always felt was the most important in his collection is a marble statue of Herakles (the Roman Hercules) which he had acquired from the Lansdowne family who had purchased it some time after its discovery near Tivoli in the eighteenth century. Thus it seemed appropriate to create a special setting for it, and in this case we abandoned the chronological limit of the destruction of the ancient

Atrium with impluvium in foreground.

villa, A.D. 79, and chose a model closer to the probable date of the statue itself, presumably during the reign of Hadrian in the second century A.D. Tivoli was the center of a major cult of Hercules Victor and, besides the great sanctuary in the town, there were numerous small sanctuaries, many subterranean, in the surrounding countryside. The most unusual was an obscure monument about halfway between Rome and Tivoli at a spot out in the country known as the Monte dell'Incastro. It had been excavated in the 1920s, but was only superficially published; I had been fortunate enough to visit it in 1957 while on a fellowship at the American Academy in Rome. My first scheme was a modified version based on an inadequate published plan and my own notes and recollections, but no accurate dimensions were available. After he had approved the design in concept Mr. Getty agreed to our having an architect in Italy prepare accurate measured drawings of it. The site was so little known that it took him two days to locate it! The circular, domed room was totally underground and was reached by a long passageway partially open to the sky and normally filled with blackberry brambles. An oculus in the center, along with a large aperture in one side of the dome, had originally illuminated the interior. The shrine was

Temple of Herakles with floor of ancient marbles reproduced from Villa of the Papyri.

Basilica of Cybele; floor of ancient marbles reproduced from Villa of the Papyri.

Author's first rough sketch for Basilica of Cybele.

lined with fine face brick with two semicircular niches flanking the entrance; these had semidomes filled with mosaic of a rinceau on a white ground while the door had been framed in travertine. The cult niche opposite the entrance had been totally ripped out, though some fragments of the travertine frame were lying on the floor. Above a molded brick cornice with dentils was the dome, completely covered with white mosaic with a small wreath of great laurel leaves around the oculus.

All these features—except for substituting plaster for brick in the cornice—were reproduced for the museum. The missing cult niche was recreated using features from the fragments for the travertine pilasters and ceiling while the interior was paneled with verde antico slabs set off by a dark red marble of the same intensity. For the floor, of which no significant traces were left on the spot, we chose to reproduce the great circular floor found in the initial discovery of the villa and were able to use the same ancient types of marble. As the room was high enough to penetrate into the second floor we were able to install a viewing balcony in a position similar to the opening in the side of the original dome which permits visitors to get an excellent view of the floor from above.

Because of the size of the original room there

Hall of Colored Marbles. Floor of ancient marbles reproduces one still in situ *in Herculaneum.*

ended up being enough space in front for an anteroom. This is square with a pyramidal ceiling and has a simple geometric floor using both ancient and modern marbles. The ceiling was suggested by that of a tomb not far from the underground shrine of Hercules.

A set of a dozen pink granite columns from Lansdowne House in London suggested the creation of a basilica to set off an important statue of a Roman matron as the Goddess Cybele. The design included marble paneled walls, an apse, and a barrel-vaulted ceiling. This, too, was approved by Mr. Getty in an initial stage, but even after the basic design was established there were important modifications in the types and qualities of marbles used, and in the end it was decided not to make use of the granite columns which had been the point of departure. The nave is floored with large inlaid marble tiles reproducing a pavement from the original villa, partly in a marvelous golden yellow marble, an antique giallo antico, combined with other antique types. The aisles flanking this have a rather severe dark grey and white floor. The columns as finally executed are of white marble but they support very unusual Corinthian capitals of four colors of marble: the bell with an incised design on it is black, while the acanthus are yellow and the florets red; the

abacus and necking are white. The paneled walls have recesses of honey-colored onyx (two have windows behind) framed in black slate with a wider border of a grey-green cipollino like watered silk. Below is a dado of lavender fior di pesco and white marble pilasters respond to the columns. Between the white pilaster capitals is a frieze of dark grey bordered in dark red. The wall scheme was suggested by rooms discovered on the Palatine in Rome in the eighteenth century. The semidome of the apse and the lunette opposite it as well as the barrel vault are decorated with superb relief plaster, including a vigorous acanthus rinceau.

A room originally designed simply as a vestibule to the basilica ended up being even more lavish in its use of marble, though its architecture is somewhat simpler. A fine geometric floor of antique marbles reproduces one still in place in Herculaneum, while the walls are paneled partially in antique marbles and partially in modern pieces taken from reopened ancient quarries. The ceiling has a fine low relief design in plaster. Fourteen different stones are used in this room, including two of the pink granite columns belonging to the set once destined for the basilica. While the color scheme there is rather low key, that of this room is very bold. Both rooms are the setting for an

Main entrance vestibule. Floor in ancient marbles using designs from a floor in Herculaneum.

especially fine collection of marble Roman portraits, though the rooms seem quite adequately furnished without anything in them at all.

The richest and most complex of the marble work appears in the entrance vestibule placed between the two peristyles. Its prominent position suggested that it should have the richest treatment. In turn, the elaborateness of the decoration precludes its being used for any sort of display. The extremely intricate inlaid floor, in four kinds of precious ancient marbles, has three different designs which are not quite interlocking but function as if they were applied, one design on top of another, in a rather curious Roman way. The richly paneled walls have inlaid designs and are articulated by unusual diagonally fluted pilasters. The floor, totally of antique marbles, is based on a fragmentary one still in place in Herculaneum while the walls use motifs from a variety of sources and combine antique and modern marbles. One wall is completely open to the interior peristyle except for a pair of slender Corinthian columns in white marble between short spur walls with marble pilasters. The ceiling with its recesses of varying sizes and shapes is decorated with paintings of grape vines as if it were an arbor above the room. Although the design was substantially established early on in the planning, the decision as to the

Detail of painted ceiling of main vestibule.

qualities of the marbles followed a lengthy hassle (with a satisfactory outcome, however) and the room was the last to be installed.

The designing and executing of the marble work was undoubtedly the most exciting aspect of the whole job and the installation the most thrilling to watch. Initially my knowledge of marbles was that of an archaeologist, acquainted with those used by the ancient Romans but not aware of what might be commercially available today. Conversely our subcontractors knew what was available now but were not acquainted with the ancient types, many of which had not been quarried in fifteen hundred years. Thus where I specified ancient types they assumed modern ones could be substituted and bid accordingly. I was not to be put off so easily, however, as my task had been to make the building as authentically Roman as possible. It then became necessary to ask Mr. Getty to allot extra sums of money to obtain the correct ancient types, and it is through his generosity that the museum possesses some of the finest marble work to be seen anywhere in the United States. In the end we compromised and used the ancient types where it seemed most important—on the four floors which reproduced actual ancient examples—while either a combination of new and old or all new ones were used on the walls since they were either adaptations or totally new compositions in the Roman mode. A fifth floor, following an ancient pattern, used new types since the background was white, and ancient material for the pattern—red—was simply not available in sufficient quantities.

We were very fortunate to have found the one firm, the Ditta Medici in Rome, both with the best supply of ancient marbles and the most experience in working with them. They have been in business since 1838 and do most of the restoration work for the Vatican. We were referred to them by Professor Raniero Gnoli, the world's leading expert on ancient marbles and the possessor of perhaps the most complete collection of samples of ancient marbles in private hands. He was also able to supply much needed ancient quarry blocks of giallo antico of exceptional quality.

The other rooms on the main floor are less obtrusive in their finishes, though some have marble floors (usually white and grey) of a simpler type, unusual Roman shaped ceilings, and Roman colors on the walls. The ceilings are especially notable in some of them and again gave endless problems to the plasterers who, however, eventually came through with flying colors.

The square inner peristyle has a colonnade of fluted columns with four-sided Ionic capitals, highlighted with color; above, the second story has plain engaged columns with simplified Corinthian capitals also picked out in color. The screen walls between have framed windows in the three center bays of each side while blind windows, filled with blue, are in the remaining bays. A row of tiles above the entablature of the lower order permits the two stories to be read separately. The walls of the main portico are in false ashlar articulated by pilasters, partly painted in ancient colors, while stone chips of the same tones appear in the terrazo floor, and these colors are used again on the coffered ceiling. The long, narrow, marble pool in the center of the peristyle is enhanced by five bronze figures of maidens who have come to draw water, replicas of ones found in the original villa. In the four corners are marble bird-baths designed after a description of the now lost originals made at the time of the discovery. The rather sober landscaping is dominated by four large matched yews.

The tablinum next to the atrium opens onto a spacious porch with its ceiling held up by spectacular Corinthian columns with spiral fluting alternately going right and left. The walls are decorated with murals of formal garden scenes while the ceiling represents the sky with birds and falling flowers. This opens onto terraced gardens dominated by fountains on two levels. The lower is in the form of a stepped pyramid, while the upper has a decorated wall with a mosaic frieze above rustic ashlar work. This upper fountain is the restoration of a very mutilated one at Herculaneum. This is flanked by two small structures, one a restaurant for the visitors, with grape arbors in front.

On the opposite side of the building is another walled garden, this dominated by a circular fountain in the center and a colorful mosaic niche fountain on the main axis. These two fountains plus the long pool in the inner peristyle, the compluvium in the atrium, and the two fountains in the west garden make a total of six water features on this axis. Here the formally laid out garden contains eight plane trees as well as laurels and a variety of decorative shrubs and flowers.

To the west of the main peristyle there is another large garden with herbs, vegetables, grape vines, and fruit trees, partly laid out in formal plots and partly on terraces with rustic stone retaining walls.

The upper floor is reserved for the collections of paintings and of decorative arts and was largely specified by the curators of those areas. My participation was limited to the design of the main vestibule with its colorful baroque marble floor and the inclusion of windows to permit views into the atrium and the shrine of Hercules as well as into the various gardens.

Many of the things dismissed here in a few words in actuality represent months of struggling, refining, and even fighting for. It was the sort of project where every detail was considered important, where one could insist on things being done right. In the very last phases when there was incredible pressure to be ready

Inner peristyle.

Portico of inner peristyle.

Inner peristyle detail.

West portico with twisted fluted columns and garden paintings.

Fountains in West Garden.

to open the museum by a certain date, a few details sneaked through unresolved and they are very obvious to those of us who lost sleep over all the others which had been resolved. In the final analysis, however, they represent an infinitesimal part of the total effect and do not really substantially disturb the impact of what "Mr. Getty hath wrought." And it is certainly clear that Mr. Getty left his mark on the design in a multitude of ways, even though he never was to visit his creation.

The initial reaction of the local critics, none capable of judging what had been done, was essentially negative, ranging from just unkind to downright vitriolic, and unfortunately their comments were picked up around the world and repeated by other equally unimaginative people. The public, fortunately, doesn't pay too much attention to what critics say and the Museum has become impressively popular with visitors. The numbers have not lessened after the first flush of excitement but rather have tended to increase and ways have had to be found to control them. It seems that this was something the public was ready for, even if the "establishment" wasn't!

Fountains in East Garden.

All photos are courtesy of the author.

A Modern Baroque Gem

The Lady Chapel in the Cathedral of the Immaculate Conception, Brownsville, Texas

by

WILLIAM A. COLES

THE Lady Chapel in the Cathedral of the Immaculate Conception, Brownsville, Texas (dedicated in 1959), is a superb example of classical ecclesiastical architecture executed within the last two decades. It was a gift of Classical America member and adviser Mr. Chauncey Stillman in memory of his great grandfather Charles Stillman, the founder of Brownsville, and his wife Elizabeth. The excellent qualities of design and sumptuous materials and workmanship in the project attest to the enduring vitality of the classical tradition, just as the gift itself gives evidence of the care, taste, and devotion of the patron.

The chapel is located in the west transept of the church, which was built in 1849 in a simple Norman Gothic style. The style of the Stillman chapel, however, is Spanish baroque, there being sound precedent for such shifts in the churches of Spain. The style is, moreover, especially appropriate for the congregation, which is predominantly Spanish, and is particularly suitable as a setting for the Murillo *Madonna and Child* which is the focus of the chapel. The architect was Joseph Sanford Shanley of New York City.

A wrought-iron screen with a gate on center marks the entrance to the chapel. This is designed in the Spanish tradition of two tiers of delicately wrought spindles forming a lace-like barrier, surmounted by a gilded and polychromed cartouche bearing the coat-of-arms of the Most Reverend Mariano S. Garriga, Bishop of Corpus Christi. Brownsville was then in the diocese of Corpus Christi, though it has since been raised to the status of a diocese, with the church as its cathedral. Bishop Garriga, who was the first native-born Catholic bishop in Texas, was himself a native of Port Isabel, the port of Brownsville. He had loved this church since his boyhood and was an enthusiastic participant in the entire project.

The floor of the chapel is paved with colored marbles laid in panels, the central one designed as a fleur-de-lys. The reredos of carved mahogany, gold-leafed, provides a rich background for the warm tones of the Murillo painting. Its salomonic columns, pediments, consoles, scrolls and finials carry the eye relentlessly and dramatically upward. The altar consists of a massive black marble mensa, supported by carved consoles of gold-toned marble.

The four slender lancet windows, two on either side wall, have been adorned with stained glass representing scenes from the life of the Blessed Virgin. These panels were made in Belgium from the designs of Joep Nicolas and are cut from the finest quality "Pot Metal" (antique glass) combined with painted miniatures coated and textured with silvery grisaille. Nicolas, a leading artist in stained glass, has depicted in a sequence of scenes the role of Our Lady in our salvation, with especial care to make her images in the glass resemble her likeness in the Murillo painting. A further function of the glass is to temper the brilliance of the Rio Grande sunlight.

The crucifix is an antique Spanish artifact of the Baroque period. The six silver candlesticks were especially made for the altar in designs of sixteenth-century character, and each is encrusted with a gold camel's head, the Stillman crest. They were designed and executed by Rambusch Decorating Company of New York City, who also produced such other furnishings as the tabernacle and sanctuary light.

The camel's head motif may be seen again in the heraldic carving of the green slate tablet on the left of the chapel. It, and the one on the right, were adapted from New England funereal stones of the seventeenth century. They were designed by A. Graham Carey and executed by Nancy Price at the John Stevens Studio, Newport, Rhode Island. The New England graveyard flavor of the tablets is appropriate to commemorate the Stillmans, who came from Wethersfield, Connecticut.

The Lady Chapel in the Cathedral of the Immaculate Conception, Brownsville, Texas. Photo: F. S. Lincoln.

The wrought-iron screen of the chapel. Photo: F. S. Lincoln.

The altar and baroque reredos containing the Murillo Madonna and Child. *Photo: F. S. Lincoln.*

A memorial tablet. Photo: F. S. Lincoln.

A memorial tablet. Photo: F. S. Lincoln.

The stone on the right reads:

OF YOUR CHARITY PRAY FOR THE SOULS OF
CHARLES STILLMAN
HIS WIFE ELIZABETH & THEIR KINDRED

the one to the left reads:

TO THE GLORY OF THE ALL MERCIFUL GOD
and in honour of the Blessed Virgin Mary this chapel was adorned in the Year of grace 1959 by Chauncey Devereux Stillman as a memorial to his great grandparents Charles Stillman 1810-1875 and Elizabeth Goodrich 1828-1910.

Mr. Stillman recalls that the rector told him that an art historian who had been traveling through Mexico, photographing and writing for a book, stopped off in Brownsville and "discovered" the chapel. He ecstatically told the rector that it was the finest in ecclesiastical work he had seen, finer than anything in Mexico proper. He was annoyed, however, and no doubt dismayed, when he learned that it was then only six months old.

In 1970 a fire bomb was thrown into the cathedral, causing smoke damage to the Murillo altarpiece (which was subsequently replaced by a copy) and damaging the reredos. Restoration has unfortunately not been up to the standard of the original workmanship. Fortunately these photographs show the chapel in its pristine glory, a modern gem of Baroque religious splendor.

The author is grateful to Mr. Chauncey Stillman for the information contained in this article.

Welfare Island Project

by

JOHN BARRINGTON BAYLEY

FOREWORD

IN 1970 the Metropolitan Museum proposed an expansion to house vast collections which it was in the process of acquiring—African and Oceanic art from the Rockefeller family, the Lehman Collection from the estate of Robert Lehman, and, in particular, the Temple of Dendur. The Museum wanted to consolidate its collections for maximum viewing and publicity. In opposition a group of citizens, deeply concerned with the pattern of growth which New York's cultural institutions were following, proposed a Museum of Man for Welfare Island.* They thought the site ideal in relation to the United Nations, and in relation to a park which might develop on the main part of the Island to the north.

At the same time city planners looked upon the Island as ripe for yet another housing development. This group thought it feasible that the museum and housing projects might be joined in a development on the southern side of the Island, preserving the open space to the north forever green.

Needless to say, these dreams were never realized, as New York society mobilized, instead, behind an aggressive expansion of the Metropolitan Museum above ground in Central Park west of Fifth Avenue.

The Island drawings can be looked upon today not only historically, but can be compared with the housing now complete which went up on Welfare Island as part of a utopian dream of New York.

What might have been a Museum of Man involving the International Cultural Community already established with the United Nations, is now an opportunity lost.

Architects were invited to submit plans which would show a museum and housing on the southern end of the Island, and their response was generous.

The drawings ran the gamut of styles. John Fulop's design had two superimposed glazed tubes containing monorails which ran around the shoreline of the island, serving the museum, housing, and shopping. His design had a great deal of glass and interpenetration of forms and recalled the early Russian experiments with modern architecture. Lawrence Randolph conceived a monumental structure like an Egyptian mastaba. The walls sloped inward and were blank. Down the middle there was a split which opened onto a series of courts. Brian Burr planned a museum for the Temple of Dendur encased in glass (similar to one now under construction in Central Park, a site lacking all sense of majesty). John Smith proposed a series of flat-roofed apartments and exhibition halls and a fine marina which had the aspect of a Scandinavian yacht club. John Barrington Bayley presented a classical solution.

It is ironic that at the moment New York unveils its new Welfare Island housing and so ends for all time the dream of open park land on the island, Vienna is creating a new channel in the Danube to form an island park.

ROBERT MAKLA

* The island is now called Roosevelt Island.

Plate I. East River Island Redevelopment Project by John Bayley, 1970. The imbarcadero and Museum of Man are at the bottom.

FIRST, I think that the name of the island should be changed from "Welfare" to "Blackwell's" Island in honor of the original owners. This is an example of *pietas* (a Roman virtue).

Blackwell's Island lies in the East River between 86th street and 53rd street to the west. This area from the East River to First Avenue is the most densely built up area in the world this side of Hong Kong. The island is thirty-three blocks long and an average cross-town block wide.

PLATE I shows the site with the towers of Manhattan on the west and the *gewerblandshaft* of Long Island City on the east. It is one of the most magnificent sites in the five boroughs.

On the prow of this island (visible to millions of citizens) would be placed the museum. The effect here would be the flat surface of the river and, rising from it and reflected in it and with reflections from it, the supreme classical form, the pedimented temple front. No other form carries as well over distances.

We have a ceremonial imbarcadero. This would be a floating landing stage attached to the terrace. The terrace is vast and meant for crowds. One can picture the busy water buses—Venetian *motoscafi*—plying from the U.N. and elsewhere, landing at our imbarcadero. Or occasions of state with the smart launches

of naval vessels discharging their precious cargoes, with flags flying and bands playing before some session of the General Assembly. Or just an old-fashioned Fourth of July with a flotilla of small craft assembled in honor of a fireworks display.

From the Terrace of Honor a monumental staircase with the easiest possible flights of steps rises to the portico of the Museum of Man. We ascend the Grand Stairway and pass between the columns of the portico—polished monoliths of Egyptian granite with Corinthian capitals. The ceiling of the porch is deeply coffered and gilt.

PLATE II. We walk through the giant portal, richly cased and reminiscent of the Pantheon, onto the floor of the vestibule figured in red, green, black, and white marbles, as is the floor of the Great Hall.

The Great Hall is not only a museum room but a civic reception room as well. The city has no proper reception suite for entertainments on a grand scale. (This is no longer true. The Custom House now provides such spaces.)

This great public building is a Museum of Man. The finest representation of the human form is in sculpture where we have the three dimensions without the adventitious effects of light so much a part of painting. In the hierarchy of the arts sculpture comes

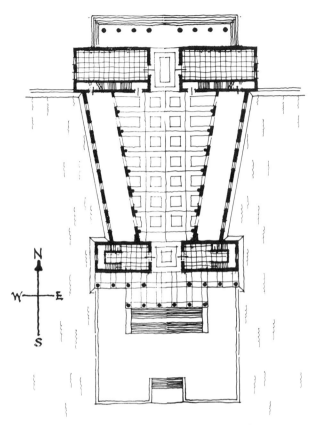

Plate II. Floor plan for the Museum of Man.

at the apex because it represents man best. The sculpture that shows man best is Greek sculpture; the Romans employed Greeks. I would propose that all the antique sculpture, including the Egyptian, in the Metropolitan Museum be brought here together with the coins, ceramics, mosaics, and paintings.

PLATE III. The Great Hall has a hung glass ceiling, or I should say that the coffers are glazed. The arcades to east and west are based on the first two stories of the Colosseum, the archetype for Roman courtyards. The room is based on the dining room of the Grand Hotel in Paris which has this same system of superimposed arcades. This room must have colossal works of sculpture. The effect of scale would be rather like the entrance hall of the Metropolitan Museum in the old days when there was scale. Let us imagine a great party. The room is thronged with people, and the statues loom over them. The courtyard of the Ecole des Beaux Arts had some magnificent effects of scale achieved with casts. We are always conscious of the great axis that runs through the room because of the colossal "portone" at either end—the great doors.

PLATE IV. The windows of the east and west walls go to the floor. The openings have a strong vertical axis. (A vertical window embraces the river and the sky, the foreground and the distance. A horizontal window fixes on the middle distance.) The

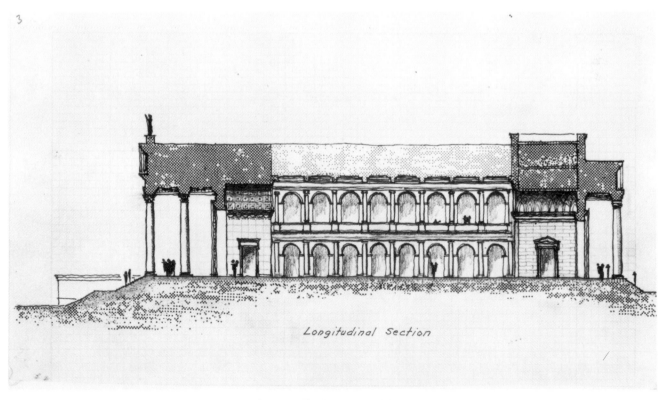

Longitudinal Section

Plate III. The Museum of Man.

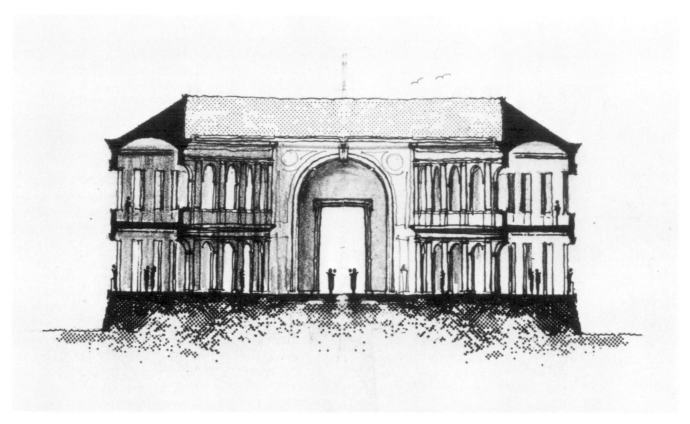

Plate IV. North portal and vestibule of the Museum of Man.

Plate V. North façade of the Museum of Man.

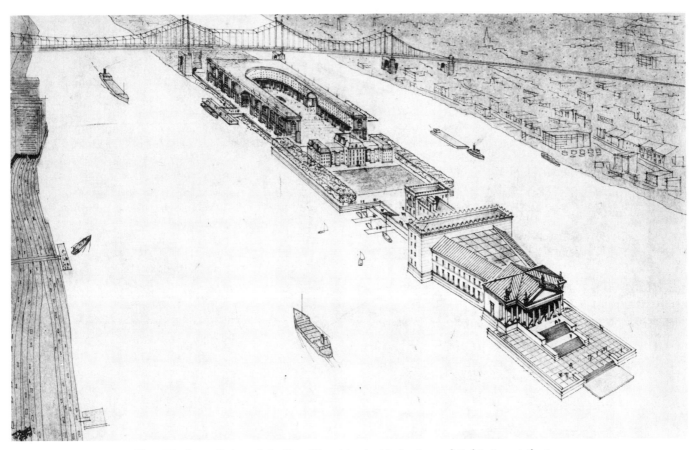

Plate VI. Over-all view of the East River island with the Area of Habitation at the top.

space between the windows is usable. The lambent reflections of light from the surface of the water would give that kind of light which can be enjoyed in the palaces of Venice or in some moated *château*—a constant lively shimmer.

The main body of the building has been given a wedge-shaped form to suggest the bow of a ship; the Ile de la Cité in Paris and the island in the Tiber have similar treatments.

We go through the north portal into the vestibule with exhibition rooms and offices to either side. The north and south vestibules have barrel-vaulted ceilings richly ornamented. They are, in fact, triumphal arches to emphasize the axis which gives coherence to the plan. (You always know where you are.)

To the north of the museum is James Renwick, Jr.'s Small Pox Hospital, a little fairyland Gothick castle, *circa* 1850, quite in the spirit of Thomas Cole and A.J. Davis. (Note: It is now a hopeless—not a romantic—ruin.)

After strolling on the lawn before this little *château d'Otrante* we turn and look to the south to the museum. Its north façade (PLATE V) is in the Dorian Mode—granitic, forbidding, and military as befits a treasure house. There are overtones from Poussin and Ledoux. The style of the structure owes nothing to the

Baroque; the site is so grand, the significance of the building so great that there have been no allowances made for charm or caprice, and the absolute ultimate in solemnity and grandeur and costliness has been employed, the architecture of Rome.

PLATE VI. This picture shows the over-all ensemble. The Museum of Man, the Renwick Gothick castle, and the second Renwick hospital of *circa* 1860.

The museum, the castle, and this hospital are all in granite. The hospital's mansard roof in copper, now a brilliant green (note: it is now being vandalized) is matched by the roofs of the museum with their gilded cresting. The hospital is set up on a *plateau* or tray. The French Second Empire design is continued in the larger rectangular *boulingrin* on the south side of the building. On both sides of the *plateau* are plantations of trees clipped architecturally with promenades beneath them. It is very agreeable to walk under a ceiling of verdure and to look at water while leaning on a parapet. Look the other way and there is the smooth green surface of the lawn ending in a line of gravel and the line of the parapet, and, above and beyond, the brightness of the distant landscape with the darkness of the clipped foliage above. This is one of the finest effects in classic French landscaping. It can be enjoyed in many places, but a particularly fine example is at Wethersfield House, Dutchess County, where you look out over a valley in just this way beneath clipped trees.

North of the *pavillons* of the hospital comes the Area of Habitation, a large interior court open on the south end to the hospital and closed on the end near the bridge by an *esedra*. In the court the first three stories have a colonnade. Behind the columns are shops, restaurants, cinemas, and saunas. Over the columns are four stories, fenestrated by high, widely-spaced French doors with balconies. On the roof there are elaborate penthouses (not shown). The façades on the river are made up of American Bays. The finest American Bays are on Grand Central Terminal. They are those large metal and glass closures in the Grand

Concourse; occasionally you will see people going back and forth on the glass-floored passages in them. This gives instant scale. There are others in the Cunard Building.

The American Bay is a device which fills in large classical openings with metal and glass, permitting a large room behind or several floors. In this case here on the Island there would be several floors with many glass-fronted loft-like apartments to each bay. There is a cross axis through the middle of the building with large arches giving onto the landing-stages for the water buses. The servicing of the building would be, as it was in so many Imperial Roman buildings, underground. There would never be a vehicle above ground south of the bridge.

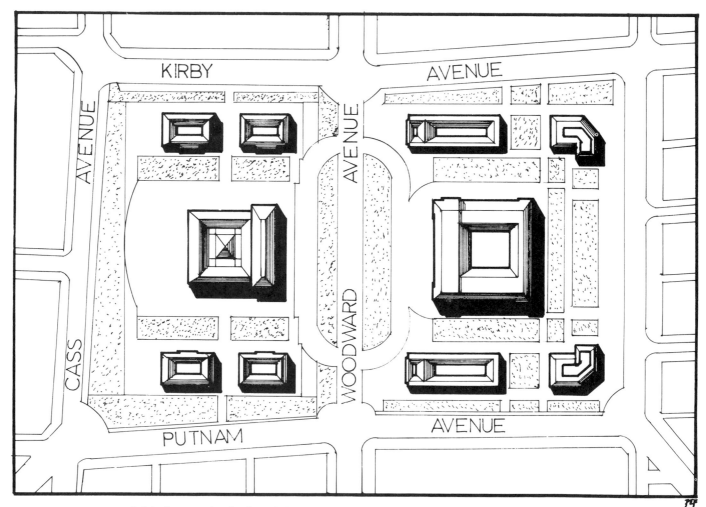

Original conception for Detroit Joint Art Center. The library was to be the first component.

The Detroit Public Library

by

PETER FEDERMAN

THE Detroit Public Library is a testimony to principles which are derived from the classicizing City Beautiful movement of the late nineteenth and early twentieth centuries. The library was designed by Cass Gilbert and, though compromises were forced in the original scheme, primarily as a result of pecuniary difficulties, the building which was constructed is marked by eurythmic unity of conception upon the exterior as well as inside. In effect, the unity of the exterior is achieved by the subordination and integration of its various components to each other, laterally and vertically, according to a symmetrical and proportional scheme; unity within is effected in each interior space by the subordination and integration of the smaller decorative units to the larger. In addition, numerous fine art forms have been utilized to adorn the library with ornament. Finally, all decoration is subordinated and integrated to the architectural setting in which it is placed. Thus the decorative elements of the library do not overly detract from nor outshine their larger environments, but rather are utilized to complement them. These then were the principles incorporated into the Detroit Public Library composition: unity of design, subordination and integration, and the use of various fine art forms of decoration. The consequent combination and use of these elements makes the library an outstanding monument both to the Beaux-Arts aesthetic and to the architectural taste of the period.

In 1901 the Detroit Board of Library Commissioners secured passage of an act of incorporation which gave it complete control over all library finances. As a result of this act, the Board was enabled, among other things, to accept gifts, to authorize the City to raise funds for library purposes with bonds, and to retain the title to property in its own name. In addition, shortly after passage of the foregoing act, the Board, by means of an intermediary, requested a gift from Andrew Carnegie. Carnegie responded to this request by granting $750,000 with the stipulation that one-half of this amount could only be spent on a "central" library.

Due to the political intrigue of the day, however, as well as to general public opposition, no Carnegie funds were accepted until 1910 and none earmarked for the main library were advanced to the Library Commission until 1917, when it received the amount of $375,000.

In the meantime, additional funds amounting to $750,000 were made available for construction of a new main library building when a Library Bond issue was passed in the Detroit general election of 1907.

After the passage of this first bond issue, however, little was done about the building of the new Main Library for some time. In fact, any definitive action towards the construction of a new main building was delayed until 1912, when condemnation proceedings were initiated which led to the purchase of a land site on Woodward Avenue between Putnam and Kirby, which extended westward to Cass Avenue. By the time the proceedings were terminated in 1913 the total cost of the site amounted to $1,194,349.72. As legal proceedings were taking place, a five-person inspection committee undertook a six-stage inspection trip in order to formulate the type of library building that should be constructed. On the tour the group was especially impressed by the St. Louis Library, designed by the architect Cass Gilbert. Apparently this structure fit the Committee's vision of a "plain, substantial structure of pleasing, dignified, and impressive appearance," that would reflect Detroit's reputaton as one of the leading cities of the United States.

After having completed its formulatory travels, the Commission retained as a consultant, Frank Miles Day, a prominent Philadelphia architect. It was Day's task to put the observations of the inspection committee into concrete drawings, specifications, and estimates. Thus, based on the Committee's desire that the library be built to house 750,000 volumes with the potential for further expansion, Day estimated that the building would cost $1 million. Additionally, Day advised a two-stage competition to select an architect for the building. The first stage was open only to Detroit architects, two of whom would then compete against four national entries. Consequently, sixteen Detroit architects submitted proposals, the most prominent among them being William B. Stratton, Malcomsen and Higgenbotham, Albert Kahn, and George D. Mason, while four national firms entered, these being Carrere and Hastings, McKim, Mead and White, H. Van Buren Magonigal Associates, and Cass Gilbert. The final choice of architect was to be decided by a three-person jury chaired by Congressional Librarian, Herbert Putnam, of Washington, and also including Paul Cret and John Mauran, both architects. The eventual result of the selection process was that Cass Gilbert of New York was awarded the contract for the library, and on June 4, 1913, Gilbert was duly notified by letter that his design was selected over the others.

As a consequence of winning the competition, Gilbert embarked on an extended trip to Italy during the summer of 1913, which lasted until November of that same year. The purpose of this expedition, as noted by a member of the Gilbert firm, was to make "several studies in connection with [the Detroit Public Library main building]." Among the places Gilbert visited were the Villa Papa Giulio, the Villa Madama, the Farnesina Palace, the Loggia of Raphael, and the Cancelleria. Apparently he often journeyed to Europe—the "Artistic Mecca," in the words of Librarian Adam Strohm—to seek inspiration for his work. It must be noted that Gilbert's journey to Europe for the express purpose of design studies was the normal practice among prominent architects of the time and of the City Beautiful movement—of which Gilbert was a noted member—for during this period the best architectural designs were based upon historical precedents.

Upon Gilbert's return to the United States, full plans for the main building were drawn up and approved by the Library Commission and during January 1915 excavation began. Excavation was completed in less than four months; however, after this point further construction did not progress so smoothly. Due to a decline in the national economy and a consequent lack of liquid funds for library construction, many commissioners doubted the sagacity of continuing the project beyond the excavation stage. However, Gilbert convinced the Library Commission to at least build the steel structure in order to take advantage of comparatively low steel prices as well as to provide employment. Thus, a contract was let out during May 1915 and by December 1915 the structural steelwork was completed.

The Commission's fears were realized however; after the framework was completed there no longer were funds available for the construction of the exterior and interior. A second bond issue had been defeated by Detroit voters in 1915. Furthermore, the Carnegie Corporation refused to release the $375,000 it had promised towards construction until that amount was needed for final completion of the structure. Hence, the library stood as a "naked skeleton of steel against the sky" until March 1917 when construction would begin again.

During the period of inactivity (1915-17) much criticism was directed at the Library Commission by politicians and the public concerning the mounting expense of the building, which incidentally had increased 50 percent from the approximate $1 million figure to $1,500,000. Out of this criticism grew proposals to cut expenses by using less expensive materials to complete the library. Nevertheless, this criticism was short lived and on November 8, 1916, a third bond issue for $750,000 was passed and then another for $250,000 in April, 1917. In addition, the Carnegie Corporation, apparently convinced that its contribution would be used to complete construction, sent checks amounting to $375,000 during December 1917.

Meanwhile, encouraged by the passage of the autumn 1916 bond issue, Adam Strohm and Cass Gilbert urged the Commission to renew work on the library building. Strohm also ordered sculpture work models from Gilbert, while Gilbert on his own initiative wrote up the specifications for the general construction of the library building.

Soon after, during March 1917, a contract for the completion of the building was awarded to the George A. Fuller Construction Company of Detroit. Various alterations of the original design were specified in a "List of Omissions" first issued during April 1917 and reissued during May 1917 in order to keep the still rising costs of construction at an acceptable level. Otherwise, work progressed successfully enough to permit an official cornerstone-laying ceremony on November 1, 1917. After this event, however, the pace of construction once again slowed, this time due to the material and labor shortages which resulted from World War I. Consequently, the actual completion of the building, including its decorations, was delayed until 1924. By mid-1921, however, the exterior façade and most of the interior spaces and ornaments had been finished. Accordingly, the Library was opened to the public on March 29, 1921, and was formally dedicated on June 3 of that same year.

Upon completion, the grounds and façade differed in various ways from the original conception. Initially, the building's main entrance on Woodward Avenue was to be approached by means of an entourage which, among other amenities, was to include a circular gravel walkway, stone fountains, statues, two seated sculptured figures by each side of the walkway, stone seats, and two stone vases one on each side of the main entrance. Also lost in actual construction was

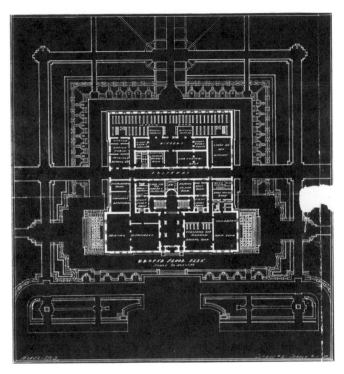

Gilbert's working design for formal treatment of the landscape.
Photo: courtesy of the New-York Historical Society, New York City.

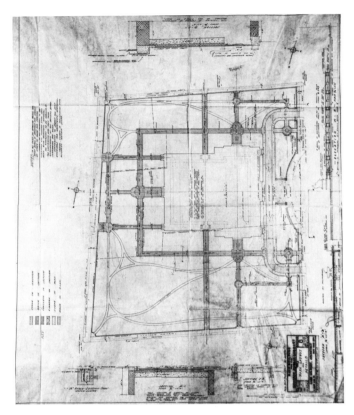

Gilbert's design for less formal treatment of the landscape. Photo:
courtesy of the New-York Historical Society, New York City.

a complete broad balustrade terrace surrounding the entire building which incorporated different brick pattern designs. In its place, two partially balustraded terraces were constructed, one on the Woodward Avenue front and the other on the Cass Avenue front. The balustrades on the Woodward Avenue terrace, however, eventually deteriorated and were replaced by metalwork. The Cass Avenue terrace was later demolished to make room for a library annex. Lastly, plans for the construction of a surrounding park layout were never executed, having been included with the other items listed on the registers of omissions dating from April and May 1917.

Upon formulation of the library plans, Gilbert had considered construction of one or two distinct park layouts. The first scheme consisted of gravel paths laid out in an informal manner with unsymmetrical curvilinear pathways. The second scheme was in a more formal Italian Renaissance style. In addition, its paths were brick as well as symmetrical and linear. Furthermore, this scheme was conceived in three dimensions, whereas the other was conceived in two. Neither of the plans Gilbert considered were used. Instead, a simple straight walkway leading from Woodward Avenue to the main entrance was constructed and still exists today. This plan did not in-

clude the construction of a surrounding park, but to Gilbert this replacement was "only temporary" and he hoped that ultimately funds would be provided for the construction of the entourage and park originally designed. In effect, Gilbert desired completion of the park layout "in order to complete the setting of the building."

The most noticeable omissions on the façade were seven statues originally to be placed in a loggia facing Woodward Avenue. Although provision was made in the completed loggia for the installation of these statues—peg holes were drilled—they were never installed, as Gilbert had come to believe that their presence would be a distraction from the façade as a whole. Also missing were various names which were to be inscribed in a belt above the main floor level. Originally there were to be at least seventeen names drawn from ancient Greek and Roman men of science and the arts, but only fourteen names on the front facing Woodward Avenue were inscribed. The last significant difference between the proposed and actual façade was the inscription over the main entrance, which was originally to read, "Free to All," but after objections from the Library Commission was changed to "Knowledge Is Power."

The façade itself is essentially Italian High Re-

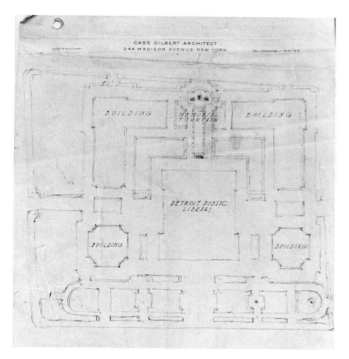

Cass Gilbert's sketch for Detroit Public Library main building with intended future additions indicated. Photo: courtesy of the Burton Historical Collection, Detroit Public Library.

naissance in style. Even the square shape of the building is reminiscent of the Renaissance; during this period it was a popular exterior shape for monumental buildings. It is important to note that the style of the edifice is not a direct copy of any one building, but rather is an individual modulation of forms within the more or less structured and methodical architectural vocabulary of the twentieth-century Classical movement. This helps to explain the light-colored stone of which the exterior is constructed: in classical design this color of material was most favored for exteriors of monumental buildings. However, though keeping to tradition in choice of color of material, Gilbert used as his material marble instead of limestone, which was more favored during the period.

The Library has four floors, although only three are visible from the frontal perspective, owing to the fact that the lowest floor is lighted solely by windows on the side elevations. The most dominant of the floors is the first one placed above the ground level. This is reflective of the Renaissance ideal of the *piano nobile*—where the first floor that is above ground level contains the most important rooms and hence is given the greatest architectural emphasis. This holds true in the case of the Detroit Public Library, as the most widely used and highly decorated rooms are located on this level. In addition the floor is a full 25 feet in height and along the exterior on three sides has a stately succession of imperial arches. The arches on the frontal façade are placed together in a group of seven, with two engaged arches detached from the central group, one on either side of the façade. There are also three groups of engaged arches at the sides. The group at the rear has since been obscured by the 1960s annex. In addition, above each of the front and the remaining side arches is a roundel in which is carved the head of some literary figure. The arches on the front and frontal side elevations are laterally complemented with pilasters that rise to the full 25-foot height of the floor.

Gilbert's original front elevation design, with loggia statues included. Photo: Burton Historical Collection. Detroit Public Library.

Loggia. Photo: Burton Historical Collection, Detroit Public Library.

Loggia, mosaic ceiling detail. Photo: Peter Federman.

Each of the two engaged frontal arches has a marble vase placed below it, while the central arcade forms a loggia. This loggia is the most distinctive feature of the Woodward Avenue façade.

The floor of the loggia is white tile with black tile inlays of Zodiac signs. Its ceiling, which was originally specified to be faced with terra cotta designs, was adorned with a mosaic pattern upon the insistence of Gilbert. Frederick J. Wiley of Detroit designed the mosaic, which was completed in the fall of 1919. By November 1920 it was installed by the famed Pewabic Pottery of Detroit, under the direction of Mary Chase Perry and H. J. Caulkins.

The subject of the mosaic decorations of the seven arches is Shakespeare's Seven Ages of Man from *As You Like It*. Each panel in the loggia measures 26 feet by 4 feet 5 inches and is divided into four sections by gold mosaic outline. Garlands and ornamental motifs connect the sections to each other, giving a sense of cohesiveness to the whole. At the acme of each arch there is a circular cartouche which contains an appropriate quotation from Shakespeare. At each side of the central cartouche is an octagonal cartouche within which are illustrated the different ages. Furthermore, within each panel are various animals and symbols which pertain to the appropriate

age. Lastly, the dark panels are separated by light-colored vaults which contain circular cartouches within which geometric shapes are inscribed. Extending from each of the vault cartouches are four projections. Two of these anchor each cartouche to the loggia sides and the other two are connected to projections from each panel. As a result of this interconnection, the loggia creates a sense of homogeneity and continuity which is "indicative of the continuity of life."

The floor below the loggia is marked by a feeling of massiveness and solidity which is created by the design of the front wall. This wall is characterized by three distinct sets of features, these being four small rectangular windows fronted by black wrought iron grilles, two rectangular faux windows carved into the marble of the façade, which are exact copies of the four small windows; and eight large, almost square windows, which are directly placed under the vertical divisions of the loggia story in order to achieve a sense of balance and continuity between floors.

The four small windows and two faux windows have been sublimated to the wall. Consequently, these features are treated more as applied ornament than architectural entities. In contrast to these, the eight larger windows are deeply recessed in order to stress

Main elevation on Woodward Avenue.

View from northeast.

View from southeast. Photo: Peter Federman.

Detail of window and urn, main elevation. Photo: Peter Federman.

Main entrance, Woodward Avenue. Photo: Burton Historical Collection, Detroit Public Library.

Detail of bronze doors, main entrance. Photo: Burton Historical Collection, Detroit Public Library.

their structural and architectural features. Thus, they function as architectonic entities. The end result of the treatment applied to the windows is a lower wall which appears to be pierced in only eight places instead of fourteen. Consequently, this treatment preserves the wholeness of the wall.

The story above the loggia is treated as an intervening frieze between the loggia story and cornice. It is pierced by square-shaped wall openings which correspond to each arch of the loggia floor. The sculptural panels set in this story are aligned one-to-one with the pilaster directly below them. The subjects of the panels are evocative of the signs of the zodiac and their equivalents in ancient mythology.

Located above the frieze is the cornice. With its exquisite spaced lion-head carvings the cornice is integrated into the entire façade rather than relating only to the frieze directly below it. This is an illustration of the careful attention which Gilbert paid to the vertical integration and subordination of the various horizontal levels. More explicitly, it is a result of Gilbert's precise and thoughtful lining up of the vertical elements within the façade in order to produce a rhythmic feeling of continuity between the levels. This vertical harmony in conjunction with the library's horizontal harmony results in the complete unity of the façade. The uppermost component of the façade is the cheneau executed in terra cotta and shaped into various white ornamental heads and designs on a gold background. The pilot-edged outline of the cheneau serves to define the crest of the building against the sky, thereby effectively crowning the façade. Visible above and behind the façade are two penthouses of yellow brick. A red tile roof called for in the original plans was supposed to cover these penthouses, but it was omitted from the design in 1917. An ajax roof was substituted in its place and though there was some desire on the part of the Library Commission eventually to install the tile roof, it unfortunately never was constructed.

At the main entrance to the building are two 15-foot high bronze doors which were designed by John Donnelly of the firm of Donnelly and Reilly, and crafted by the Polachek Bronze and Iron Co. in 1918. The design of the doors was influenced by the style of Donatello. Their theme was the five modes of ancient Greek and Roman literature—epic, tragic, lyric, philosophic and comic. Each of the two doors has five panels in bas relief, scarcely half an inch above the surface. The panels, with their simple detailing, are designed to be viewed from a distance as part of the edifice. Thus despite the significance of their theme, the doors are intended to be decorative rather than pictorial. This further stresses the importance of subordination and integration in the over-all design of the library's exterior.

In front of the main entrance is a terrace, which runs the full length of the Woodward Avenue façade. In the initial scheme there were fourteen bronze candelabra placed along four balustraded terraces. Only six candelabra were installed, however, two in lieu of marble vases on each side of the main entrance. Of the remaining four, two are located at each end of the terrace and two flank the entourage stairs.

The two main entrance candelabra are more elaborate than the others, owing to their greater height and more intricate design, consisting of floral motifs, vines, and classical-inspired bucranea. Each of these candelabra is further distinguished by the placement of windows with black iron screens behind them. The other four possess a similar but less intricate over-all configuration and lack the bucraneum motif. Each candelabrum is anchored on a lion-paw base and topped by a white glass globe.

Each of the two candelabra by the main entrance and its corresponding window is a balanced and harmonious unit owing to the design of the windows, whose dimensions are such that they do not detract excessively from the visual integrity of the candelabra. In addition, the candelabra were designed to oxidize to a black patina. Juxtaposed to the flat black window screens behind them, the black candelabra are another example of the principle of subordination and integration in the design of the library.

This principle can be seen working among all the components of the façade. In general it takes place along both horizontal and vertical lines, the former being achieved through the use of symmetry, and the latter by means of rising interrelation.

Initially, the Library had an automobile concourse which ran from Putnam Avenue through the lowest floor to Kirby Avenue. The purpose of the driveway was to facilitate pickups and deliveries from and to the Library. At each driveway entrance were two hand-forged bronze gates which, along with the driveway, were subsequently removed during construction of the later addition.

Ingress to the Library is gained by passing through the main doorway into a small entrance vestibule. At either side of the vestibule are entrances to two rooms; on the left the Newspaper and Periodical Room, and on the right, the Children's Reading Room. Beyond the vestibule is the entrance hall which at one time terminated in a statue niche. Eventually, the niche was removed in order to connect a new addition to the main library structure. The entrance hall now leads into a walkway which transverses the length of the building.

Ascending at right angles from the floor level of the entrance hall at its west terminus is a double stairway to the second floor, known as the Main Stairs. At the second-floor level is a large barrel-vaulted chamber—the Great Hall—which arches over the whole of the stairs and which also divides the building along its width.

Parallel to the eastern edge of the Great Hall is a long corridor. At the northern end of the corridor is the opening to the Music and Drama Room, while at the southern end is located the opening to the Civics Room. Bisecting the east wall of the corridor is the gateway to the Fine Arts Room.

Along the length of the western edge of the Great Hall is the portal to the Delivery Hall. Through the Delivery Hall entrance access can be gained to the Reference and Reading Room, the Open-Shelf Room, and the stacks. The accesses to the first two rooms are along the south and north walls, while the stack opening is directly opposite the Delivery Hall portal.

All of the public rooms of the Library with the notable exception of the Stack Room, are embellished with various types of applied interior decoration. In conformance with the ideals of the *piano nobile,* however, the rooms on the second floor are the most important and hence most lavishly ornamented. Likewise, as a result of its importance, the entrance hall on the first floor is accorded a similar application of artistic adornment. Also various key interior spaces are faced with pink-grey Tennessee marble stonework which was carved by the John Donnelly Co. Foremost among these is the entrance hall, which has a marble floor and marble walls. More significantly, the entrance hall contains twelve marble columns of Roman Doric style. Of these, four are engaged while the remaining eight are free-standing. In addition, until the erection of the new annex, there was a sculpture niche at one end of the entrance hall. Originally, a larger-than-life-size statue of Minerva was specified to be placed there; but it was on the 1917 list of omissions. Instead, a small bust of Commodore Perry was substituted in Minerva's place. Nonetheless, Cass Gilbert hoped that the Minerva figure would eventually be acquired and installed in the niche. In Gilbert's opinion, a Minerva, Goddess of the Arts would be highly appropriate in his "municipal temple to the arts."

At this end of the entrance hall are the twin portals from which the Grand Stairs ascend. The walls of the stairs, as well as the steps, bannisters, and balustrades are executed in Tennessee marble. In addition, above the first landing of each stairway is a carved panel faced with an angel motif. The walls of the Great Hall and the long corridor are also sheathed in marble up to their vaults. In addition, the wall separating the stair hall from the corridor is pierced with three large arched openings. The central opening is flanked with detached pilasters of marble. Each of the two other openings is flanked on its outer edge by an engaged

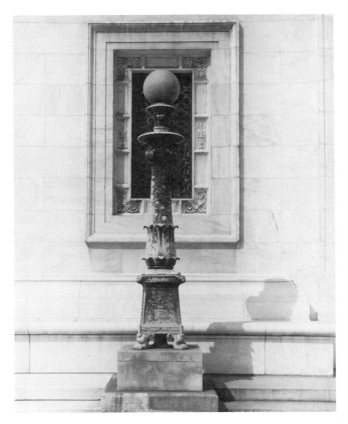

Bronze lamp standard and window with wrought-iron grille, ground story. Photo: Peter Federman.

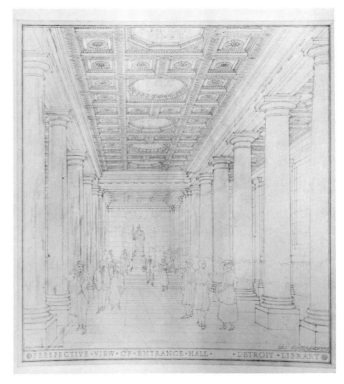

Main entrance hall with original end wall niche and intended statue of Minerva. Photo: Burton Historical Collection, Detroit Public Library.

Detail, vaulted ceiling, Grand Stair Hall. Photo: Peter Federman.

Original rendering for Grand Stair Hall. Note the architect's intention for lighting fixtures and conception of wall and ceiling decorations. Photo: Burton Historical Collection, Detroit Public Library.

pilaster. This pilaster arrangement is repeated along the opposite wall of the Great Hall and along the long corridor; however, in these cases all four pilasters are engaged.

Marble is also used at other locations. On the first floor the portals marking the main entrances into the Fine Arts Room and Delivery Hall are decorated with carved designs inspired by Italian Renaissance antecedents. Lastly, the Delivery Room is faced in grey Bedford Indiana stone. Twelve arched openings are provided, nine for windows and three for mural decoration. Between the arches are shields placed upon elliptical backgrounds which further enhance the ornamentation of the room.

Two basic methods in the decoration of the library's ceilings have been employed. The method used is contingent upon the structure of the ceiling. In rooms where the ceiling surface is flat and square or rectangular a design consisting of repeated geometric patterns is used. On the other hand, in rooms where the ceiling surface is vaulted with arches, the soffits, spandrels, architraves, and demi-lunes have received more elaborate and distinct treatment. All modeling for the ceilings was executed by the Donnelly and Reilly Company, and they were erected by McNulty

Brothers of Chicago. All ceiling painting was executed by F. J. Wiley.

In order further to acquaint Wiley with the style of ceiling ornamentation to be installed in the library, Cass Gilbert sent him to Italy during the winter of 1920-21. In Rome Wiley stayed at the American Academy, which was the center of Beaux-Arts activity. Among the sites Wiley studied were the Borgia apartments in the Vatican, St. Peter's Cathedral, the Loggia of Raphael, and the Villa Madama.

Consequently, Wiley's decoration of the Delivery Hall—where a large 75′ x 75′ flat ceiling surface was available—is modeled upon the symmetrical arrangement of caissons and rosettes in the small nave in St. Peter's. The octagonal caissons of the Delivery Hall are formed by light neutral grey beams. Along the beam soffits are molded plaster ornaments on pale green backgrounds and at each beam intersection is a gilded rosette. The ornamental moldings of the caissons are gilded and accented with deep reds, blues, and violets. In addition, at the center of each caisson is a large gold rosette in high relief against a dark blue background. Lastly, in order to make the transition between the elaborate ceiling and the comparatively severe stone walls, an intervening blue frieze with gold

Grand Staircase. Photo: Peter Federman.

Detail, Grand Staircase. Photo: Peter Federman.

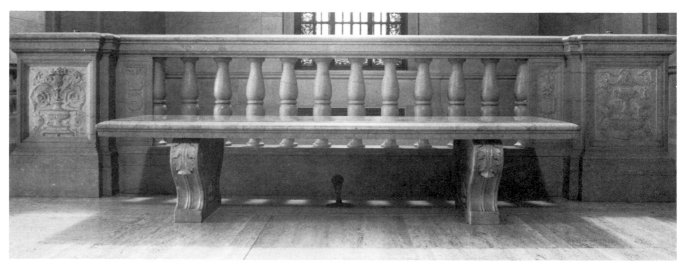

Marble bench, Grand Stair Hall. Photo: Peter Federman.

Entrance to Fine Arts Room from Main Hall. Wrought-iron door grille by Samuel Yellin. Photo: Peter Federman.

Delivery Hall ceiling detail and chandelier. Photo: Peter Federman.

letter inscriptions runs along the four sides of the room. In other rooms where the ceilings are decorated in a symmetrical manner, the applied ornament is less brilliant and ornate, but subtle coloring similar to that in the Delivery Hall has been used in them for effect.

The entrance hall ceiling is divided into three main sections by the columns. Each section is further divided into octagonal and square panels by flat beams ornamented with a Greek fret broken at intervals by rosettes. The octagons are alternated with squares and contain figures in low relief, grey-white on a red background, which are accorded cameo-like treatment. In each square is an ornamental composition which is relieved with gold and detached against a blue background. Gold is also used with grey on the ornamental moldings and white is used in some of the small square panels. As a result, the over-all effect of this room is rich and quiet.

The design for the ceiling of the Fine Arts Room is derived from the Church of Santa Maria Maggiore in Rome. The walls are capped with a frieze which is made into panels by pairs of brackets equally spaced about the room. Each panel is filled with delicate arabesques that are suggestive of the designs of Pompeian grotesques. The ceiling is divided into squares by beams which are decorated in relief and rosettes are in the centers of many of the squares. The walls are a

soft mulberry tone whereas pale yellow and grey-blue are used in the frieze. The beams are colored blue and green, ornamental rosettes and moldings are pale yellow and grey.

The ceiling of the Music and Drama Room is reminiscent, in its general design, of the Ducal Palace in Mantua. It is divided by beams into octagonal areas and at each beam intersection is a gilded lyric mask relief. Many center panels contain blue colored rosettes, and the ceiling is colored dull-grey which is relieved with shades of gold, red, and green. The walls are painted a subdued shade of blue.

Patterned after a ceiling in the Doge's Palace in Venice, the ceiling of the Civics Room is divided into oblong squares by a four-inch round molding of floral character. The intersections of the molding are marked by a rosette. At the center of each square is a larger rosette and in place of the four central squares is a large picture of "Wisdom Counseling Statesmanship." Along the frieze below the ceiling is a series of semicircular drums separated by triangular modillions which connect the ceiling to the yellow walls. The frieze is further decorated with arabesques and circles containing portrait heads. The ceiling is colored blue, light-grey and gold, the gold being used on all moldings and rosettes and the grey on the other ornaments.

The ceilings and walls of the Open Shelf and Reference Reading Rooms are very similar to each other. The ceiling of each consists of a pattern of hexagons and small triangles defined by a thin, round molding; in the center of each hexagon and triangle is a gilded rosette. A grey, flat band runs on either side of the molding. The background of the rosettes in the squares is grey, while the background of those in the triangles is red. The general hue of the ceilings is yellow-grey.

By far the most imposing and most important ceiling in the Library is the barrel-vaulted ceiling of the Great Hall above the Grand Stairway. Here, four wide bands of ornamental relief divide the ceiling into five main sections. These bands cross the vault from east to west and are consequently subdivided into oblong panels separated from each other by round or hexagonal cartouches. These cartouches contain bookmarks, printers' devices, emblems, escutcheons and various other ornaments with a bibliographic theme. In the dividing bands are four oblong panels, each of which contains a seated figure symbolizing some form of arts or letters.   The interlace ornament which forms part of the four bands follows the intersection of the pendentives. It is executed in relief and gilded over a background of color. The three middle sections into which the vault is divided follow a similar pattern of subdivision. Each has an ornamental octagon modeled in relief and edged with gold in the center of the group. A gilded fret on a blue background surrounds this

Drama Room ceiling detail. Lighting is a later addition. Photo: Peter Federman.

Civics Room, ceiling detail. Lighting is a later addition. Photo: Peter Federman.

central panel and serves as a border to rectangular panels, which are flanked by cameo-like cartouches of Pompeian flavor. In the panels of the center section are the inscriptions—LETTERS, ARTS, HISTORY, SCIENCE. The panels of the two lateral sections contain the seals of the United States, the State of Michigan, The University of Michigan, and the City of Detroit.

The main sections to the south and north of the room contain large rectangular panels bearing an inscription and smaller panels on either side with the names of distinguished authors.

The arched vault has six penetrations, three on each side. Four of these are adorned with ornaments in relief. Each of the two side vaults on the east contain a vase in the center typifying the fountain of Pirene, flanked by the winged horse Pegasus. Each of the central penetrations contains a single figure. On the west wall is "Inspiration" seated on an eagle, and on the east "Genius" on a winged horse. The color is predominantly green-blue with gold ornamental lattice work and deep antique gold colored moldings, relieved with shades of grey.

The ceiling of the Long Corridor—located east of and parallel to the Great Hall—is integrated with the ceiling of the Great Hall by the use of a common color scheme. The corridor ceiling consists of seven sections separated by arches. Each section has four triangular panels formed by the intersecting vaults, the groins of which are ornamented with the same latticework used in the decorations of the barrel vault.

The four panels of each section at the north, central, and south ends are ornamented with architectural frames in stucco relief. Each panel contains a seated representative figure. Each of the remaining four sections in the corridor shows two standing figures in architectural frames. Additionally, each of these four sections has two ornamental torches with two standing figures.

The seven broad and two narrow arches—one at each end—which divide the corridor ceiling into its seven parts are themselves subdivided into three distinct panels by two hexagonal shaped roundels. The hexagonal roundels at the south and north ends contain painted allegorical figures, and the roundel designs upon the remaining arches alternate between allegorical figures and panels. The walls of the corridor have figures modelled in low relief over the doors to the Civics, Fine Arts, and Music and Drama Rooms. The general color of the walls is a red-pink.

In effect, the many and varied ceilings within the Library constitute a combination of form and color that is reflective of the spirit of the Roman, Florentine, and Venetian schools of the sixteenth century. During this period, the practice of combining relief surfaces

produced by stucco, with flat surfaces ornamented with painted compositions, came into favor. Also during this time, soffiti ceilings were extremely popular.

Successfully incorporating the ideals of this period, the ceilings of the Library are subtle and rich in design. Their beauty, however, lies not only in their fine and subtle ornamentation and coloring, but also in their controlled restraint. Every ceiling is subordinated so as not to be too distracting or overbearing in relation to its surroundings. As a result each ceiling is coordinated into its total environment. In essence, the use of reserve, subordination and coordination in ceiling designs is derived from Italian Renaissance architectural canons which were incorporated into the American school of Beaux Arts architecture.

During November of 1920 Gilbert recommended to the Library Commission that Edwin Blashfield, the most prominent mural painter of the day, and the well-known Detroit artist Gari Melchers be used to execute murals for placement in the Great Hall and Delivery Room. As a result, on December 20, 1920, invitations were extended to Blashfield and Melchers and by December 23, 1920, both had received and signed contracts to do their respective murals.

Blashfield eventually painted five murals for the Library: one in a lunette over the portal leading into the Delivery Hall, two in arched tympana on the west wall of the Grand Hall, and two in the lunettes at each end of the Grand Hall.

The canvas over the portal is titled "Joining Of The Ways." In the foreground are two figures clasping hands. The one on the left is representative of the region of the Great Lakes and the one on the right is Detroit. Behind the figures stands the symbolic figure of the City of Detroit with the shield of the City against her knee.

The northern tympanum symbolizes music. In its center is ecclesiastical music: a monk leading a choir of boys. Above this is classical music and below, opera.

The other tympanum panel symbolizes the graphic arts. In the center a man and a woman—Greek and Gothic architecture—respectively hold models of the Parthenon and the cathedral of Chartres. Above them, a spirit on Pegasus flies upwards as two other figures throw wreaths and palms to a group of artists standing below. In this group from left to right are: Giorgione, Donatello, Titian, Raphael, Rembrandt, Rubens, Michelangelo, Tintoretto, Velasquez and, seated, Durer.

The canvas in the south lunette symbolizes poetry. In the corner stands a Muse before whom stand two children who hold an inscribed tablet. To the Muse's left are the poets Pindar, Virgil, Dante, Petrarch, a troubadour symbolizing the beginning of modern poetry, St. Francis of Assisi, Spenser, Corneille,

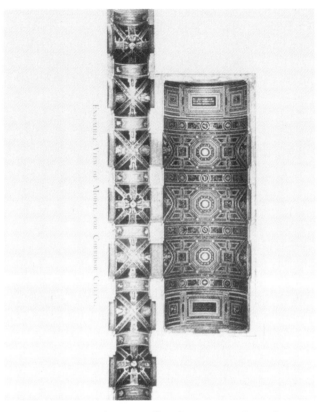

Design for Grand Stair Hall and Main Corridor ceiling.

Main Corridor.

Main Corridor ceiling detail. Photo: Peter Federman.

Main Corridor ceiling detail. Photo: Peter Federman.

"Joining of the Ways" mural by Edwin Howland Blashfield in Grand Stair Hall. Photo: Peter Federman.

Racine, Victor Hugo, Shelley, Tennyson, Wordsworth, Browning, Poe, Whitman, and Longfellow. To the Muse's right are Chaucer, Shakespeare, Milton, Molière, Calderon, Goethe, Schiller, and the musicians—Bach, Handel, Mozart, Beethoven, Rossini, Verdi, Gounod, and Wagner.

The north lunette picture depicts prose. Like poetry, a Muse with two children holding an inscribed tablet—LETTERIS ARTIBUS—occupies the center of the composition. To the right of the Muse are Galileo, Newton, Rabelais, Luther, St. Augustine, Erasmus, Boccaccio, Rousseau, Voltaire, Stevenson, Dickens, and Thackeray. Across the bottom are Dumas, Balzac, Stendhal, Emerson, and Carlyle. To the right of the Muse are Aristotle, Plato, Plutarch, Leonardo da Vinci, Montaigne, Bacon, Cervantes, La Fontaine, Macaulay, Gibbon, Michelet, and Howells.

Across the bottom are Fielding, Defoe, Johnson, Swift, and lastly, Scott.

In two of his three panels, all of which are located on the east wall of the Delivery Hall, Gari Melchers pictures actual events in the early history of Detroit. The panel on the left is entitled "The Landing of Cadillac's Wife" and represents the arrival of Madame Cadillac and Madame Tonty at Fort Pontchartrain in 1703. The right panel depicts "The Conspiracy of Pontiac," an event where the great Indian chief was blocked in his attempt to massacre the British garrison at Detroit. The two pictures show events from the French and English rule in Detroit.

The central panel is entitled "The Spirit Of The Northwest." Instead of being historical it is somewhat allegorical and romantic. In its foreground stand the pathfinder and the trapper. In the background is a belt

"Poetry" mural by Edwin Howland Blashfield, Grand Stair Hall. Photo: Peter Federman.

"Prose" mural by Edwin Howland Blashfield, Grand Stair Hall. Photo: Peter Federman.

"Music" mural by Edwin Howland Blashfield in Grand Stair Hall.   Photo: Peter Federman.

"Graphic Arts" mural by Edwin Howland Blashfield in Grand Stair Hall. Photo: Peter Federman.

of the Detroit River, the tip of Belle Isle and the Canadian shore. A birch bark canoe is the central figure of the gilded laurel border at the bottom of the picture. In addition, hovering in the midst of the picture is Sainte Claire; on St. Claire's Day La Salle, who navigated the first vessel through the Great Lakes, entered a lake and named it Lake St. Claire in appreciation for his safe passage. Though they have always been popular, the Melchers murals are less purely decorative in character and more narrative or illustrative. In color, too, they lack the warmth and richness of Blashfield's work.

Each entrance to the Delivery Room culminates in an ornamental entablature. Within each entablature is a frieze decorated with the following motifs: a cow's skull; a book, representative of knowledge; a lamp, typifying enlightenment; an owl, illustrative of wisdom; a torch in combination with books, symbolic of enlightenment as well as knowledge; and the following printer's marks: Thielman Kerver, Paris, 1488; Johann Gruninger, Strasbourg, 1483; Foulis Press, Glasgow, 1740; Aldus Manutius, Venice, 1494; Chiswick Press, London, 1811; and the New York City Coat of Arms, 1733. In addition, every entrance is composed of three openings, which are separated by elaborate bronze pilasters and columns crowned by Corinthian capitals. The motifs found on the frieze are also used to decorate the pilasters and columns. Also within the Delivery Room are nine large arched window openings which are surrounded by bronze work decorated with a lamp motif. Below each opening are three grills which incorporate floral, shield, and fish ornamentation. The mullions of each opening are decorated with a rope network, with a rivet placed at each intersection. Every piece of bronze work exhibits low relief and dark color. The over-all mood of the bronze work is very low key—subtle, soft, and delicate.

The main entrance of the Delivery Hall parallels that of the Fine Arts Room. At the Fine Arts Room entrance is a wrought iron gate of delicate workmanship styled in the tradition of the Italian Renaissance. The gate was designed by Samuel Yellin and fabricated by the John Polacheck Bronze Co. in 1920.

Initially most rooms in the Library were lighted by suspended chandeliers which have now been replaced by recessed lighting panels. The panels are less distracting than the chandeliers because the ceilings in these rooms are too low for rows of hung chandeliers to appear aesthetically pleasing. The recessed lighting panels help to preserve the lines and integrity of the rooms in which they are placed. Areas, however, where chandeliers remain and do complement their rooms are the Delivery Hall, Entrance Hall, and Long Corridor. Chandeliers which also remain but detract from, rather than complement, their room are found in the Great Hall, which initially Gilbert desired to have lighted by four pedestal lamps, one on each cornerpost of the stairway, and where he always opposed the placement of chandeliers. In effect, at this location the chandeliers are intrusions into the general decorative harmony of the Hall; besides obscuring the Blashfield murals and some of the Wiley decorations, the light cast by the chandeliers is uneven, either placing the ceiling ornaments in light too brilliant or too dull. The installation of the pedestal lamps which Gilbert specified would have produced a more even and acceptable level of illumination for the Great Hall, producing the "Perfect lighting for the murals [and ceiling ornaments]" that he desired.

Additional illumination in the Great Hall is achieved by means of two large windows, one at each end of the Hall. These windows were originally plain glass, but as they permitted views of the blank brick walls of the light courts behind them, they were deemed inappropriate. In fact, in a letter dated June 28, 1920, Cass Gilbert wrote to Adam Strohm:

> The large windows in the Grand Stairway are unsatisfactory in appearance. It was my intention to provide stained or leaded glass for said windows. . . plain glass was substituted in place thereof.
>
> It is my opinion that whatever is done should be done properly and no compromise adopted. Using frosted or slightly colored glass would hardly improve matters, due to the very simple lines in the frames and muntins.
>
> The windows are in a prominent location and leaded or stained glass of a suitable design should be provided. . . .

As a result of Gilbert's desire, F. D. Wiley was authorized to draw up and submit plans to the Library Commission for new windows during October 1920. The only restriction put upon Wiley by Gilbert was that the windows, "Should be simplified. . . so that they should not compete with Mr. Blashfield's decorations," but rather should complement them. Consequently, funds were made available for the windows and on December 21, 1920, the window proposal was formally accepted by the Library Commission.

By the end of 1921, both windows were completed and installed. Technically, the windows are designated as "vitrals" after the French word *vitrail*. The term "vitral" defines a bay which admits light into a building through a mosaic of colored glass sutured by lead. The vitrals of the Library are "quarry" windows, made of painted glass cut into squares in the Italian Renaissance manner. The design of these vitrals was inspired by Italian Renaissance precedents (especially by the windows in the Audito del Colloquio in Florence by Giovanni da Udine) and includes adaptations of decorative motifs treated in bronzework, which are found in the marble work and mosaics of the Library. Both vitrals are framed with a rich border composed of picture panels. In the center of each window is an oval cartouche set in an ornamental frame. Garlands of ornamental laurel descend from the composition.

The north vitral portrays Study, Art, Music, and Painting in the side panels and contains the inscription "Conata Perficio" in the panel at the bottom. The central cartouche is surmounted by two amorini and supported by a winged angel.

The south vitral portrays Meditation, Sculpture, Music, and Geography in its symbolical inserts. In its bottom section is the inscription, LABORE VINCES. As in the north vitral, the central cartouche is surmounted by two amorini but here it is supported by two females as well as a winged angel.

These vitrals were very well received. Adam Strohm commented to Gilbert that they were "like an illuminated title page from the 17th Century." In fact, they were so popular that the Library Commission decided that vitrals should also be installed in the Delivery Hall. As a result, a contract for the installation of clear cathedral glass in the Hall's nine windows was canceled and F. D. Wiley was authorized to draw up designs for nine vitrals in their place.

The first two windows were ordered on March 14, 1922, and by December 1922, they were installed. The remaining seven vitrals were erected and installed as funds periodically were made available for them. In order to preserve a unity of design, Wiley was retained as sole artist.

Of the nine vitrals, the three on the west wall are presently bricked over on the exterior and obscured on the interior by a hideous and banal canvas mural dating from the 1960s. The other six, three each on the north and south walls, remain intact. In harmony with the architecture of the rest of the building, the vitral designs are likewise inspired by Italian Renaissance precedents.

The middle north vitral is bordered with the classical egg and dart molding, broken by four panels at the top, bottom, and at either side. In its center is a cartouche set in an architectural frame of sculptural effect, with the base and top sections brought together by arabesques and uprights suggestive of the wrought iron grilles, or rejas, common to Spanish cathedrals. In addition, decorative attributes of the Renaissance, such as peacocks, griffons and sphinxes are used in the side pilasters, lintels, and bases. The cartouche represents an old wood-cut with medieval personages illustrating the verse:

O Truant Muse, What Shall Be Thy Amends For Thy Neglect Of Truth In Beauty Dyed?

The central vignette in the north right vitral contains a representation of the Muse Erato. Like the other Muses depicted, Erato resides within an architectural design of lintel and plinth with columnar uprights. Below the Muse are the symbolic figures of

Stained-glass window, Grand Stair Hall, by F. J. Wiley. Photo: Peter Federman.

Aquarius, while above her is a depiction of Apollo driving the horses of the sun through the clouds. At the top arch is an inscription by Shelley, "I walk upon the mountains and the waves."

Thalia is the Muse depicted inside the central vignette of the north left vitral. The figures of the zodiac presented here are Sagittarius and Capricornus; the top inscription, by Milton, reads, "And Cynthia checks her dragon yoke."

The central vitral of the south wall exhibits border and central cartouche treatment which is similar to that of the north central vitral. The central cartouche here contains a composition of woodcut effect illustrating the verse:

With Them The Seed Of Wisdom Did I Sow,
And With My Own Hand Sought To Make It Grow.

Above the cartouche, in a sculptural setting capped by an angel, is the inscription "Aspiro." Below the cartouche, seemingly inscribed on book bindings, is, "The greatest consulting room of a wise man is a library."

The vitral to the right contains the Muse Uterpe in a central architectural setting. Toward the top Venus is pictured seated in a chariot drawn by doves. Beneath Uterpe are the signs of Gemini and Cancer. The

Original conception of Delivery Hall without stained glass windows. Photo: courtesy of the Burton Historical Collection, Detroit Public Library.

Stained-glass window by F. L. Wiley, Delivery Hall. Photo: Peter Federman.

inscription vaulting the top is by Shelley, "Make me thy lyre even as the forest is."

The left south vitral is devoted to Melpomene, the Muse of tragedy. Above her is Mars in his chariot being drawn through the clouds by the dogs of war. The signs of the zodiac which are present are Aries and Taurus, while the inscription at the top is, "Let gorgeous tragedy in sceptred pall come sweeping by," by Milton.

The dominant color of the vitrals is the light grey of their plain glass. However, black-green, dark blue, yellow and red colored glass are used in the compositions in each vitral. The subtlety of the windows is in accordance with the stateliness of the Delivery Room where the main effect is of majesty and repose. The completion of the vitrals marked the end of further decoration done to the Library as desired by Cass Gilbert.

In effect, within the interior of the Detroit Public Library are found the same principles of subordination and integration that are present upon the exterior. Each unit of interior structure or adornment is purposely designed to be subtle and hence in no way to distract from its environment as a whole. Furthermore, each interior ornament is intended to fit only

Interior, Delivery Hall, with stained-glass window by F. L. Wiley and bronze portal. Photo: Peter Federmun.

into the space where it is installed. Essentially each unit is thought of as a complement of the larger composition in which it is set, ultimately culminating in the unit of the entire interior. Subordination and integration are employed to reinforce and cultivate the effects of refinement and control which are present in the interior spaces of the building.

The subordination and integration which so mark the design of the Detroit Public Library were also intended to be applied to a larger cultural complex. During 1913, when plans for the library were first drafted, a Joint Arts Center Committee was organized to study the feasibility of erecting a huge Joint Arts Center along Woodward Avenue with the library as a major facet of the grand plan. The committee's final design called for eleven buildings. Besides the library and an art museum on the east side of Woodward Avenue there was also to be a School of Design, a Philharmonic Hall, a School of Music, a Historical Society, a Horticultural Society, and four buildings for "Learned Societies." In addition, four buildings were to be grouped around the library and five about the art museum as annexes. The essential principle behind the design of the center was that each individual building would be subordinated to a dominating, all-embracing architectural plan. Consequently, the result would be the integration of each structure within the whole. Furthermore, according to a master plan for Detroit, the arts center was to be linked to the rest of the City by two major diagonal boulevards, one to Belle Isle Bridge and the other to the new Michigan Central Railroad Station. Such planning would not only have improved communication within the city, but would have resumed the baroque intentions of the city's original Woodward Plan. However, efforts to enact this master plan were fruitless.

Monumental and stimulating as this plan was, it was initially delayed by the 1913 recession, which prevented its financial backing, and by the time World War I had ended, its existence had been all but forgotten by civic leaders in Detroit. Unfortunately, no facets of the scheme were ever carried out, although the Detroit Institute of Arts was constructed across Woodward Avenue from the Library, but in a style which did not fully complement the design of the Public Library. An even greater misfortune is the two extensions that were added on to the Library in the early 1960s. Though designed by Cass Gilbert's son—Cass Gilbert, Jr.—they are totally unsympathetic to the style of the original building. In effect, they are mere shadows which do not stand up either to the restrained beauty of the Library or to the extensions which had originally been planned to complement the Library in the design of the Joint Art Center.

An important factor in the determination of the final form of the Detroit Public Library was the architect/client relationship. Gilbert's image of the library was not just as a large storage vault for books but rather as an illustrated example of culture itself. To stress the importance which he read into the library as a symbol, Gilbert naturally wanted only the best of everything, be it marble for the elevations or the foremost artists of the day to decorate the interiors. Importantly the librarian Adam Strohm was sympathetic to, and understanding of, Gilbert's preconception of the library building as a symbol and illustration of culture. Thus, the combination of Gilbert and Strohm was able to sway the Library Commission from any action which might have "cheapened" the final outcome of the library. Unfortunately the values toward buildings which Gilbert and Strohm held and which were indicative of their time did not persist until the new wings were added. If they had, the new wings undoubtedly would have been more successful in complementing Gilbert's original building in terms of decorative qualities.

POSTSCRIPT

Cass Gilbert's Public Library shares in the sickness that blights Detroit today. That sickness is not simply poverty and a dwindling population, which might have allowed the stately edifice to settle into a picturesque and benign neglect, like some marvelous grand Italian palazzo. Grime might then sink into its fabric and chinks and cracks appear in its worn stones. It could wear the scars of time proudly. Ours, however, is not an age of inactivity. We are never too poor simply to rest. We must be about—not our Father's business— but some sort of monkey business. Old libraries these days don't just fade away; they are kicked and prodded and tormented.

When the new wings were added to the Detroit Public Library, they were not merely unsympathetic in style but even more so in planning. Gilbert's plan brought the Library's users through noble bronze doors, past a stately and noble hall, up a sumptuously decorated staircase, and into the most magnificently proportioned and adorned space in the city. Here were the catalogues and access to the books. And along the way there was also to be absorbed a full course in monumental aesthetics and civics for which the neighboring Wayne State University might well have granted three credit hours. The only real luxury of civilization is beautifully adorned space. Detroit has plenty of empty space, very little of it beautifully adorned. And yet this prime example of luxury and visual splendor, for which its librarian had labored long, was now deemed superfluous. The remodeling of the Library, which pushed a corridor through the sculpture niche at the end of the entrance hall, carried users into a stripped-for-action, low-ceilinged card catalogue room, where they might briefly pause while in transit from the front to the back door. They might, that is, get the books without the "culture," at least without the heavy load of seemingly "corny" culture designed by the architect. This lesson the city of Detroit has learned only too well.

Robbed of all function, the Delivery Hall today stands empty and desolate. On one side Gari Melchers' murals evoke a simple, quaint, idealistic past. On the other side a grotesque, post-remodeling mural, concocted presumably by a sign painter, ominously suggests that the city—or civilization—is in the hands of some demon monster of transportation. At least the Wiley vitrals, however, are still behind the plaster board, awaiting excavation by a more enlightened age. Meanwhile, the Delivery Hall might make a sumptuous setting for official civic functions—a mayor's inaugural ball or the reception of whatever distinguished visitors come to Detroit today. Instead, however, its walls are often covered over with temporary display hoardings, and book fairs and other clutter functions set up their tents within its walls.

The entrance hall, too, knows no repose. Its bronze doors have been masked by a flimsy year-round wooden storm door. Ugly booths, dispensing all sorts of leaflets and litter abound on both sides of the hall, destroying the impact of Gilbert's colonnades. And the usual array of ephemeral handbills disfigure the walls. All of this clutter announces the fact that the Library is an "information" dispensing center, not merely a repository of books and civilized culture. These functions could, of course, be adequately discharged from a suburban warehouse, and no doubt they soon will be, if Detroit's librarians have their way.

In the area originally conceived of as the Joint Arts Center, there also has been activity of late. All additions, both to the Library and to the Art Museum were, of course, made in styles and plans differing from the original conception of the architects and planners of the Center. Other buildings in time were erected surrounding the monumental core, some not unattractive in themselves. However, no continuing and consistent thought has been expended to achieve a co-ordinated and unified scheme. Recently, in spite of the city's near collapse, an art school and a science museum have been erected in the area, brought there, no doubt, not by any lingering nostalgia for a Beaux-Arts forum of the arts, but to huddle close to the older institutions for comfort in the modern municipal wasteland. In place of the still-born boulevards which might have brought visitors into the area in leisure and elegance, expressway spurs have bulldozed their way through the surrounding decay to whisk suburban visitors in and out of the collected institutions. There is no temptation to linger when one's business or cultural errand is done. And nothing to do if one had such a perverse desire.

In tormented, "problem-oriented" Detroit today there is, it would seem, little time for the visions and ideals of the past. They would probably be dismissed as the affectation and dead cultural machinery of a repressive upper-class ascendancy of former days. Civilization there is not cumulative but discontinuous. "Renaissance" in Detroit now refers not to the style of Gilbert's library but to the towering glass chimneys of a development precinct clustered by the river in which the city vests its hope for survival. The word "renaissance" is a misnomer here. These towers, huddled behind a fortress wall, recall not the opening up of civilization in the Renaissance but the medieval castle fortress, barricaded against barbarian onslaughts from without. In such an atmosphere Detroit today needs to retrieve not information but wisdom and values. It could do worse than to commence that task of reconstruction and reconstitution by attending to the words, images, ideas, and ideals emblazoned upon or shining forth from Cass Gilbert's Public Library.

THE EDITOR

A garden room with trompe l'oeil decorations by Hight Moore. Photo: John Bayley.

A Trompe l'oeil Flower Room

by

HIGHT MOORE

WHEN I first saw the room it remained as designed in the late 1930s for one function—to arrange cut-flowers from the garden—and was called, appropriately enough, the "flower room." It was a small room, only nine by eleven feet, with access from the garden through french windows. It had an attractive brick floor, the only furnishings being a copper sink set into an oak work counter which was balanced on the opposite side of the room by an eighteenth-century Bavarian stove of superlative quality.

Through the years the room retained its function but had become a catch-all when the owner asked me what could be done to make it more cheerful. He had a concept of what he wanted and it was only a question of bringing it into actuality. Starting with the playful rococo of the existing stove and the owner's love of the eighteenth-century villas on the Brenta, the design

of the room was an easy collaboration of patron and artist.

As is appropriate for a *trompe l'oeil* room, it was all done with paint alone, with no structural changes or embellishments. The only actual three-dimensional detail on the wall is the pre-existing door frame, a single half-round molding at the top of the illusionistic cornice, and a chain rail. The end result is a room of a light and happy character and part of the active life of the house.

Color plays an important part in the scheme of the room. Against the white of the walls, the *trompe l'oeil* architectural details, i.e. the dado, cornice, ceiling panels, etc., are in a pale mauve, with the actual door frames and back splash of the sink in *faux marbre* of mottled lilac. The rocaille-and-vine motifs are in a strong green, as are the rocaille frames of the two

The painted door frame in faux marbre *surmounted by a painted relief in a rocaille frame. Photo: John Bayley.*

113

Detail of the rocaille-and-vine- motif panels. Photo: John Bayley.

reliefs, the one over the door and the other over the sink. The details of the reliefs are white, like the stove, against a soft terra cotta background which echoes the brick floor. The colors of the room make an easy transition from the colors of the garden outside, just as the formalized foliage makes the transition from the actual foliage of the garden.

The relief over the door represents a pair of rustic nymphs, of water and woods. Over the sink, where the flowers are arranged, the relief is a garden scene of a harvest of flowers.

The Bavarian rococo porcelain stove, backed by rocaille and vine panels. Photo: John Bayley.

A painted relief panel and frame. Photo: John Bayley.

Horace Trumbauer, Elkins Park, and Classicism

by

ANDREW M. WALLERSTEIN

ELKINS Park, Pennsylvania, has never been an average town. When Charles II's land grant brought English colonists to Pennsylvania, the village was among the first to be established. In 1682, the same year as the founding of Philadelphia, the future Elkins Park was settled nine miles to the north. Germans soon joined the English and gave the name of a leading local family to the place, which thereafter was to be long known as Shoemakertown. Its importance increased in 1764 with the opening of the highway now called Old York Road, passing through Shoemakertown en route from Philadelphia to Elizabethtown Point, New Jersey, where travelers boarded the ferry for Manhattan, and which was the main road between New York and Philadelphia into the present century.

Following the Civil War, Elkins Park became the country home of Philadelphia's new money. None of the first arrivals among the town's millionaires was wealthier than Jay Cooke, the financier; a common expression in America at the time was "as rich as Jay Cooke." During the 1860s, Cooke designed and built for himself the prototype of any Elkins Park mansion, his idea of a French chateau. It had a mansard roof, heavy stone walls, and too many Victorian features for it to be termed classical. The immense structure, no longer standing, was named Ogontz after an Indian chief who was a friend of Cooke's father. Shoemakertown soon changed its name to that of the estate.

By the turn of the century, the community abounded in the vast mansions of the rich, along with the big houses of the well-to-do. When the Reading Railroad erected the present station in 1899, the stop was renamed—over his objections—for William L. Elkins, a local resident and director of that company. In a few years, the town also adopted the new name, for by the time Cooke died in 1905 (and was buried there), Elkins Park had even richer and more famous inhabitants.

Today Elkins Park remains one of Philadelphia's most beautiful suburbs. The charm of the town derives not only from its natural setting but also the taste over the years of its dwellers and the artists in their employ. Fitting into both categories was Horace Trumbauer, one of the most important architects of the American Renaissance, who more than any other person contributed to the appearance of the place. In 1878, when he was nine years old, his family moved to Jenkintown, a village immediately adjoining Elkins Park. Although he much later took up residence outside the area, he never from the beginning of his private practice in 1890 until his death in 1938 ceased to design structures for Elkins Park and its surrounding towns, such as Abington, Glenside, Jenkintown, Oak Lane, and Wyncote. In fact, Trumbauer's entire development as an architect can be traced in the more than fifty buildings, all within walking distance of each other, that he created for the neighborhood, an unusual living architectural museum that also contains the work of such divergent architects as Carrère and Hastings, Charles A. Platt, Ralph Adams Cram, Frank Lloyd Wright, and Louis I. Kahn, to name only a few.

Although this article follows Trumbauer's development as a classical architect, a frank admission must be made that throughout his career he designed his country architecture, including that at Elkins Park, in not only the classical but also a variety of other traditional styles. Gothic, Elizabethan, and Tudor he found as well-suited as classical to rural settings beyond the formality of cities, where he used the classical almost exclusively. The nonclassical styles in the mainstream of Occidental architecture were being revived along with classicism; it was the Victorian secessionists and precursors of modernism on whom the designers of the new age were turning their backs.

When at age twenty-one Trumbauer opened his own office, which was in Philadelphia, the American Renaissance was even younger than he. The decisive switch to classicism was not to come until 1893 with the World's Columbian Exposition, held in Chicago. Trumbauer's early buildings in and around Elkins Park show him setting aside the romantic notions earlier prevalent for the new classical movement. At this stage, however, neither he nor American architects as a whole were yet making use of many classical elements.

Trumbauer's "big break" came about, oddly enough, through the destruction of one of his own works. The Glenside home of sugar merchant William

Grey Towers Castle. Photo: courtesy of Beaver College, Glenside, Pennsylvania.

Welsh Harrison, which the architect had thoroughly remodeled, was destroyed by fire in 1893. Harrison decided—probably with Trumbauer's prodding—to replace it immediately with Gray Towers, now the main building of Beaver College. The exterior of the mansion is Gothic, based partially on Alnwick Castle in England. Gray Towers contains some beautiful classical interiors, such as the Rose Room and the ballroom. The first of his residences of the scale and splendor for which the era is noted brought the architect to the attention of many rich potential clients, whose special admiration for the classical rooms was quickly recognized by the young Trumbauer, who had a talent for business as well as design.

His medium-size residences of this early period are usually without classical touches, except for occasional features in interior woodwork. Bend Terrace, the Wyncote house he had designed in 1892 for H. K. Walt, is Richardsonian in the solidness of its stonework. The large, sharply-sloping roof and the zig-zag decoration at certain eaves are probably due to the influence of Frank Furness, whose fame must have appealed to his younger fellow-Philadelphian.

These commissions were too important to experiment with, so Trumbauer tried his hand at the emerging classical style with small houses. In 1892, the same year as Bend Terrace, he had designed a house for Howell Bean far more advanced than its neighboring homes in a Victorian section of Elkins Park. Although a clapboard house, the over-all shape of the structure, with its blanketing roof and octagonal tower, brings to mind the shingle style, which was then in fashion. The classical features appear on the porch, where a cornice with rather anemic dentils is supported by well-formed Tuscan columns.

The house built in Wyncote in 1897 for Morris Hoover was of local stone, and resembled in its general form many other residences in the area, but the important difference was the addition of fine classical detailing, fashioned of wood. The building is as utterly suburban as any of Trumbauer's earlier works in the romantic styles, but while equaling their relaxed atmosphere, it also had a stateliness those styles could not provide. Over the years, Trumbauer was to re-create the Hoover house in numerous variations, as in Twin Maples, the 1904-5 Charles Schmidt residence in Elkins Park.

The Hoover house is a country residence with classical features applied to it, while Elstowe, a mansion designed only a short time later, was a thoroughly

Rose Room, Grey Towers. Photo: courtesy of Beaver College.

Ball Room (Mirror Room), Grey Towers. Photo: Beaver College.

Bend Terrace, Residence of H. K. Walt, Wyncote, Pennsylvania.

Morris Hoover Residence, Wyncote.

"Elstowe," William L. Elkins Residence, Elkins Park, Pennsylvania

classical country residence. It was built at Elkins Park in 1898-1900 for William L. Elkins, the traction magnate, whose son George, in 1896, had ordered from Trumbauer a large Elizabethan home—Chelten House—for an adjacent site; both houses now are a Dominican retreat for women. The visitor to the Italian Renaissance house proceeds through the porte-cochère, through the magnificent front doors of soft steel, and then into the house's Great Hall, which is Elkins Park's best interior. After viewing such beautiful rooms as the breakfast room and the library, he can go outdoors again at the garden front with its profusion of terraces and plantings below one of the mansion's two huge side bays.

Across Ashbourne Road from Elstowe stands Lynnewood Hall, one of Trumbauer's best known designs. This was built in 1898-1900 for Elkins' partner in the trolley business, P. A. B. Widener, and is now a seminary. Despite its grandeur, the 110-room mansion was planned for practical living. Widener, who was a widower, occupied, with one son and his family, the west wing's second story, while the other son and his family lived on the second floor of the east wing; the first-story rooms, such as the dining room and the salon, were shared by all. A third wing, projecting at the rear of the house, held the Widener art galleries, whose contents now make up a large proportion of the collection of the National Gallery in Washington, D.C. The three wings of Lynnewood Hall meet at the two-story Great Hall. Jacques Greber, the French landscape architect and the designer of Philadelphia's Benjamin Franklin Parkway, later redesigned the mansion's grounds, and at the same time, sculpture was added to the pediment, where before had been a fanlight window. Trumbauer, who in earlier residences had more or less puttered with classical design, emerged as a master of the style with Elstowe and Lynnewood Hall.

Philadelphia has a tradition of fine ironwork, and Horace Trumbauer accordingly designed many beautiful gates and fences for his estates, such as the wonderful Elstowe gate and the mile-long fence around Lynnewood Hall. Among his most elegant gates are those for Latham Park in the town of Oak Lane, just south of Elkins Park. Latham Park, developed in 1911 by William T. B. Roberts, is a park of deluxe residences. An allée of greenery separates two roads along which are the plots for houses. Surrounding the whole is a very long fence, culminating in the double gates fronting Old York Road. The fences and gates are painted black, with details on the gates in gold.

After Jay Cooke's bank was forced to close in

Great Hall, "Elstowe." Residence of William L. Elkins, Elkins Park.

1873, his mansion became the much-respected Ogontz School for Girls. In 1916 the school moved to Abington and new quarters Trumbauer had designed for it; today those structures hold the Ogontz Campus of the Pennsylvania State University. The stone main building may best be called Georgian, but is the most rural Georgian imaginable, as befits its woodland setting. The interiors are just as casual, and even the exterior's most formal feature, the main doorway, was eventually carved with a detail hardly from the classical tradition, the head of chief Ogontz himself.

One of Trumbauer's last mansions of largest size for the area was the 1922-25 brick residence of John C. Martin in Wyncote. Here the architect is seen adapting classicism, the style in which he was now so comfortable, to a new era. The entrance portico is reduced to a modest, though handsomely decorated, one-story porch; white marble keystones between slanted bricks replace the former all-stone lintels; a wide, plain stringcourse, the exterior's most dramatic feature, shoots across between the two principal stories. The architects of the 1890s would have made the mansion ponderous and elaborate, but Trumbauer was keeping in step with the times, and so creating Georgian architecture no less imposing than its predecessors, but streamlined for the 1920s.

An ideal building to demonstrate Trumbauer's power as a mature classicist is the 1924-25 Jenkintown

Garden Front, "Elstowe," Residence of William L. Elkins, Elkins Park.

Lynnewood Hall, P.A.B. Widener Residence, Elkins Park. Photo: Raymond D. Entine Collection.

Pedimental Sculpture, Lynnewood Hall, P.A.B. Widener Residence.

Art Gallery, Lynnewood Hall, P.A.B. Widener Residence.

Dining Room, Lynnewood Hall, P.A.B. Widener Residence.

Latham Park Gates, Melrose Park (Oak Lane), Pennsylvania.

Ogontz School, Main Building, Rydal, Pennsylvania.

Trust Company, now a branch of the Industrial Valley Bank, in Jenkintown, a few blocks from Trumbauer's home of many years. The building is one of countless American Renaissance banks that became, in fact, a type. Like those other banks, the Jenkintown Trust was meant to suggest strength and security. Under other architects, however, the devices of giant Ionic columns and the high and multilayered attic might have appeared oppressive. Trumbauer avoids heaviness by an uncanny sense of mass and proportion and with enlivening decoration, such as the griffins on the attic frieze and the acroterion over the entrance. The bank points out a basic truth about Trumbauer's work: accepting and working in established modes he made his place in architectural history by doing what everyone else did, but doing it better.

Other buildings in the vicinity by Trumbauer include a movie theater, a train station, a grocery, a pharmacy, a church, a Masonic temple, two schools, and many private houses. It is virtually impossible for a resident to go through a day without encountering a building by the architect. Horace Trumbauer's reputation is far-flung, but no neighborhood benefited more from his ability than did the area in and around Elkins Park.

Pediment of Doorway, Ogontz School for Girls, Abington, Pennsylvania. Central Medallion carved in 1925.

Residence of John C. Martin, Wyncote, Pennsylvania.

Jenkintown Trust Company (Pennsylvania).

The Architecture of Raymond Erith, R. A.

by

WILLIAM A. COLES

THE death of Raymond Erith in 1973 brought to an end the career of the most distinguished English classical architect of the post-World War II period. These were not days of classical grandeur for Great Britain any more than they have been for the United States. There, as in our country, the traditional system of architectural education had collapsed, and the abstract and futuristic redevelopment schemes of architects and planners wreaked havoc upon the townscape. Financial stringency and social change further compounded problems. The former almost seemed to licence the gimcrack and shoddy; the latter to have banished grace and style. The swinging Londons, Liverpools, and Birminghams rose from the ashes of "commodity, firmness and delight."

Perhaps because Great Britain is at heart a traditional, close knit, and good humored society, the disenchantment with this visual humbug has been relatively swift and remorseless. Modern architecture there is thoroughly detested and virtually at a standstill, except where some *retardataire* council or local authority has not yet gotten the popular message. The new Jerusalem is revealed as the old Babel and the word architect — now seen as a compound of two four-letter words joined by a small "i" — is synonymous with sham. The legacy of Carlyle, Ruskin, and Arnold would seem to have proven too strong for intellectual deceit, spiritual aridity, and aesthetic anarchy.

In this thoroughly unpromising atmosphere Raymond Erith pursued an architectural career marked by carefulness, sureness of taste, and an uncompromising concern for the traditions and amenities of the environment. His work is not the sort that is celebrated today in textbooks, and doubtless most American critics have never even heard of it. But I daresay none of Erith's clients has ever had cause to regret his choice of an architect or to lament the pleasure, beauty, and comfort he has purchased.

Fortunately Erith's accumulated knowledge and experience continue. His former pupil and partner Quinlan Terry carries on the office at Dedham, a town whose unspoiled charm Erith was largely responsible for maintaining. *Classical America* had intended to do

an article on Erith's work in a previous issue, but arrangements could not be completed in time. Since then the Royal Academy has given him a memorial retrospective exhibition in the fall of 1976, and, through the kindness of Mrs. Michael Archer, the architect's daughter, and Mr. Quinlan Terry, materials for this tribute have been made available to us.

It is most important that American classical architects be in touch with their counterparts abroad. Work in different countries will always differ according to local tastes, materials, and traditions of building, but the experience of classical design is a precious accumulation which must be shared if it is to continue and to prosper. Our President Mr. John Bayley and Mr. Quinlan Terry have both spoken of the essential uses of experience in architecture. Mr. Bayley, during his work on the Frick Museum extension, remarked to me that for a design problem which he had to solve laboriously, a McKim or a Trumbauer would most likely have had a solution at hand because they had encountered the problem before.. So much for the myth of rote copying from the past. Mr. Quinlan Terry, in a remarkable diary he kept of the design process for Kingswalden Bury, makes a similar point: "a knowledge of Vitruvius is fundamental, but knowledge tempered by experience is essential to avoid amateur results. It all points to the fact that among the many qualifications necessary to be an architect one must also be middle aged!" It goes without saying that when Mr. Terry says architect he means a classical architect. His partner Erith wrote to me two months before his death a sentence that can usefully gloss Mr. Terry's: "I will not start to tell you now what we think about classic architecture, but as a short cut I could say we think modern architecture is not architecture at all, but anti-architecture; which explains why it is unprincipled, irrational, false, and brutal."

Among Erith's work we will see houses that blend effortlessly into country towns or urban streets, collegiate buildings that will give pleasure long after the glass and concrete blobs that disfigure the back gardens of other colleges have been forgotten, mature country houses for mature landscapes and even more mature tastes. Erith's work makes us better able to

Great House, Dedham, Essex, 1937-38. The house replaced a Georgian house burned down in 1936. Originally designed with two stories and an attic. A third story was added at a late stage of the design at the client's request. Photo: courtesy of National Monument Record.

Three small houses in Aubrey Walk, Campden Hill, London, 1951-52. Because of the difficulties of the site, there are few windows on the front elevation.

Aubrey Walk, back view.

Moreley Hall, Hertfordshire, 1955-57, before remodeling.

Moreley Hall, after remodeling.

Moreley Hall, R.A. drawing of the design for remodeling.

Constable Memorial Hall, East Bergholt, 1957-59, a "deliberate attempt to design a 'compact and simply constructed building' out of cheap materials."

The Pediment, Aynho, near Banbury, 1956.

Croquet Shed, Aynho; the garden building is of a later date than the house.

appreciate how unsatisfactory is much that passes for conservation and preservation architecture in this country. It frequently lacks culture, understanding, and conviction. Our National Trust could learn much from Erith's example, as could our burgeoning university preservation programs.

Our introduction to Erith's life and career can most appropriately come through the account prepared by his daughter Lucy Archer for the Royal Academy exhibition brochure:

Raymond Erith was born in London on 7th August 1904, the eldest son of Charles Erith, a mechanical engineer. At the age of four he contracted tuberculosis which led to twelve years of intermittent illness and left him permanently lame in his left leg. As a result of this invalid childhood he had practically no formal education and developed a habit of independent thought, with a tendency to question received ideas, which remained with him for life. From a very early age he enjoyed drawing careful plans and elevations as well as painting in watercolours, inspired by both his father's engineering magazines and his mother's copies of *The Studio*. In 1921, at the age of seventeen, he entered the Architectural Association where he had a successful career, winning the Howard Colls, A.A. and Henry Florence Travelling Studentships as well as the Alec Stanhope Forbes prize. He had first visited Italy in the summer of 1921 and these prizes made further European travel possible. He completed his training two terms early and went to work in Morley Horder's office for Verner Rees who had been one of his teachers at the A.A. During his three years there he was employed on the working drawings for the London School of Hygiene and Tropical Medicine.

Provost's Lodgings, Queen's College, Oxford, 1958-60. Traffic noise in the lane limited windows on the front.

Provost's Lodgings, Queen's College, Oxford, garden view.

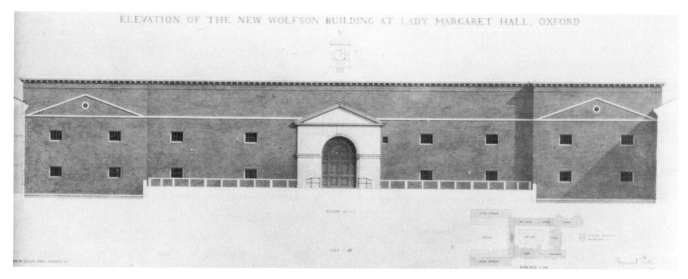

ELEVATION OF THE NEW WOLFSON BUILDING AT LADY MARGARET HALL, OXFORD

Wolfson Residential Building and new entrance gate for Lady Margaret Hall, Oxford, 1963-66. R. A. drawing, "deliberately designed for an effect of 'simplicity and repose' as a rest from the ubiquitous windows of the University."

In 1928 he set up his own office in Bridge Street, Westminister and was joined in the following year by Bertram Hume, with whom he had trained, at a new office in Warwick Street. Their partnership lasted until the war. Their practice consisted mainly of small domestic jobs and alterations, most of minor interest; however, Erith's work already showed his superb handling of detail, for example in the shop front for A. Bide of Conduit Street. He also entered numerous competitions and in 1933 Hume & Erith won (jointly with two other foreign competitors) an international competition for the replanning of the Lower Norrmalm area of Stockholm. Since the competition was held with the intention only of collecting ideas and suggestions, their plans were not carried out but their success brought considerable acclaim.

In 1934 Erith married Pamela, younger daughter of Arthur Spencer Jackson. She too had trained at the A.A. and worked for a while in his office. They soon decided to move out of London; Erith had always disliked the suburban atmosphere of Sutton in Surrey where he grew up and had a deep love of the country. He had already got to know the Cotswolds and also Suffolk which had a particular appeal for him since his family traced its origins back to the Eriths who were numerous on the Essex/Suffolk border in the seventeenth and eighteenth centuries. In 1936 he bought a house in Dedham, near Colchester, a beautiful unspoilt village and near enough to London for him to travel regularly to a new office in Bishopsgate. This move led to his lifelong involvement in the cause of the preservation of the countryside; he was a founder member and life-long supporter of the Dedham Vale Society and was its President at the time of his death. Living in the country gave him more opportunity for studying vernacular architecture from which he drew inspiration with increasing understanding and skill for the rest of his life.

During the remaining pre-war years Erith had only two major commissions: Great House, Dedham for his father-in-law and a pair of lodges at Royal Lodge, Windsor for King George VI, both built in a simple austere style with an emphasis on proportion and fine detail which characterized all his work. Since he was not eligible for active service he decided on farming as his war effort and moved in 1940 to a farm at Little Bromley about five miles from Dedham. He and his wife had four daughters and the family stayed together throughout the war years. In spite of his disability he was very active and enjoyed the way of life so much that he was tempted to abandon

architecture altogether. However he had thought and written a great deal about architectural theory and still hoped for the chance to design worthwhile buildings; so in 1945 he sold up and returned to Dedham where he continued to farm about 80 acres..

In 1946 he opened an office in Queen Street, Ipswich, moving to Arcade Street in 1953. Through the period of post-war shortages and building restrictions he gradually built up a practice which he described as consisting of "dozens of odd jobs, bathrooms, smoking chimneys, leaky roofs and the rest—I am a real market-town architect". But he had not weakened in his resolve to fight for the survival of classicism and embarked on a series of drawings for the Royal Academy Summer Exhibitions of those of his designs which interested him most. As soon as it was possible he began to travel abroad again, first of all to Vicenza to look at the work of Palladio. What spare time he had he devoted to his family and a succession of vintage Bentleys. By 1955 he was getting more work than he could do and was no longer so dependent on his local practice; so in 1958 he moved his office to the Old Exchange in Dedham just opposite his house. From now on he was able to do more of the sort of work he had been waiting for—houses both large and small and larger buildings such as the Library and Wolfson building for Lady Margaret Hall, Oxford, Jack Straw's Castle on Hampstead Heath and the new Common Room building for Gray's Inn. In 1958 he was appointed architect for the reconstruction of Nos. 10, 11 and 12 Downing Street, a job in which he was able to make full use of his thorough understanding of eighteenth-century houses and his appreciation of the importance of their later history.

In 1959 he was elected an Associate of the Royal Academy and became a full Academician five years later. In 1960 he was appointed to the Royal Fine Art Commission on which he served until 1973. As a result he became even more involved than before in efforts to protect threatened buildings, a cause to which he gave a great deal of time and devotion. But he found it more and more depressing and wrote to a friend in 1971: "Please do not think I have lost heart. I have not; but sometimes I find it difficult not to: my hatred of the destruction of beauty begins to eat into my love of it, so that I find myself becoming a husk like the husks modernists make of Georgian terraces."

In 1969 he took into partnership Quinlan Terry who had been working for him since 1962 and the firm became Raymond Erith R.A. and Quinlan Terry which it still is. When he died very suddenly

New quadrangle, Lady Margaret Hall, Oxford, "designed in the same manner and tradition as the earlier buildings by Sir Reginald Blomfield." The Library (1959-61) is at right.

Library interior, Lady Margaret Hall, Oxford.

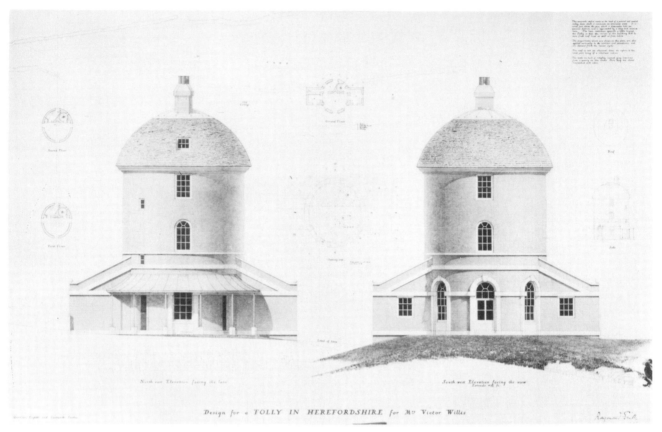

The Folly, Gatley Park, Herefordshire, 1961-64, a building designed to be "at once practical and 'fantastical.'" R.A. drawing.

The Folly, Gatley Park.

on 30th November 1973 at the age of 69 he was still at the height of his powers as an architect. Indeed much of his most important work belongs to his later years when he was able to put into practice the accumulated ideas of a lifetime.

As a young man he was already greatly concerned with the theory of architecture, as was his partner Bertram Hume, and read widely about Greek and Roman construction. He would copy lengthy passages from books and then analyse them and reach his own conclusions but he finally decided that "It is impossible to get much out of the books except muddle. All the authorities avoid the origins, or disagree about each other's theories . . . It seems that I shall have to do my own thinking." And so he did, writing about both the theory and the practice of architecture on and off throughout his life and always intending one day to publish a book. But apart from one or two articles and a very few lectures he did not make his ideas public, though he discussed them often with his family and friends, both in conversation and in letters.

Where he disagreed with modernism was in its theory which had, he felt, led to the shoddiness and brutality which he hated in contemporary architecture. "All our troubles, as I see it, arise out of an incomplete conception of what it is that makes building into architecture." The defect of the modern theory is "that it does not allow for the fact that architecture is an art as well as a science. It confuses beauty, which is one thing, with the object in which we see beauty, which is another . . . It has left us aimless. . . . Yet architecture has in its new materials, especially reinforced concrete, problems and possibilities of a sort it has never had since the invention of the arch." Speaking to students at the R.I.B.A. in 1955, he emphasized the need for a perfect balance in architecture of the Vitruvian principles—Firmness, Commodity and Delight. "I follow the classic tradition", he had written earlier "because it is the tradition of these principles. I will admit that the classical tradition has

Wivenhoe New Park, near Colchester, Essex, 1962-64. The garden was an essential part of the design.

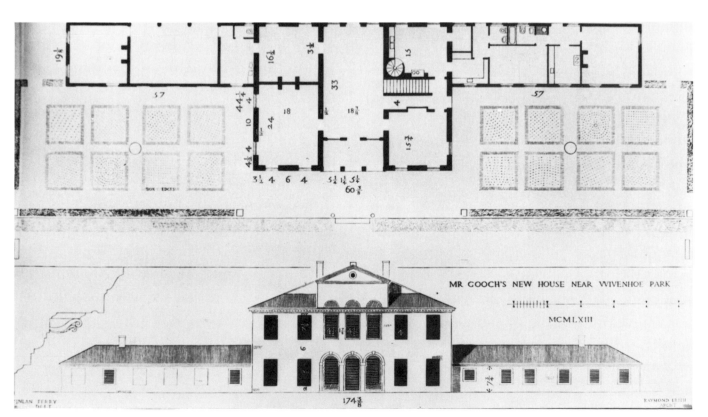

Wivenhoe New Park.

Jack Straw's Castle Public House, Hampstead, 1963-64. Faced with a utilitarian and clumsy plan that could have been a masterpiece of ugliness, the architect "wanted to demonstrate . . . that a malformed modern building built with traditional materials in a traditional way might be more bearable."

become so debased that it needs a certain amount of moral courage to take this attitude. I think however that tradition, if it can be purified and restated, still has its place in architecture." He was keen to emphasize that "by classic tradition I do not mean classical style. I think the traditionalist architecture of the present time (1930s), Wrennaissance and all the rest of it is just awful . . . . What I think should be taught is the general classic tradition, in other words the classic principles." He did not advise students to go straight back to the Orders but "to accept tradition in principle and certainly to stop avoiding traditional forms and methods . . . because the rejection of tradition is a dead end that is leading nowhere and can lead nowhere. The only course which can possibly have any future is to accept the broad stream of tradition as a whole and then enlarge and expand it" for as he later wrote "modernism is too restricted. The restriction is negative in the sense that modernism is completely tied to tradition by its determination to avoid it. It only makes sense, or rather it only becomes understandable, if one sees it in the context of the architectural revolution i.e. as the negation and inversion of historic architecture.

He considered it vital that a building should be intelligible and wrote in 1966: "That, architecturally, is the main point about my buildings; they are what they look: if you see a stone pier or wooden column it does in fact do what it appears to do; they are not casings to steel or reinforced concrete framing. In other words nothing is sham." So his architecture was as much practical as theoretical and it was by a direct approach that he had sought to look back to the point where he felt that the classical tradition had been lost. In 1959 he wrote: "My aim has always been to recapture the essential

quality of architecture, by which I mean the quality which began to disappear sometime during the eighteenth century and which had practically vanished before 1805 . . . . I do not pretend to know the whole answer but by studying old buildings I have managed to get a fairly clear view of the thing itself and I think I have found the method, or a method, by which it was produced." So his classicism was rooted in the vernacular and it was this which gave his buildings their particular sense of originality with a feeling of pleasant familiarity so that they seem always to have been there. Nevertheless he was not opposed to innovation though he treated it with circumspection: "There is no reason to encourage a change of building technique, with the idea of producing something fresh, if the established method will do as well. This does not argue that change or improvement should be resisted: merely that change for the sake of change is undesirable"; and he was convinced that the classical tradition could be adapted "to an expanding knowledge of the means of construction and of comfort". He wrote of Soane that his aim was "to make classical architecture progress and absorb in itself the new needs of a new age" and he longed himself for the opportunity "to knock the idea that for a big building there is *no alternative* to the established (1970s) style of architecture".

All his buildings testify to his belief in classicism as a living tradition and to the sort of man he was—modest and affectionate with a delightful sense of humour. Not long before his death it was suggested to him that he had at least kept the lamp of classicism alight. Characteristically he replied "Not alight, but smouldering"; however in a letter written in 1971 he put into words his enduring faith: "All my life I have been waiting for the revival of architecture.

Jack Straw's Castle, inner court.

Jack Straw's Castle, inner court.

Knight's Hill, Buntingford, before restoration.

Knight's Hill, restored 1964-66.

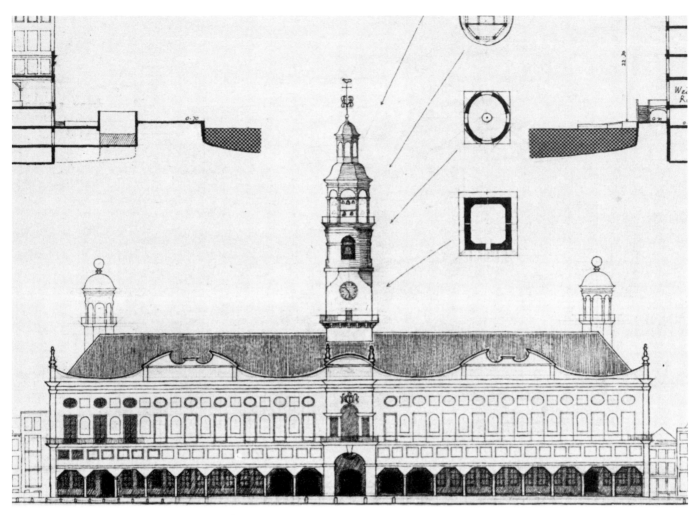

Amsterdam Town Hall competition sketch. The style of old Amsterdam, Erith felt, was perfectly suited to modern building.

I do not think it *will* happen but if the right idea could be put out at the right time I think it could happen. The world could be beautiful again. And nothing, really, but a blind spot stops it.''

Erith's partner Quinlan Terry, wrote an account of the working practices of Erith's office for the Royal Academy exhibition. It is especially helpful for an age like ours which generally receives its opinions from critics who often lack the most rudimentary knowledge of the actual methods of a professional office:

It was said of Palladio that he was obliging and reasonable; this might just as well have been said of Erith. There was nothing eccentric or whimsical about him. He was sound, imaginative, reliable, courageous and always practical. He had a distrust of genius and prima donnas; to him architecture was much closer to the stonemason's yard and the joinery shop.

His office was really like a master-builder's workshop in a group of timber-framed Tudor cottages refronted in the eighteenth century with sash windows and stucco. The drawing boards were all antiquarian size on low tables. Erith was insistent that each board should be placed under a window so that the drawings could be prepared in good daylight. All working drawings were to antiquarian size and there were strict rules on hatching for brickwork and stonework as well as size and spacing of lettering for titles, sub-titles

and notes. Italic and lower case lettering were not encouraged. The drawings were prepared in 3H pencil, ruling and mapping pen; needless to say Rapidographs, electric rubbers, felt pens, stencils or Letraset could not be of any use. Erith had incredibly sharp eyesight; he drew superbly and expected the same standard from all of us. He was not charitable to anyone who drew an eighth scale drawing with 4½-in. brickwork measuring 5 in. on his ivory edged scale. The assistants, usually about six in number, were all local and most of them stayed with him for a great number of years. They succeeded in so far as they were willing to apprentice themselves to him irrespective of their previous qualifications, which he regarded as of marginal value. This apprenticeship took about ten years, and it led to perfection in draughtsmanship, sound understanding of construction and intelligent use of source books. The books were an essential part of equipment. Most frequently in use were *Palladio's Quattro Libri*, the 1825 Paris edition of *Palladio's Works*, the 1832 Venice edition of *Sanmicheli's Works*, *Letarouilly's Five Books*, as well as more standard works on the Orders and measured drawings of ancient Rome.

The official working hours were 9.00 a.m. to 5.30 p.m. but it was unthinkable to arrive after 8.50 a.m. and considered bad form to leave before 6.00 p.m. If you stayed beyond 6.30 p.m. the work would continue less formally over a glass of sherry in Erith's drawing room across the road. When it came to site visits and surveys Erith was indefatigable. A typical surveying day started before 6.00

New houses at Walsham-le-Willows, Suffolk, 1967-68, commissioned by a client to prevent any redevelopment which would spoil the village. Front view.

House at Walsham-le-Willows, front view.

House at Walsham-le-Willows, back view.

House at Walsham-le-Willows, back view.

Terrace of nine houses at Canonbury Place, London, 1969-70.

a.m., went on relentlessly until dusk and usually finished with a slap-up meal on the way home. It was invariably on these occasions that Erith came out with his best statements on art and architecture. He liked talking and by process of discussion would simplify and reduce a problem to its irreducible minimum. He was very quick to see the main point and was often talking about the "general physique" of a building. He always started with the plan and ruthlessly discarded charming ideas that were not germane to the design. When he was more-or-less satisfied with the plan he would begin to work up the section and last of all he would reflect the plan and section in the elevation. He was remarkably quick in seeing the fundamental strength or weakness in a design but very painstaking and thorough in working up the details. It was at this stage that he looked for precedents and searched through classical examples in books and buildings around him to see how Palladio, Inigo Jones or the local master-builder got over the same problem. Invariably the answer had to be adapted and worked on and so became his own but the classical language and principle remained. This process took place over everyone's board in turn; no drawing ever left the office without his real and practical imprimatur. It was in these board to board discussions that we learned from his powers of observation and judgement how to practise the art of building in the way Alberti described. "It is the business of architecture, and indeed its highest praise, to judge rightly what is fit and decent: for though building is a matter of necessity, yet convenient building is both of necessity and utility too: but to build in such a manner, that the generous shall commend you, and the frugal not blame you, is the work only of a prudent, wise and learned architect."

And finally, a memorial address, delivered by Sir John Betjeman at St. Mary's Church, Paddington Green (a church restored by Erith) on 15 January 1974,

Tower of the Winds, a ventilation shaft for London Transport, the Victoria Line, Gibson Square, 1968-69. A design for a garden was part of the scheme. Linocut by Quinlan Terry.

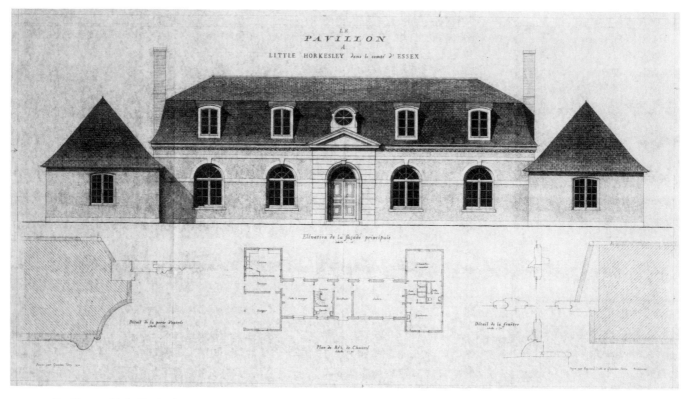

Pavilion at Little Horkesley, Essex, 1969-70. The commission was for "a house in the French manner." R. A. drawing.

offers an affectionate yet true assessment of his work and character:

His best-known work is, I suppose, the restoration of Nos. 10, 11 and 12 Downing Street after the last war. Here the charm is in the interiors. Then there is No. 10 South Square, Gray's Inn, which is *more* than neo-Georgian, it is Raymond Erith and the most distinguished new building in that delightful square. I say Raymond Erith because he had his own style, like Lutyens. He wasn't sham Georgian. I have chosen some London examples. The first building he did which I looked at in detail was the Provost's lodging at Queen's College, Oxford. He did this in 1956. It was a vital site in the tenderest, most time-worn and stately part of Oxford University—crumbling domestic Tudor of New College with its towers and bells and pinnacles; the fantastic, almost-Chinese twin-turrets of All Souls' by Hawksmoor; the great dome of the Radcliffe Camera beyond. In Queen's College itself there is the glorious length of the library looking over the Fellows' garden. The site of the Provost's lodging was in New College Lane, a narrow, walled thoroughfare of ancient, undisturbed back-yard Oxford, the sort of place where if you looked through a doorway you might see a cobbled courtyard with lean-to sheds and perhaps a brewhouse or a tool-shed or a coach-house of the days when the Heads of Houses kept a carriage. This was just the sort of thing Raymond liked and instead of following the fashion and building a glass tower or a concrete abattoir to show that he was up to date, Raymond built for the Provost of Queen's a very plain rectory whose entrance was let in to New College Lane walls and blended with them by the use of rusticated stone. The inside was like a comfortable Georgian rectory with slender staircase, domed entrance hall and windows looking on to gardens. It looked as though it had always been there and perhaps that is why it is never mentioned at any length, if at all, by the writers of guide-books to modern Oxford. His other Oxford work is quite different because it is in the red brick 1860 Gothic leafy suburb of North Oxford where the dons' wives used to live. It is the library and entrance-arch to Lady Margaret Hall. The library is brick and plain Palladian outside, and inside the joinery of the stairways and bookcases are part of the design. The new main entrance gateway to the College itself is an imposing climax to a winding and romantic Victorian suburban road. It is like the triumphal archway entrance to a private park, a deliberate classic contrast with its surroundings. Standing in this archway and looking out into suburban Oxford the whole district is pulled together and ennobled by the lengthening vista. The building which Raymond most enjoyed designing was Kings Walden Bury, Hertfordshire, which was illustrated in *Country Life*. This may well be called the last great Palladian country-house to be built in England *so far*—because the tide is turning.

Raymond was brought up in Sutton, Surrey, and he didn't like the place at all. In his childhood he and his brother used to go to Cavendish and Clare in Suffolk, where the family originated. To them it was Arcadia. They liked people and they liked farming and Raymond had been on his back ill for eight years and thus had the inestimable advantage of not going to school. This set him free from modern clichés and trendy stylism and gave him plenty of time to study the books of Palladio and of acquatinted illustrations. He knew that he was born to be a Classic architect.

All photos are courtesy of Mr. Quinlan Terry.

Pavilion at Little Horkesley, front view.

Pavilion at Little Horkesley, back view.

Three houses in Dedham, built to prevent unattractive development in the village, front view.

Houses in Dedham, back view.

Raymond Erith, R.A. 143

Kingswalden Bury, Hertfordshire, 1969-71, north front. Though inspired by Palladio, this house turned out to be baroque in nature. It was built on the site of an earlier house in a mature park.

Kingswalden Bury, north front, center pavilion.

Kingswalden Bury, south front, center pavilion.

Kingswalden Bury, under construction.

Kingswalden Bury, Hall.

Kingswalden Bury, staircase.

Kingswalden Bury, Hall, the module of the house is the Venetian foot (1 ft. 2 in.) to give a more generous and more Italian scale.

Two cottages at Britwell Salome, Oxfordshire, 1972.

Gray's Inn, 1970, before Erith's building.

New Common Room Building (center), Gray's Inn, 1971-72.

Gray's Inn, 1970, before Erith's building.

New Common Room Building (center), Gray's Inn, 1971-72. The new common room links Gray's Inn Square with South Square by joining the buildings in each into one continuous frontage.

New Common Room Building, Gray's Inn, and "Tudor" Buttery (1972) attached to the Hall.

Proposed design for a new Museum of Heraldry, the College of Arms, Queen Victoria Street, London, 1972. R. A. drawing.

St. Mary's Church, Paddington Green, designed by John Plaw, 1788.

Interior restoration of St. Mary's Church, Paddington Green, 1972-73. The church was not merely restored but improved, with new box pews, brass chandelier, reglazing and repainting, and a marble and stone floor.

St. Mary's Church, Paddington Green.

St. Mary's Church, Paddington Green.

Design for a new organ case, St. Mary's Church, Paddington Green, by Quinlan Terry, 1976.

First design for a new Baha'i temple, 1973. R. A. drawing, 1975. The building will be as large as St. Paul's Cathedral, on a vast tract of land, with numerous other subsidiary buildings planned.

Baha'i temple, south elevation.

Baha'i temple, elevation of south front.

Baha'i temple, elevation of a typical porch.

Baha'i temple, elevation of the dome.

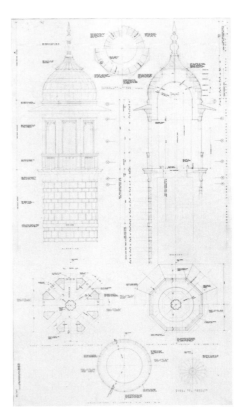

Baha'i temple, working drawing of a minaret.

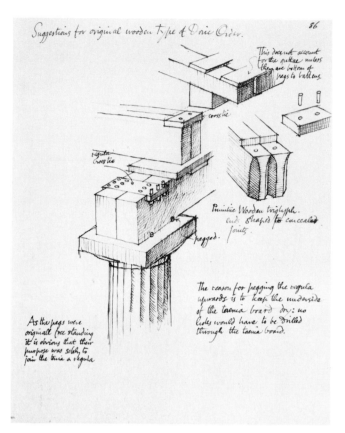

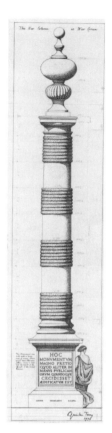

A page from an Erith sketchbook.

A monument for a park by Quinlan Terry, 1976.

Design for a garden wall fountain by Quinlan Terry, 1976.

The Enigma of John Sargent's Art

by

R. H. IVES GAMMELL

IN the course of his working life John Sargent devoted his energies to several kinds of painting. He painted portraits and figure pieces and mural decorations. He sketched all sorts of subjects in watercolors and in oils. He devoted some of his time to sculpture and not a little of it to designing textiles. He made portrait studies in charcoal. Though he took up these various activities at widely separated periods of his existence it is notable that, generally speaking, his earliest productions in each of these several fields remained superior to anything he subsequently produced in the same form.

The work of no other eminent painter falls into a similar pattern. Pictures painted in the later years of an artist's career often show a decline due to physiological changes or to illness. Some painters, overwhelmed by the press of orders, have entrusted the execution of their pictures to assistants, with unfortunate results. Some have been spoiled by success. Others have prostituted their talents for the sake of gain. In Sargent's case none of these causes were operative.

Throughout his life the sincerity and humility of his attitude toward painting was recognized as one of his outstanding characteristics. He was never much interested in financial gain. Except when painting portraits, he chose his own subject matter and worked on his own time schedule. His faculties continued to be unimpaired until the day of his death and his physical strength declined far less than that of most men. The baffling thing about Sargent as an artist is that we can discern no completely dominant motive behind his urge to paint. His was not an art of self-expression, as was that of a Delacroix, of a Puvis de Chavannes, or a Burne-Jones, for instance. Nor was it in essence an art of conviction, dedicated to an ideal principle of interpretation and workmanship, as we recognize the art of Manet, of Degas, or of Whistler to have been. Sargent's approach was akin to that of these last-named men, but his fidelity to a particular concept of painting was less complete and uncompromising than theirs. It was precisely this absence of a deeply felt guiding principle which puzzled the serious artists of his time and kept them from giving their wholehearted admiration to the work of a man whose great talent and

obvious sincerity they could not fail to recognize.* The first murals seemed to herald the development of something resembling an art of self-expression but the promise was not fulfilled by the later decorations. Only a few of Sargent's canvases, and all of those were painted early in his career, achieve the full dignity of great impressionist art. The majority of his pictures are apt to suggest a disinterested display of virtuosity rather than devotion to a high artistic ideal.

If, after studying Sargent's mural decorations, we re-examine his output as a whole we may feel justified in hazarding an analysis of his elusive personality. Everything we know of his working procedures indicates that Sargent's creative thinking took place in his subconscious mind to an extent very unusual in a painter who has proved himself capable of acquiring a high degree of professional skill. Subconscious mental activity does play an important role in all artistic creation, of course. It is, however, characteristic of the art of painting that, once an idea has been conceived and its general orientation has been established, translating that idea into effective pictorial terms requires very clear thinking and the judicious application of much acquired knowledge. In Sargent's case an unusually large part of these later operations seems to have been worked out in the earlier subconscious processes. To a bystander, and quite possibly to Sargent himself, his pictures may have appeared to take shape spontaneously in very nearly their final form. The gropings and the experimental studies whereby artists ordinarily arrive at their final results are relatively rare in Sargent's work. When he made a failure it was a poor picture from the start and it remained so. The tricks of patching and altering or of reconstructing an unsuccessful composition, which most painters consider an indispensable element of their craft, were apparently scarcely known to him. He seemed incapable of telling

* Sir William Rothenstein, who was on friendly terms with the leading English and French artists of the period, wrote: "We all acknowledged his [Sargent's] immense accomplishment as a painter to be far beyond anything of which we were capable. But the disparity between his gifts and our own we were inclined to discount by thinking that we had qualities which somehow placed us among the essential artists while he, in spite of his great gifts, remained outside the charmed circle. I was used to hearing both Whistler and Degas speak disparagingly of Sargent's work. Even Helleu, Boldini and Gandara regarded him more as a brilliant executant than as an artist of high rank." (*Men and Memories*, Coward-McCann, 1931.) Jacques-Emile Blanche voices a similar attitude (*Propos de Peintre*, III, 1929) and much the same opinion was held by many American painters at the time of Sargent's greatest success.

anyone how he had arrived at a given result. He presumably was only vaguely aware of it himself. The necessary brain work had been largely subconscious, or so rapid that the artist appeared to have been guided by instinct rather than by reasoning. A painter able to work in this fashion often seems to have no very clear idea of what he is trying to do because it has never been necessary for him to formulate his aims to himself.

When this kind of mental activity is basically responsible for the quality of a work of art the artist can do comparatively little to control it. He can toil assiduously, of course, as Sargent certainly did. But his work will only reflect the full measure of his capacity when the faculties dormant in his subconscious are aroused to their maximum activity. At other times his painting will tend to be a routine version of what he produced in his "inspired" moments. An artist of this type probably has very little idea of how his mind functions. He simply goes on painting as best he can until some external stimulus awakens the forces of his psychic being to intense creative activity. Only at such times is he likely to produce his finest work.

If we feel justified in assuming that John Sargent's psychic mechanism conformed to some pattern of this kind we naturally will wish to ascertain what sort of stimulus served to set it in motion. In this connection a comment made to me by his niece comes to my mind. It seemed to her that her uncle was attracted to his chosen subject matter by virtue of the very difficulties which it presented to him as a painter. And here we perhaps have the key to the riddle. Apparently something in Sargent's inner nature responded in an unusual degree to the challenge of an exceptionally difficult technical problem. The challenge aroused no mere impulse to demonstrate his skill, as it might have in a lesser nature. In Sargent's case it seems on occasion rather to have engendered a series of reactions involving all the resources of his extraordinarily gifted personality, focusing their activity on the problem in hand and releasing emotional drives usually quiescent. Is it not reasonable to suppose that the subconscious of this reserved, inexpressive man, whose emotional life seems never to have found an outlet in any personal relationship, was dominated by an exceptionally powerful compensatory urge to assert his superiority? A peculiarity of his nature made it extremely difficult for him to express himself in speech or action and whenever possible he evaded occasions for so doing. In this he was aided by circumstances, for he received as his birthright many things which most men obtain only with effort: education, financial independence, and access to the most desirable society. His cosmopolitan existence released him from the duties of citizenship, and he never assumed the responsibilities

of family life. His inability to deal with practical matters was proverbial. Serious illness and love passed him by. He even lacked the capacity for vicarious experience which ordinarily marks the creative artist.* Had he not painted, John Sargent would have passed for an amiable, cultivated though colorless man of the world. But he happened to be endowed with a prodigious talent for painting, coupled with an exceptional receptivity to art, literature, and music. All his otherwise unexpended energies were concentrated on the exercise of this dual gift.

No painter can have practised his own art more constantly than did Sargent, and he found his relaxation chiefly in music, in reading, and in looking at works of art. His extraordinary talent, developed by ceaseless industry and tempered by continuous contact with the best that the human mind has produced, kept his work on a high artistic level at most times. But Sargent attained his maximum potential, as it would seem, only when his subconscious will to power was aroused by an opportunity to assert his superiority through his art. The challenge of a fresh and exceptionally difficult artistic problem apparently induced a catalysis whereby all the latent forces of his immensely gifted personality and the accumulated store of his impressions merged into a single creative effort.

Let us glance briefly at the record. The admirable portrait of Carolus-Duran (1877), executed by a young man of twenty-one under the critical eye of his master whose presence obviously put the boy on his mettle, is almost as fine in workmanship as anything he was later to paint. Two years afterwards came the spectacular *El Jaleo* (1881), a *tour de force* if ever a picture was, which, in spite of certain defects of drawing apparent in the secondary figures, might perhaps be taken as the most complete expression of his characteristic qualities that Sargent ever achieved.† In the following year (1882) he painted the lovely *Lady With A Rose* and finished the *Boit Children,* a composition in which the difficulties always attending on the painting of children were compounded by problems of rendering light and atmosphere on a vast scale. Faced with this inordinately difficult subject which inevitably evoked comparisons with Velasquez' *Las Meninas,* Sargent created a masterpiece. It was followed by the portrait of *Madame Gautreau* (1884). The difficulties presented by this portrait were no less real, though they

---

* A doctor, well acquainted with Sargent and who also had occasion to see him frequently at the time of the artist's visit to the battlefront in 1918, told me that he was convinced that this aesthetically hypersensitive man remained largely unaware of the grim realities with which he was in daily contact during those weeks.

† Mr. George Harold Edgell, then director of the Boston Museum of Fine Arts, told me that, one afternoon when as a young man he was calling on Mrs. Gardner at Fenway Court, he found himself in her company with John Sargent. The three happened to pass the *El Jaleo,* then recently installed, and Edgell expressed his enthusiasm about the picture, saying he did not believe Sargent had ever painted anything greater. In Mr. Edgell's own words, "Sargent's reply was to look at me rather sadly and to say, 'Young man, do you know that I was a student in Paris when I painted that picture?' "

Portrait of Carolus-Duran. Photo: courtesy of Sterling and Francine Clark Art Institute

"El Jaleo." Photo: courtesy of Isabella Stewart Gardner Museum, Boston.

The Daughters of Edward D. Boit. Photo: courtesy of Museum of Fine Arts, Boston.

are less obvious. The subject was a conspicuous "beauty" of the time, very much in the public eye, and an uncooperative sitter. Hers was a singular type of beauty, emphasized by makeup, which even a slight exaggeration or understatement of form could turn into ugliness. As was his way, Sargent made things harder by electing to paint the lady in an attitude suggesting arrested motion. Once again he was triumphantly successful. The four last-named pictures belong in the great line of impressionist painting, each one in its particular way on a level which Sargent never quite reached again. When he finished *Madame Gautreau* he was twenty-eight years old.

Almost immediately an entirely new set of pictorial problems gave a fresh impetus to his creative activity. At this epoch painters were increasingly preoccupied by the problems of plein-air painting, the chief of which consisted in making accurate color notations of the transient effects created by ever-changing light and weather out of doors. Once more we find Sargent attacking a new problem in its most complex form, heaping Ossa upon Pelion to increase the obstacles he proposed to surmount. He chose the most illusive lighting conceivable, the brief moment of twilight between sundown and dusk. He created an additional complication by introducing the artificial light of candles seen through Japanese paper-lanterns. Again he took children for his models, dressing them in white frocks which assumed hues of exceptional delicacy in the gloaming. He surrounded these young models with flowers whose shapes and colors were scarcely less elusive than those of the children themselves. The result was *Carnation, Lily, Lily, Rose* (1886), a picture unique in the vast output of nineteenth-century plein-air painting. Sargent never again attempted anything of this kind.

The particular qualities which make these pictures great do not recur in Sargent's subsequent work in a comparable degree. The portraits painted during the next twelve years included some of his most brilliant achievements. Remarkable as they are in characterization and in handling, and occasionally as pictures, even the best of them somehow fall short of being classed with the world's greatest portraits. Whereas the best canvases of the eighties elicited comparisons with Velasquez and Hals, the portraits of the nineties were more often praised for being superior to Boldini's and Laszlo's or as perhaps rivaling those of Sir Thomas Lawrence. We still find Sargent seeking difficulties as if they provided a dram for his genius. He sets the Duke of Portland to playing with his collies, paints Mrs. George Batten in the act of singing a song, groups Mrs. Carl Meyer and Mrs. Edgar L. Davis in complicated attitudes with their restless children. The results are amazing and exciting but in some ways less

Madame X (Mme Gautreau). Photo: courtesy of The Metropolitan Museum of Art, Arthur H. Hearn Fund, 1916.

satisfying than many portraits by far less gifted men. After the turn of the century Sargent's portraits rarely reach the level established earlier by his own best work.

Between 1890 and 1904 mural decoration provided Sargent with another artistic adventure capable of drawing out all his latent capabilities. He responded to this fresh challenge in the two great lunettes at the Public Library, in the frieze of the prophets, and in the Astarte. The new problems brought into play previously untapped resources of his imagination and of his literary background, enabling Sargent to create masterpieces fully as remarkable in their way as his finest achievements in the field of impressionist painting.

Venice - I Gesuati. Photo: courtesy of Museum of Fine Arts, Boston.

From then on it is disappointing to follow the progressive decline of his later mural work which reaches its lowest point in one of the Widener Library panels.

About 1906 Sargent began exhibiting watercolors, and during the following decade his most brilliant work was done in that refractory medium. It is, in point of fact, the most difficult and unmanageable of all mediums for an artist bent on precise color-notation. Sargent rapidly made it his own, becoming almost immediately the most accomplished watercolorist which the world has yet seen. We find him successfully rendering subjects that would baffle the skill of almost any other painter even in the less difficult medium of oil; linen hung out to dry in flickering sunlight, white marble buldings silhouetted against white clouds, ladies resting on windswept hilltops, oxen and donkeys and alligators. Many observers have thought that the watercolors painted in the first decade of the century were his best, but he continued to turn them out until the end of his life with little apparent decline, perhaps because by their very nature they made few demands on his inner being. In this art

everything depended on sheer dexterity and brilliance, on "making the most of an emergency," as he himself defined painting a watercolor. With this phrase he consciously gave the best characterization of his entire approach to art. He loved to make the most of an emergency and the greater the emergency the more he was usually able to make of it.

My interpretation may answer another question frequently raised in connection with John Sargent. Why did this brilliant, many faceted artist continue for so long to accept portrait orders? By the early nineties he had accumulated a considerable fortune and enjoyed international celebrity. The professional portrait painter's task is notoriously exhausting, frustrating, and thankless. Sargent himself complained of it to his friends. I had it from a man who in his youth had consulted Sargent as to whether he should take up painting, that the most sought after painter in the world adjured him to avoid portraiture. "It ruined me," said John Sargent. Why then did he go on for another decade accepting orders from all and sundry? Because, perhaps, each unknown, unsolicited sitter

Villa di Marlia, Lucca. Photo: courtesy of Museum of Fine Arts, Boston.

presented the fresh challenge which his nature required, an unexpected, unpredictable artistic problem demanding a solution.

This brief review of Sargent's career would seem to lend considerable support to the hypothesis I have outlined above. More than a hypothesis such an analysis could not pretend to be. Any attempt to describe the creative processes of a great artist is useful only insofar as it may help to understand and appreciate the artist's work. The art of John Sargent has puzzled both his admirers and those to whom it makes no appeal. Even the most appreciative have realized that it was strangely lacking in some fundamental quality of feeling. But this deficiency, which may perhaps be attributed, as I have suggested, to the emotional poverty of Sargent's initial creative impulse, should certainly not cause us to undervalue the intellectual power and technical brilliance of the resulting art or to doubt the sincerity of the artist.

Gustave Flaubert maintained that an artist, to achieve lasting fame, needs must either chisel a Parthenon or amass a pyramid. John Sargent stands with the pyramid builders. Perhaps no painter of comparable artistic stature has ever, unaided by assistants, been as prolific. The magnitude and variety of his output staggers the mind. The two outstanding characteristics of his art are vitality and a certain element of surprise. While the pervading sense of life captured at full swing still animates the best murals, canvases, water colors, and drawings, familiarity has perhaps dulled our appreciation of what were once startlingly novel presentations of familiar subjects which amazed and sometimes shocked his public. To take the full measure of Sargent's originality one must restudy the art of his own time whose wilder manifestations look more and more like the eccentricities of minor artists hampered by their inadequate technical command. Sargent both knew his trade and kept to the main line of the western tradition, but his originality is manifested in everything he did. His work was uneven in quality, no doubt. His splendid contribution may be likened to that of a torrent which gushes headlong down the mountainside bearing, together with minerals of lesser value, nuggets of the purest gold.

This appraisal of Sargent's genius is the final chapter of a still unpublished book ''The Mural Decorations of John Singer Sargent'' by Mr. Gammell.

The Library of Congress Today

by

PIERCE RICE

THE idea of the Capitol Grounds is a powerful one: the great palace itself, the Plaza, Olmstead's magnificent terraces, the Grant Memorial at their base, the flanking pair made up of the Cannon Building and the Senate Office Building, the Dome and the East Portico serving as the culmination of East Capitol Street, the axis of which, resumed on the west by the Mall, is vertical to that of the Capitol. But it has remained an idea, never fully realized, and in many ways departed from.

Damage has been done within the recent decade by putting up the Rayburn Building and the New Senate Office Building, related to the plan but destructive of it. An earlier violation was the Longworth Building, the product of a time when people ought to have known better. But even before the devising of the McMillan Plan, which represents the inception of the larger concept of the Capitol Grounds, a decision was taken that would forever be an obstacle to achievement of the symmetry of the scheme, which is its heart. This was to raise, east-south-east of the Capitol, and hence off center to it, quarters for the Library of Congress. A generation later the seal was put on this error by the erection of the Supreme Court, directly north of the Library; in scale, in style, in material, utterly out of harmony with the Library, and by its presence making impossible the completion of the Capitol Grounds on the original principle. The path dictated by conditions would have been to raise alongside it the Library's duplicate, after the fashion of the Ministry of Marine and its own identical neighbor on the Place de la Concorde. The effect would have been almost too dazzling to contemplate, but no alternative arrangement could be other than disagreeable. What is to be remarked on is that there is no record of even the faintest advocacy of this nothing-less-than-mandatory course.

The Library, accordingly, by its very existence is unsettling, however unaware the spectator may be of the reasons for the dissatisfaction certain to be felt when, in an aggressively symmetrical situation, a disastrous contradiction is apparent. The greater the attractiveness of the Library and the impact of its sheer bulk, above all the force of its own symmetry, the more this wrongness is pointed up.

Viewed for itself, the Library is, after the Capitol, the most absorbing structure in Washington. We may prefer others, but no single building is the match of the Library in what it offers, in plan, in elevation, and in the intricacy of its interior, the Capitol alone excepted. Any of these aspects would provide pleasure and reward inquiry and be instructive as an example. But the special distinction of the Library is the enrichment of its surface, both inside and out. Dramatic and splendid when viewed in full, its impressiveness only increases on close inspection.

The Library is a product of the Nineties, and its seventy-fifth anniversary was celebrated in 1972 by giving over in that year the October number of its own *Quarterly Journal** to the story of the Library's conception and construction.

The Library was no exception to the rule that controversy presides over the birth of great buildings, and the *Journal* describes the struggle between architects and librarians, architects and builder, architects and Congress, and architects among themselves. If these are unedifying, they testify to the intensity of interest aroused in the project. There had been a competition, with quarrels (of course) over the results. The successful contestants, John L. Smithmeyer and Paul J. Pelz submitted, to placate complainers, designs in various styles, all handsome. The two deserve every credit, though our guess is that at that stage in history whatever went up would have been substantially similar to what was finally decided on, a work picturesque in its masses, Classical but out of harmony with the Capitol, and elaborate in detail. Smithmeyer and Pelz had a standing dispute with the builder, Brigadier General Thomas Lincoln Casey, over authority and honor. Our sympathy in these cases is invariably with the artists, but it is hard not to acknowledge that seeing the job through was the great thing here. The chief wonder is that the vast pile came into being; the form given it is secondary. General

* Available from: The Superintendent of Documents, Government Printing Office, Washington, D.C. 20402.

160

The Library of Congress. Photo: courtesy of The Library of Congress.

Casey was the Titan in the matter. That he replaced Smithmeyer and Pelz with his son Edward Pearce Casey can hardly be passed over without notice, but the change, justice apart, probably contributed little to the Library's detriment or advantage, although the new architect's youthfulness accounts for the interior being a little more up to date than the fabric.

As with the structure itself, the marvel of the Entrance Hall and the Reading Room is less their design than their limitless embellishment. These things are hard to measure, but our guess would be that there is more color here, in tile, in mosaic, in varieties of marble, in gilding, in metallic hue, above all in oil paint (if we take into account the Corridors and Pavilions) than is to be found under any other single roof in the United States. And to the eternal credit of the Library this color is so distributed that the painted panels are simply incorporated into the system, not made the heart and soul of it. The blend here of the ornamental arts is unique of its kind.

The Reading Room is less lavish that the Entrance Hall in that the variety of decorative devices is limited; but not so much from simplicity, which hardly could apply here, as from greater concentration, the artistic effect is all the stronger.

Only at the famous national expositions is it likely that anything like the number of painters and sculptors was employed as at the Library. But interest is misdirected if we turn it toward the eminent among this assemblage. Famous names appear on the Library's extensive roster of artists. The Library's beauty, however, can be credited to none of these, because no individual achievement dominates or even makes itself conspicuous in either of the two great rooms. To two men, whose work on it was the major accomplishment of their lives, are due the chief honors for the realization of the Library's interior as we know it. These are Albert Weinert, who supervised the infinite quantity of modeling and carving, and Elmer Garnsey, who was responsible for the color. Each, in addition to the task of conception for this immense project, or rather pair of projects, was in charge of an army of painters or sculptors. With General Casey and Bernard Green, the engineer, who completed the Library after Casey's death, they are responsible for what is most to be marveled at, the Library's scope.

The richness of the relief is revealed only by inspection. We are struck, in the coffered ceiling of the Reading Room, by the pattern of the coffers themselves, with their golden rosettes set in blue rectan-

Neptune, the dominant figure of Hinton Perry's fountain in the forecourt of the Library. Photo: courtesy of The Library of Congress.

gles. But the background for these rectangles is an extraordinarily intricate field of stucco ornament, not at first apparent, made up of almost the full range of Classical motifs. What initially appears to be the simple repetition to be expected—and seems on further study the very opposite of this, a sea of random ornaments—is, of course, the rhythmic scheme required, but composed of (the record, not our eye, tells us) almost four dozen motifs. In the Hall, the pilaster capitals, nominally Corinthian, turn out to be a forest of original designs in matched pairs. The charm of these comes from the substitution for volutes of the creatures of the Classical zoo—griffins, harpies, eagles, winged horses, and cats.

Garnsey had no less than twenty-five painters at his disposal, and these were in addition to the considerable number that contributed medallions and lunettes. That the pictorial decoration, though everywhere to be seen, asserts a relatively modest claim on attention might be attributed to a degree of commonplaceness in the skill and judgment displayed throughout much of it. But it is one of the great virtues

of Garnsey's elaborate system that shortcomings and merits alike are secondary to the role individual parts play in the over-all scheme. Much of the painting is actually of a high order. John Alexander's episodes of what would now be called communications history alone are too illustrative to qualify as decoration. (For what it is worth, it should be noted that this is the set most touted by the Library itself.) All told, there was so even a distribution of the various sets and series that none is put ahead of any other by place, and it would almost go contrary to the spirit of this concept to single out instances of particular merit.

In the way of an exception, there was a sort of assignment of honor; the crown of the whole affair. This was the so-called Collar of the Dome and the Eye of the Lantern, entrusted to Edwin Blashfield. But as this is in the Reading Room, it does not bear on the general effect described.

Of the sculpture in the round, most attention over the years has been given to the Ethnological Heads that form the keystones of the windows of the corner pavilions and to the portrait figures that line the balcony of the Rotunda. This is probably because the first group is a curiosity, and the second is what the reader at his desk (who has hurried through the Entrance Hall) sees every time he raises his eyes from his book. The actual masterpieces are the brilliant fountain outside the building, by Hinton Perry, and the balustrades of the staircases within, by Philip Martiny. Perry's fountain is a composition of giant nymphs, Tritons, sea-horses, frogs, and turtles, presided over by Neptune, swirling in a degree of volcanic movement very foreign to prevailing American practice—a spirit shared within the Library only by William De Leftwich Dodge's ceiling for the North-West Pavilion. The balustrade is a cascade of marble babies symbolizing the Continents, the Arts, and the Occupations, descending to newel posts that are the pedestals of bronze female lamp bearers. Martiny's figures are full of animation, though of a more restrained liveliness that those of the fountain.

There is a fourth item, neither painting nor sculpture, that shares at least prominence with the other triumphs listed here. That is Elihu Vedder's mosaic, *Minerva*, which caps the mosaic scheme that covers the ceiling of the first floor. This upright single figure is impressive, but Vedder expressed his own dissatisfaction with it, and this was not just diffidence, because he was quick enough to describe his lunettes as the only paintings in the building that "look as if made for the place they occupy." This judgment is over-simplified, though it is fair enough to put Vedder on the top·of the scale on which Alexander placed lowest.

What sets the Library apart from other lavishly appointed structures in Washington is that it is not by its opulence that the viewer is most struck. Across the street, in the Supreme Court, surface and scale account for the impact. The glow of the marble, the height of the columns, their reflection in the floor, are what impress us there and in the Archives and the Rotunda of the National Gallery. In the Library it is the order into which these things are put that is the factor; not shine, but thought, is what has moved us. At first glance around the corridors outside the Hall the visitor is overwhelmed by the quantity of gold. That is because the vaulted ceilings are so low that the rosettes, themselves very beautiful, seem to be within arms reach. But the patterns they follow, and the painting and stucco work against which they are foiled, outweigh the primitive appeal of the gilding, which in the circumstance is not subdued by the juxtaposition but made all the more brilliant.

All this is the merest sketch. The relation, for example, between the schemes of the floors and those of the ceilings could be inquired into. But the Library defies detailed examination, except at infinite length. All that can be conveyed is flavor. Perhaps we could settle for that and rest content in satisfaction that such a jewel belongs to the nation.

Unhappily, the matter cannot be left at that. After three-quarters of a century the care shown the Library is no less than such a treasure deserves, and any overt threat to its continued existence is unimaginable. But what has been described here is only to be enjoyed as a fragment of its original self. For it has been the Library's fate to be cherished by all except its occupants. It would be unfair to assume that the librarians dislike the building. It may well be that they are fond of it. But the view held by the profession is that its task is of more consequence than the setting provided for that task. In that light, it would be illogical for appearance to flourish at the expense of function. And conscientiousness has not allowed this to happen. Work comes first, with the praiseworthy evidence of this everywhere.

The gorgeous corridors described here were long ago closed to the public. And it was long ago that room for a desk or two was found in a corner of the Entrance Hall balcony. By now there is not even a corner of the balcony that a visitor could so much as edge onto. The upper staircase alone is kept free, this leading to a look out on the Hall. All else is given over to offices, partitions, and shelves. The deprivation of the tourist is not the issue; it is the monstrous disfigurement caused by thousands of feet of plasterboard. Moreover, not only is this ugly in itself, but it conceals by its height acres of the Hall. The two beautiful sets of ceiling medallions by Frank Benson and Robert Reid, with their rich attendant ornament, are barely to be made out in the dark, and must be searched out at

The Great Hall of the Library, in its present state. Photo: courtesy of The Library of Congress.

an angle from the stairs, with the adjacent walls completely hidden. The warehouse effect has also been carried into the Reading Room, with masonite lining the full circumference of the balustrade, except for the Visitors' Gallery. The irony here is that this defacement was introduced immediately on the heels of the Room's refurbishing. The Room was allowed to shine forth briefly in almost (but not quite) its original splendor; then this scar appeared across its surface.

If the brightening up of the Reading Room is more than welcome, it is balanced by the restoration undertaken in the Entrance Hall. There, the result was disastrous. Restoration is keyed to cleaning, which, more often than not, reveals the original tone and color, because oil paint does not, of itself, tend to darken. Where there has been outright deterioration, fresh paint can bring the damaged portion into key with the cleaned area. Sixty years of dust and grime have made the painting in the Library a perfect candidate for this treatment, which would have made the Hall positively glow. Instead, the painting of the South Corridor, a

Edwin Howland Blashfield on the scaffolding beneath the eye of the dome in the Reading Room of the Library. Photo: courtesy of Richard Murray, National Collection of Fine Arts.

beautiful series of lunettes by H. O. Walker given over to *Lyric Poetry*, was subjected to a course of reconditioning which amounted to the spreading of house paint within existing contours. The delicacy of Walker's modeling and the fusing of his outlines with the background have simply vanished. The procedure followed has been the crudest of all restoration techniques, the painting of new pictures over old.

It is only fair to add that the Library seems to have been struck with the enormity of what was done here, because the rest of the Hall has been spared similar attention (and at the same time the necessary cleaning), but the South Corridor has been ruined forever.

The clerical and storage facilities crowded into the Entrance Hall and Reading Room are not the only intrusion. Display cases fill up the remaining floor space, interfering in their own way with the designers' originally intended effect. The material so shown is literary, historical, but as often as not bibliographic or

artistic, in short, cultural. But this testifies to the odd twist of a librarian's mind, that it should seem reasonable to exhibit posters, manuscripts, rare volumes, examples of typography, in short, the periphery of one art—writing—at the price of the concealment of another—design.

To cap all this, it has been years since the magnificent Neptune Fountain spouted any water.

There is, of course, an Annex east of the Library, connected to the main building by a tunnel, but related in no way artistically, and hence disagreeable in effect whatever its merits, which anyway are slight. Presently there will rise to the south the Madison Memorial, which will be similarly unrelated to either existing structure, and by its location play further havoc with the symmetry of the Capitol Grounds. This is supposed to give Madison his due, alongside the Memorials to Washington, Jefferson, and Lincoln, but nothing of the sort will be accomplished. The building will be Annex No. 2, and remind us of the fourth President only if we happen to glance at the inscription over the entrance.

The *Quarterly Journal* article strikes a note different from these few paragraphs. It sticks to the facts, handing down little praise or blame. We learn from it the remarkable circumstances that the building came in at a cost below the estimate, and we are told something of the range of General Casey's concerns, and of the scale on which Weinert and Garnsey operated. It is instructive, too, to read that, in resistance to the idea of the Library as a kind of reliquary of learning, the most penurious and backward members of Congress were joined (even that long ago) by the professional librarians to a man.

It is not too clear how far from that attitude the *Journal* itself has come. But in its emphasis on the physical side of the great task, the judgment conveyed, though not directly expressed, is that there is more to be astounded at than to admire. And there is a whimsical undertone to the account of General Casey's single-mindedness and the Bohemian undependability of the artists, which suggests that the real charm of the Library of Congress is its quaintness.

It is proper enough that a librarian's first loyalty is due to the (his) library as an institution, that is, a systematic collection of books, his responsibilities being the constant refinement of that system, the increase and protection of the collection, and the making available of the books themselves, in about that order. Accordingly, the aspect of building that is of interest to him is its adaptation to the purpose listed. This is so notoriously, by the librarian's own continued insistence, his view of the matter, that it is unfortunate that the community has not, from the beginning, accepted it, and maintained its own control over what is admit-

The North Staircase of the Great Hall, at the time of its creation. Photo: courtesy of Pierce Rice.

tedly of no concern to the librarian—architecture, which is the aspect of building that has to do with appearance. The Library of Congress is only the most prominent example of the denizens of a public palace, which is allowed them as an accomodation, behaving as if they were its owners.

A New Paneled Room in Dutchess County

by

JOHN BARRINGTON BAYLEY

THE house in which this room stands was built *c.* 1939. The house is Episodic-classical: a gable with outside chimney and two little windows will recall any of the local farmhouses (1750-1850). The front porch with a perfectly executed Order in brownstone is our Greek Revival. The bay-windows with pelmets in wood suggesting tents and the cast-iron porches could be Regency Britain, and so could the triple-hung windows to the floor and the French doors. The oculus dormers are Directoire. The gardens are Lutyensesque with long narrow rills or Rhines planted with water lilies and reeds; the lawn at the house is circular, and walled on two sides with a garden house in the corner—but, alas, there are so many delights that we are carried from our subject.

Inside the house the same genial eclecticism holds sway. The rooms on the ground floor range from an eighteenth-century pine-paneled drawing room, through a Venetian painted and marbled garden room

to a superb ''Salon de Compagnie'' (see your Wharton-Codmans) with a fully frescoed vaulted ceiling above an entablature of Portuguese marble on pilasters of the same, the whole parcel gilt.

The bedrooms have lowish ceilings and a general air of sophisticated simplicity—the woodwork is far above the usual. The room which we are talking about originally was papered in blue and white. It was decided, however, to bring the owner's collection of pictures relating to Washington from the National Gallery and to hang them in this room, and hence to give the room more consequence.

The owner said to me that he wanted a rather countrified Virginian room of the Pre-Revolutionary period. I got out two copies of *The Mansions of Virginia—1706-1776* by T.T.Waterman. I cut them up and made a big scrapbook. All the different types of fireplaces on a page or so, then a page of baseboards, one of cornices, rails and stiles, and so on, so that we

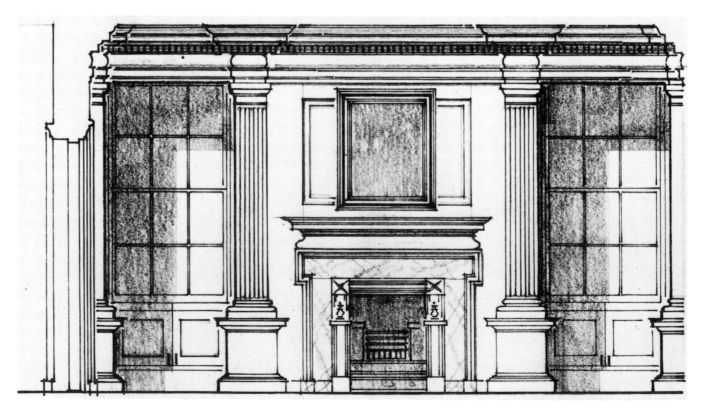

Plate I.

could decide what was best. Lots of drawings were made because we had to shoe-horn the pictures into place. There wasn't much space left over.

PLATE I shows one of the first designs bodying forth the "simple country look." I tried for the unsophisticated look by using "Harewood" in West Virginia as a prototype. The owner: "I may want a simple country look, but I am not Squire Western." I had gone too far in the hound-dog-asleep-on-the-porch direction. I felt, as did the owner, that anything is better than the "Lake Forest" look which has deluged so many Virginia houses with forests of lampshades.

PLATE II is a working-drawing. I know of no way to study architecture except with large precise scale drawings in ink. Although it would drive an office manager mad, it is the only way I know to really see what a thing is going to look like.

PLATE III shows the west wall of the room, and one of our most brilliant decisions. The door you see was an existing door. If we had paneled around it and accepted it as a part of our composition then the panels around it would have been suburban in size—like somebody's den—and the door itself all wrong, dating from, say, about 1803—Late Regency and not the 1770s we were projecting. Instead of this we decided

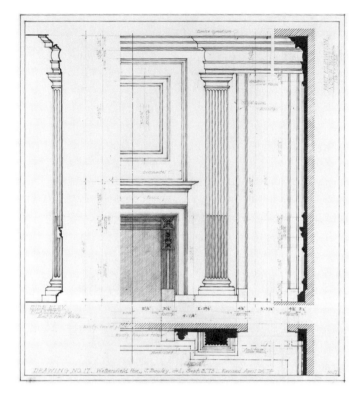

Plate II.

Plate III.

Plate IV.

Plate V.

to pretend that we had a 1770s room which had been *modified* in the 1830s. The door is a later modification; a new wing was added to the house. The very blank looking slots over the door have been covered by Chinese frets in brass.

PLATE V shows the east wall, some of the pictures *in situ,* and a blind door. Ogden Codman and Edith Wharton in *The Decoration of Houses,* a book which all members will be receiving shortly, deal *in extenso* with the *odium theologicum* which has been leveled at these doors by partisans of "The Ethical Fallacy." A magisterial inquiry into this widely held heresy will be found in your copies of *The Architecture of Humanism,* Chapter Five. Suffice it to say here that the blind door, the door that lies, is in somewise an emblem of classical architecture.

You will note on the right hand side of the picture a window in the Regency manner. This is one of the "modifications" made to the room in 1830.

Plate VI is sheet twenty-one, I note. This means that twenty sheets of study preceded it. Classical architecture is not necessarily an endurance test; the fact that so much work has been done doesn't say that it is good. However, as none of us were raised in the classics it is, alas, necessary. I think anything is preferable to the use of the rather flaccid standard details repeated over and over again by the manufacturers of millwork: doors, door enframements, windows, chimney-pieces, and lighting fixtures. If they had been good in the first place it would be different, but they generally try to look more expensive than they are and are skimped and under-scaled and truly vulgar. If one were reared in the tradition one would have been doing these things for thirty years or so, and one would have a whole bag of tricks, but there is no such person today. The old boys that I have known were brought up in the days of the classical decline and were busy watering down classicism. (Cornices instead of projecting at forty-five degrees were made to project less, all reveals were put on a starvation diet, and the small town Georgian library or Fire Station resulted.)

It may be true that every generation has to do things all over again from scratch, and that the only people at the *present* who can do good classical architecture are those who have *been through* the Modern Movement.

PLATE VI was originally full-size. The procedure is that the cabinet-maker then takes all the profiles shown, breaks them down into manageable components, and has knives made which fit to the curves of the profiles. These knives revolve at high speed in machines. Pieces of wood are fed to them, and emerge with the proper profile. A molding like the large bolection would probably take five different knives.

I had never done a paneled room in this style

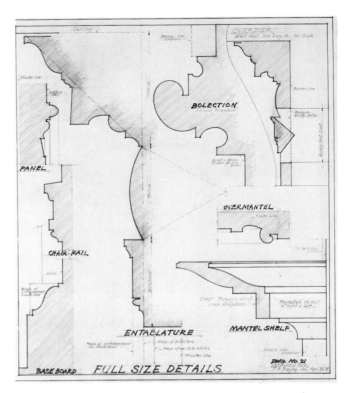

Plate VI.

before, and these were some of my discoveries made by studying Waterman and by trips to various rooms in museums. Baseboards are extremely heavy and extend into the room, chair-rails are flat and massive, and the whole entablature very big. When I say "big" or "heavy" or "massive" I mean in comparison with run-of-the-mill Georgian or Colonial Revival. Another surprise was that the masters of yesteryear used Doric pilasters with, as here, an Ionic frieze. An Ionic frieze is plain, except for the sculpture on it. It sometimes has a curved outline (as it does here), as if ready to be carved, and is then said to be *pulvinated,* from *pulvinar,* a bolster, which it much resembles. The pilasters have Attic bases. This base is shown in *The American Vignola* belonging to the Ionic Order. The flutings in the Doric Order are separated by an arris, a sharp edge. The flutings here as in the Ionic are separated by a fillet of about one fourth their width. The corona, the flat part of the cornice, which lies between the cymatium—here a cyma recta—and the bed mold, instead of having a right angle corner has a corner at a more acute angle, as should be done in interior cornices, though never in exterior. (This bandying about of architectural terms will be less tiresome after you have become familiar with *The American Vignola.* Eventually all members of our Society will be provided with a copy of this book. The architectural vocabulary falls between Roman, Greek, and Gallic stools, and there are synonyms galore, so that termin-

Plate VII.

ology will always be a problem.) A bolection molding covers the joint between two members with different surface levels. The delight in this molding is to make the undercutting of the torus as dramatic as possible, so that you can grip it with your hand. In this example the undercutting is carried about as far as it ever is outside of Italy, and it makes a very fine shadow around the fireplace opening. A minor bolection frames the over-mantel. The drawing of the mantel-shelf shows a tricky situation where a molded surface has to project more on one side than on the other. The corner angle can't be at forty-five degrees, and the curves have to be adapted accordingly.

PLATE VII shows some of the things just described, and raises a final point. As you can see on PLATE VI at the top of the cornice—the cymatium *or* cimaise—there is a gap between the ceiling and the cornice. This is called the shadow line. It is essential to use this if the paneling is installed after the ceiling is in place because the plaster is wavy and the wood is straight, and never the twain shall meet. Even when the wood goes in first I feel that there should always be a dark shadow separating the two materials.

The room was designed by John Barrington Bayley and built by Max Grammer.

Drawings and photos by John B. Bayley

A Design for a Pavilion in Fairmount Park

by

JOHN BLATTEAU

The design which is published here was created for a show in the fall of 1976 at the Langman Gallery in Jenkintown, Pennsylvania. The architect is John Blatteau, who is head of the Philadelphia chapter of Classical America. The idea of the show was to design a house for the site of the existing historic mansion Mount Pleasant in Philadelphia's Fairmount Park. Mr. Blatteau's choice of a formal French classical solution to the problem was noticed by Progressive Architecture *and the* Philadelphia Inquirer *with an interest which several years ago would have been unthinkable. His design might be compared with John Bayley's Dinsha House, featured in previous issues of* Classical America, *and with Raymond Erith and Quinlan Terry's Pavilion at Little Horkesley, shown elsewhere in this issue. Blatteau's project is, of course, an ideal conception, like those formerly designed for Beaux-Arts competitions.*

Mr. Blatteau accompanies his drawings with the following commentary and three quotations which, for him, contain the essence of the classical spirit.

THE EDITOR

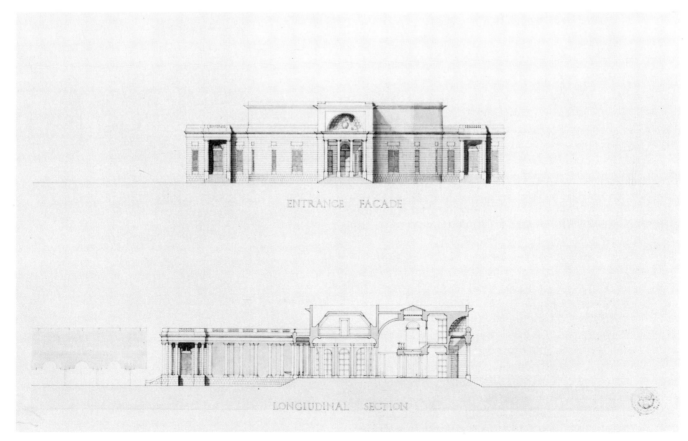

John Blatteau, "Mount Pleasant," a design for a pavilion in Fairmount Park; entrance façade and longitudinal section.

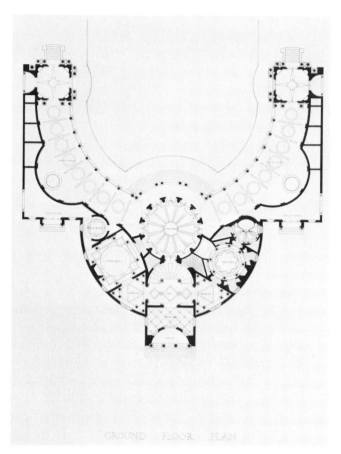

"Mount Pleasant," ground floor plan.

THE Mount Pleasant Show, of which this house is a part, was a response by several architects in Philadelphia to the need for a creative opportunity in architecture outside the customary restraints of client and budget. The design problem, selected for its universal appeal, was a residence, a simple challenge that every architect could respond to without special preparation. The site, Mount Pleasant, a real and existing mansion, one of several located in Fairmount Park, was chosen because of its natural beauty and its easy recognizability by the people of Philadelphia.

The theme of this house, Mont de Plaisance, is basic to the site itself. Fairmount Park has a rich tradition of sharing in the civic life of the city. In addition to being the first and largest major piece of land to be dedicated to park use within a city, it was the site of the city's first major water works. The first Zoological Garden in the New World opened in Fairmount Park. America celebrated its centennial in the park. And for the Bicentennial the city has restored many of the park's eighteenth-century mansions. Within this context, one could hardly introduce a private residence, yet a public residence seemed absolutely appropriate. A residence in the park, free from the historical connotations of the existing mansions,

open to the pleasures and desires of the citizens of Philadelphia, seemed a most real and practical addition to this civic tradition so strongly established.

Since the house is to be a permanent addition to the park setting, it strives to eliminate the specific and to amplify the general. The house is at once a collection of ideal rooms and a collection of rooms organized into an ideal whole. Each room is made into a clear and recognizable place with its shapes, its patterning and its structure expressing and enhancing the generic aspect of the function it contains. The house as a whole, with its totally open garden façade and its relatively solid entrance façade, simply states its contrasting private and public needs. Finally, in detail, as well as in composition, the house has a universal quality. French Neoclassical in style, a style thought most appropriately to embody the spirit of a public residence for the park, the house uses architectural elements traditionally. The columns, walls, windows, and parapets, have undergone no process of creative interpretation or transformation. They are what they appear to be, traditional architectural elements used literally and more or less correctly.

The Show also represented an important opportunity not only to practice the theory of traditional architecture, but also to exercise the drawing skill required of the traditional architect. By this concrete example, it is hoped that Classical Architecture and the point of view it represents will in some way be advanced.

I know that to speak of tradition now is to be far behind the times; the present tendency is to scorn tradition. That means to despise long efforts continued through centuries by industrious generations preceding us; to seek generally to conceal ignorance by affecting to scorn the unknown in order to avoid the effort necessary to know it. Preserve yourselves from this error! Progress is slow and must be sure. Whoever proceeds slowly is sane, and whoever is sane goes far. Do you know what is very strong and original? It is to do very well what others have merely done well. The finest epochs are those in which tradition was most respected, when progress was continually perfecting, when there was evolution and not revolution. Never has there been spontaneous generation in art. Between the Parthenon and the temples preceding it there are only shades of difference. Furthermore, tradition is especially precious for studies. To dare to become free from it one must judge it, and to do this it must be known. Tradition is a patrimony; to dissipate it independently, one risks wandering at random and must at least know how to find himself another shelter.

JULIEN GUADET

Our destination is uncertain and directions nonexistent. Not only has the cord of continuity broken, depriving us of all native and subconscious impulse, but fifty years of quite unexampled architectural degeneracy have undermined any inherited taste we might have had. We have not it in us to create great things, for the sequence of power has been broken and we drift at loose ends. Moreover, technological, democratic, materialistic civilization, with its mass production, parliamentary government, phrenetic movement, religious sectarianism, spiritual indifferentism and

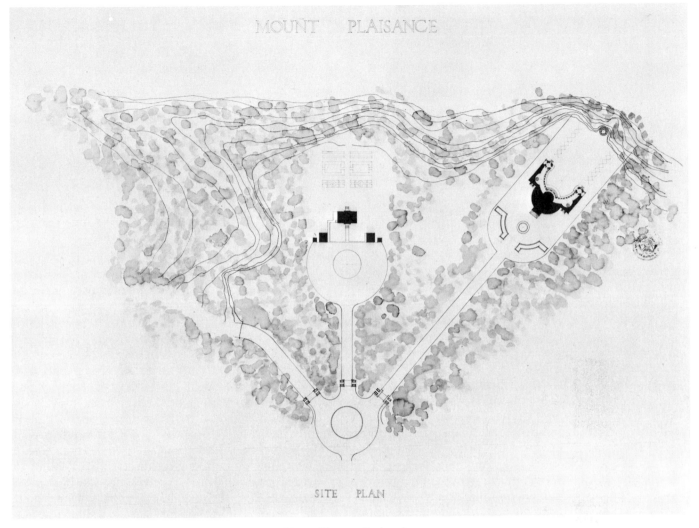

MOUNT PLAISANCE

SITE PLAN

"Mount Pleasant," site plan.

philosophical pragmatism do not provide the soil in which vital art grows spontaneously or the mental and corporal environment which foster it. We look for the "change beyond the change" and in so looking we dig and delve in the ruins of a great past, salvaging what we can of beauty and significance and using this as efficiently as we can.

RALPH ADAMS CRAM

The Classic Spirit is the disinterested search for perfection, it is the love of clearness and reasonableness and self-control; it is, above all, the love of permanence and continuity. It asks of a work of art, not that it shall be novel or effective, but that it shall be fine and noble. It seeks not merely to express individuality or emotion, but to express disciplined emotion and individuality restrained by law. It strives for the essential rather than the accidental, the eternal rather than the momentary—loves impersonality more than personality, and feels more power in the orderly succession of the hours and the seasons than in the violence of earthquake or of storm. It loves to steep itself in tradition. It would have each new work connect itself in the mind of him who sees it with all the noble and lovely works of the past, bringing them to his memory and making their beauty and charm a part of the work before him. It does not deny originality and individuality—they are as welcome as inevitable. It does not consider tradition as immutable or set rigid bounds to invention. But it desires that each new presentation of truth and beauty shall show us the old truth and the old beauty, seen only from a different angle and colored by a different medium. It wishes to add link by link to the chain of tradition, but it does not wish to break the chain.

KENYON COX

Karl Friedrich Schinkel: Berlin as the City Beautiful

by

JAMES ALLEN VANN

BERLIN at the end of the eighteenth century was a confused jumble of disparate buildings, tangled waterways, and crooked streets. It lacked the splendid parks that made London so pleasant a capital, nor did it have the grandiose monumentality that brought tourists flocking to Rome, Paris, and Vienna. The island of Cölln, about a mile in length and shaped by the flow of the Spree River and one of its minor branches, formed the center of the city. There the royal palace and the cathedral stood on the scraped clay of a military parade ground whose borders were a haphazard clutter of vending booths, storage warehouses, and factories. Beyond the island governmental buildings jostled private dwellings and commercial enterprises on a network of rambling streets, sliced arbitrarily by boulevards leading nowhere in particular and lined with monotonous barrack-like constructions.

Karl Friedrich Schinkel, who was active during the first decades of the nineteenth century, struggled to transform this undistinguished urban ambiance into a harmonic unity. He designed a series of buildings, avenues, monuments, and parks for the city that aimed to accommodate the needs of the citizenry and yet provide that sense of ornamentation so essential for civic pride and pleasurable living. What he understood by ornamentation was not excessive embellishment or extraneous clutter but rather that the creation itself must stand as an ornament to its area. It must be pleasing to the eye, of noble proportions, and of a grand scale. His decoration was always in tune with the structural limitations of his creation (which is by no means the same thing as saying that his decoration was always structural!). From this harmony of the general scheme of decoration with the building and of the details of the decoration with one another sprang the rhythm distinguishing his work and imparting to it a beauty at once sumptuous and arresting.

Born in 1781 at Neuruppin, an important garrison town in the Mark Brandenburg, Schinkel came to Berlin at the age of thirteen. Four years later he entered the atelier of David and Friedrich Gilly, Berlin's champions of German Neoclassicism, to "devote his life to fine arts and architecture." His subsequent rise

to the post of Royal Architect was relatively steady. After five years as apprentice to the Gillys, he traveled extensively in Italy, France, and Austria, studying the art and architecture of Europe's classical, medieval, and Renaissance past. Returning to Berlin, he became interested in the new phenomenon of panoramas and published a series of optical-perspective paintings that in some cases depicted remote, exotic places and in others romanticized timely events such as Napoleon's burning of Moscow. Intensifying the visual and psychological impact of his panoramas by back-stage choirs and hidden lights, Schinkel evoked a religious feeling, bordering on emotionalism, in the masses who flocked to view these spectacles. Despite reservations felt by the more sensitive viewers, these extravaganzas were extraordinarily successful, and they assured Schinkel an important place in the affections of the Berlin populace. More important, the shows attracted the attention of the intensely patriotic Queen Louise, who saw in them a possible way to enflame popular sentiment against Napoleon. Schinkel's appointment as a civil architect in 1810 was apparently in large part due to the Queen's personal interest in his panorama presentations. Once appointed, his unquestioned architectural and artistic ability carried him forward until in 1816 he was named official architect and planner for Berlin.

In their comprehensive scope and in their overt commitment to the city as an object of beauty, Schinkel's plans for Berlin bear a striking resemblance to the monumental vision for Chicago presented at the turn of the twentieth century by Daniel Burnham and Edward Bennett. Schinkel, like his later American counterparts, spoke to all facets of urban life; he worked to solve the problems of commerce, industry, and traffic flow as well as those of residential building, monuments, and parks. In 1817 he presented King Frederick William III with a master plan for the city, a set of drawings addressed to the transformation of the entire corps of the capital so as to eliminate "an intolerable hodge-podge of organization." Besides the erection of new churches, the creation of imposing city squares, and designs for a series of elegant residential

The Gendarmenmarkt, with the National Theater (Schauspielhaus) in the center of the plaza. Photo: the Collection of the Institut für Denkmalpflege, Berlin.

gardens and buildings, Schinkel's plan provided for consolidated medical facilities and a totally new shipping and storage center: a harbor basin whose bridges, cranes, and L-shaped complex of customs warehouses would streamline the economic life of Berlin. Inefficient canals were to be closed, river traffic was to be redirected, and a series of spacious parks, charmingly planted and adorned with statuary, was to be opened in the very heart of the city.

Schinkel's plan was never fully implemented. Frederick William proved a patron of limited vision, a man whose artistic concerns centered most directly on matters of cost and immediate practicality. He possessed neither the aesthetic nor the material resources necessary to support a large-scale project such as Schinkel's. No record indicates that he even responded officially to this comprehensive proposal. But if he ignored the broader plans, the king did support his architect in a series of more restricted building ventures. By the time of his death in 1841, Schinkel had produced in Berlin some of the most notable architecture in the Germanics. Furthermore, he had maintained steadfastly his commitment to the ideal of

the City Beautiful, seeking always to integrate a particular project with its surroundings and to produce an architecture that was both practical and attractive. He demonstrated a constant concern for the quality of urban life, for creating a well ordered, convenient city that offered the best possible conditions of living. To this end he insisted that principles of function and purpose should soar beyond those of mere expediency and rationalism; that a spirit of beauty should facilitate and enhance the more subtle psychological needs and aspirations of the inhabitants. He never identified the "duty" of exposing structural forms—that obligation weighing so heavily upon the conscience of the modern architect. Rather, he thought first of adapting his buildings to the uses for which they were intended and then of decorating them in such a way as to give pleasure to the eye. The maintenance of that relation which the eye exacts between main structural lines and their ornamentation was the only form of sincerity which he knew or cared about. In his words, "The beautiful stands as one of the bases of existence upon which rational life is built. Without this foundation one struggles with barbarism." And beauty for Schinkel

Portico and clerestory of the Schauspielhaus. Photo: the Messbildarchiv, Berlin.

could never be achieved by relying solely upon "structural honesty" and on a relentless order of repetitive modules.

A detailed look at two of his completed projects, the Schauspielhaus and the renovation of the island of Cölln, will point up Schinkel's contribution as a city planner and provide a historical model against which to measure our contemporary architectural standards and by which to refine our expectations in urban design. The National Theater, or Schauspielhaus, illustrates Schinkel's determination to create a civic art whose end was harmony, good order, and beauty. At the same time it illustrates his belief that a civic center depended for its effectiveness on the character of the architecture displayed in the buildings themselves, in their harmonious relations with one another, and in the amount of space in which they are placed. No isolated, contrived façade is permitted to monopolize a single, highly intellectualized vantage-point; rather Schinkel was concerned that a building be seen and experienced from points of view other than the obvious and conventional ones. Similarly, his treatment of the Lustgarten and his ingenious arrangement of the system of warehouses behind this great plaza demonstrate his

ability to coordinate the component elements of the city—the practical, the decorative, the old and the new—into a single unity of formal, spatial, and visual relationships that successfully reconciled a set of specific functional requirements to sweeping grandeur.

Our own need for such models is acute. The universities, alas, fail all too often to instill in their graduates an ability to articulate or even to formulate personal standards of taste. The result is that the men and women who sit on committees to decide the aesthetic fate of our cities often feel uncertain and ambivalent in assessing arguments of design. They lack the technical terminology that would enable them to define and defend an artistic criterion, especially in confrontation with an architect or construction firm urging a particular shopping center or "renewal" scheme. Discomfort often drives the city fathers to sanction plans for housing and buildings that they feel instinctively to be repellent, faddish, and unsatisfactory. Brave indeed is the man or woman who speaks out on the council board against such banalities as the recent Detroit project for an eighteen-million-dollar "Renaissance Plaza," a concrete expanse centering around a cloud-creating, computer-operated fountain of four posts, whose waters are to symbolize "the American Indians, the flight of birds, and jet planes."

Schinkel's work suggests an alternative approach to the city from that of the Detroit planners. His approach, moreover, is eminently applicable today; in his efforts to beautify Berlin he was confronting many of the same problems that plague our modern cities. Like so many designers today, Schinkel was forced to develop his proposals within the constraints of an already established urban complex, one, moreover, that was suffering from haphazard planning and rapid growth of population. In the seventeenth century Berlin had mushroomed from a small provincial capital of about 56,000 inhabitants to an important European center of some 200,000 souls, a population equal to that of Rome or Madrid. Much of this demographic growth was concentrated in hastily erected, unappealing quarters on the periphery of town, cut off from any creative participation in the life of the dispirited inner city. Frederick the Great, who ruled Prussia from 1740 to 1786, had loathed his capital and, by setting up his residence at Potsdam, drew out of Berlin many of those forces that might otherwise have acted to invigorate the old city. Add to this situation the desperate state of post-Napoleonic Prussian finances, and the modern urban parallel is complete. Expansion and renovation were essential if Berlin were to accommodate the return of the government; but funds were as limited as the architectural propensities of the monarch and his entourage.

In meeting these problems, Schinkel showed both talent and vision. Equally important, he approached his work with a sympathetic appreciation for the importance of the grand scale in urban life. He saw that the only worthy purpose of architecture was the creation of such beauty as would elevate and inspire the beholder. Through a skillful use of scale, setting, ornamentation, and formal unity, he sought to create an architecture that would typify the permanence of the city, record its history, and express the aspirations of its people. In this task he included not only external decoration and landscape, but even detailed interior treatment, extending to wall decoration and furniture. "To be an architect," he wrote, "means to be a man who elevates all aspects of human life. Within his sphere of creative effort he must embrace all branches of the fine arts. He fuses sculpture, painting, and architecture into a single expression of art, according to the demands of man's moral and rational life." The end result was to be a completely harmonious presentation.

In this emphasis on unity and symmetry, Schinkel stands squarely in the tradition of classicism; his emphasis on ultimate repose is equally Greco-Roman in

A view taken in 1928 from the steps of Schauspielhaus onto one of the two italianate churches of the Gendarmenmarkt. Photo: Klaus Beyer, Weimar.

inspiration. But though the art of antiquity unquestionably proved a source of inspiration for Schinkel, it would be a mistake to view him as drawing exclusively from classical or neoclassical models. Even his earliest drawings reveal a conscious effort to avoid the frozen quality produced in the works of his architectural mentor Frederick Gilly by a rigid and overly zealous application of these rules. Rather than commit himself to a single style, Schinkel sought to manipulate forms and spaces according to the dictates of practical need, symbolic association, and his own uncommon sense of beauty. Gothic forms, for example, fascinated him and often seemed to offer scope for the movement and vitality that he found lacking in the neoclassicism of his contemporaries. Maintaining as he did that design should be an outgrowth of function, he believed that in one structure function might dictate a Gothic solution and in another a classical one. In this regard, Schinkel is more profitably regarded as an inventive eclectic than a highly innovative genius. Werner Hegemann—though he quite misses the totality of Schinkel's urban vision—correctly describes his artistic career as "a swing back and forth from classical to gothic forms in an effort to develop a new artistic style."

The doors to the Berlin Schauspielhaus opened on

Lateral view of the Schauspielhaus. Photo: Klaus Beyer, Weimar.

26 May, 1821, admitting a curious public into a theater already acclaimed as one of the most significant pieces of architecture in nineteenth-century Germany. Those attending the opening night performance of Goethe's *Iphigenie auf Tauris* faced a backdrop that pictured all the goals of the builder. To underscore the dramatic effect of his theater, Schinkel had created on the stage a panoramic view of the new building in its total architectural setting, a perspective that graphically illustrated his ethic of grandeur in the magnificent square of Gendarmenmarkt which the Schauspielhaus helped to form. From the beginning Schinkel had struggled to integrate his building with the two massive Franco-Italianate churches that dominated the Gendarmenmarkt, feeling that a correlation with these older buildings whose structure and function was so different from that of his theater was an absolute essential. The end result was an extraordinary square whose monumental elegance expressed the civic pride of a capital that was coming increasingly to dominate the Germanies and whose beauty added an important element of inspiration to urban life.

Their common classical orientation was the most obvious bond between the new building and its neighbors. Freestanding pedimented porticoes, symmetrical balance of masses, and emphasis on a central axis were basic to his design. But the point must be stressed that his unity was not the result merely of Schinkel's adaptation of neoclassical motifs. His inventive transformation of classical elements resulted in a building that was indeed new, readily distinguishable from its neighbors, though it retained, like the churches, a classical repose and a noble proportion. Convinced that the theater should dominate the plaza, Schinkel chose a pyramidal composition for the main façade, repeating the triangular pediment of the portico above the clerestory. He crowned this second pediment with a bronze sculptural group, counterbalancing the vertical emphasis of the domed churches flanking the square. He additionally elevated the theater on a rough stone podium which framed the huge staircase leading up to the main portico. The treatment of this mammoth portico echoed that of the two churches, thereby drawing the three sides of the square into a formal unity.

The dramatic effect of this ensemble was enhanced by a more subtle set of relationships between the churches and his theater. Schinkel properly perceived that the principal feature of the two churches was their three-sided porticoes. He therefore designed his building so that in approaching the square along one of the connecting streets, one's eye was led by the multiple porticoes around the projecting mass of the church into the square and up the raised porch of the Schauspielhaus. The sense of the coherence was further stimulated by a repetition, on the lateral wings of the theater, of the pediments that crown the three principal façades of the churches as well as the central façade of the theater. Finally, he ornamented each wing of the Schauspielhaus with a complex rhythm of vertical supports and window openings, placed so as to echo the line of the porticoes.

The majestic dignity that characterized the Schauspielhaus found an even more dramatic expression in Schinkel's renovation of Cölln, the island home of the royal palace, the cathedral, and the Port of Berlin. Through a combination of landscape, sculpture, and architecture, he transformed the parade ground flanking the palace into a magnificent urban plaza known as the Lustgarten. Beyond the Lustgarten, he reorganized the buildings of the Port Authority so as to consolidate the city's principal commercial offices into an efficient complex. The end result was that buildings as diverse in their uses as an armory, a palace, a cathedral, an office complex, and a warehouse were drawn into a harmonious unity that imparted a spacious magnificence to the inner city of Berlin.

The commission to create a museum to house the Hohenzollern art collections—one of the first public museums to be constructed in Europe—provided Schinkel with the architectural rationale for enclosing the parade ground and for separating the palace from the commercial area of the port. He placed his building directly across the parade ground from the northern entrance to Slütter's great baroque palace, so that the museum was framed on the east by the cathedral and on the west by a canal separating the palace from the Royal Armory that Slütter had built a century earlier. In designing the museum Schinkel was careful to choose a composition that would harmonize with these three important buildings already standing on the square. He conceived an exterior for the museum that was complementary in geometric form to the palace and the Zeughaus, both of which were horizontal rather than vertical in architectural emphasis. At the same time he produced for the principal façade a modified version of the colonnade on the cathedral, a building whose vertical thrust had become a foil to the lower, broader structures surrounding it on the plaza.

Schinkel's façade for the museum anticipated the strikingly similar one of the British Museum, constructed some twenty years later in London. The resemblance between the two buildings was so startling that Smirke, the English architect, actually had to defend his drawings before a nervous museum committee who feared that he had "taken over the design

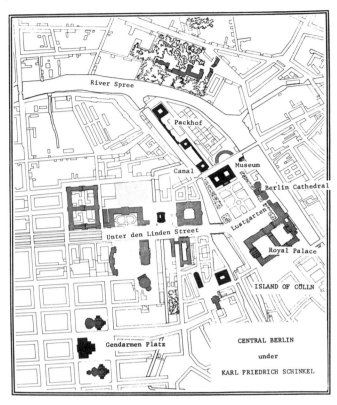

A map of Central Berlin.

from Schinkel." But while the similarities were pronounced, important differences underscore some of the creative variations possible within the classical vocabulary. Smirke's façade is that of a typically Palladian building whose recessed center and projecting wings place it squarely in the eighteenth-century tradition. Schinkel's façade is bolder, more innovative. Its absolutely straight sheer front, with one giant order running throughout, is entirely uncompromising. No pediment breaks the central unity and the whole is crowned by a heavy architrave and cornice. The treatment of the staircase is equally original. The stairways at each side of the façade are enclosed at no point by walls, remaining open to the colonnade and culminating in a semi-enclosed vestibule with a dazzling view onto the Lustgarten and, beyond, to the city itself.

In addition to the formal relationships, spatial relationships also operated to make the Lustgarten a visual unit. The central spatial element was the plaza itself, where a simple but elegant arrangement of planting linked the civic, royal, and religious buildings. To create an impression of spectacular dimensions within the plaza, Schinkel set the museum as far back from the palace as possible, filling in an old canal in order to extend his setting. His imaginative use of sculpture and shrubbery endowed the area with geometric balance and more intimate charm. Precise arrangements

A view from the canal onto the Hohenzollern palace on the Island of Cölln. To the left of the photograph the Lustgarten façade is visible. The entire complex was destroyed in 1944. Photo: Klaus Beyer, Weimar.

The Berlin Cathedral as seen from the steps of Schinkel's Museum. Today the Cathedral stands in ruins. Photo: Klaus Beyer, Weimar.

of trees and bushes, punctuated at key points by examples of elegant garden statuary, disguised the fact that the façade of the cathedral and that of the palace did not lie on a perpendicular axis to the museum and that the façade of the museum—by express order of the sovereign—did not run parallel to that of the palace. At the same time, the planting of a double row of chestnuts along the canal and to the right and left of the cathedral allowed Schinkel to screen out those buildings whose sites and exteriors did not support his over-all plan.

Quite apart from the spaciousness of the square itself, the citizens of Berlin delighted in the variety of vistas and the handsomely controlled visual experiences that Schinkel provided. Through a skillful use of right angles and axial alignments he had brought organization to what might otherwise have been a group of unrelated elements: while planting, sculpture, and ground plan carried the eye across the sweep of palace, church, and museum, oblique angles offered tantalizing glimpses onto the plaza and the city beyond. Wherever the eye wandered—within the Lustgarten or looking out from it—the vista was one of beauty. When it was opened to the public in 1830, the Lustgarten took a proud place among the city plazas of

The Museum as viewed from the Lustgarten, 1928. Photo: the Collection of the Institut für Denkmalpflege, Berlin.

Europe and gave Berlin a central focus worthy of its rank as a major European capital.

The Lustgarten might well be regarded as one of the last great urban squares, ending a tradition of city plaza development that had begun in sixteenth-century Italy and that had organized urban living since that time. Certainly it was the most successful such plan executed in nineteenth-century Germany. Neither Leo von Klenze's contemporary work in Munich nor Fredrick Weinbrenner's plans for Karlsruhe so successfully combined monumental splendor with harmonic movements as did the Lustgarten. While the former projects remained rigid and static, Schinkel's square evidenced a dynamic, picturesque quality that delighted by its orchestrated power but charmed by its warm, graceful landscape and by its carefully controlled architectural vistas.

Once he had completed the museum and the Lustgarten, Schinkel turned his attention to the remaining areas of the island, to the warehouses, vending booths, and offices of the Port Authority. Between 1829 and 1832 he built a series of connected buildings that transformed the existing jumble into an efficient complex successfully serving the commercial, storage, and shipping needs of the inner city. The Packhof, as the development was called, is most readily envisioned as a set of three principal structures, joined by lower architectural elements and placed in an effec-

The portico and principal staircase of the Museum. Photo: Klaus Beyer, Weimar.

tive arrangement along the quays of the northern end of the island. At the foremost tip, the entrance into the Berlin Harbor, Schinkel erected a five-story warehouse. Known as the Magazin, the building was a miniature version of Slütter's Italianate Zeughaus so that, despite its strictly functional purpose, it possessed the same majestic grace as the offices of the municipal government. The two other main units of the Packhof, the Customs House and the Offices of the Port Authority, were equally pleasing. Schinkel saw to it that their commercial function did not preclude their being distinguished. Believing as he did that ornamentation and monumentality were entirely compatible with efficiency, he spoke to this conviction in creating sculptured pediments and gracefully balanced façades to adorn this set of eminently functional buildings. For nearly a century the Packhof served the commercial needs of the city. Not until 1906, when the population had risen to almost two million, did the complex cease to function adequately. At that point, it was razed and two Imperial museums, the Pergamon and the Kaiser Friedrich (now Bode Museum), were erected on the area.

Looking today at Cölln, one can identify only the barest outline of Schinkel's creation. The great museum still stands, carefully restored by the East German government, but its surroundings have undergone drastic and devastating change. Instead of a magnificent monument that once formed but one element in a splendid plaza—a plaza whose unabashed aim was to create in the beholder a sense of and appreciation for the beautiful—one now finds only the splendid façade of an isolated building. The planting has gone, and the Marx-Engels-Platz now covers the ground where the palace once stood. The cathedral has been transformed out of all recognition, and the Packhof, of course, has vanished. Starkly functional buildings housing the government of East Berlin and the foreign ministry of the DDR crowd into what once

was a carefully organized panorama of balanced harmony and elegance.

Quite apart from the disaster of war, a portion of the blame for the startling impermanence of Schinkel's Lustgarten lies with the architect himself. One of his most exciting characteristics—his deliberate use of planting and sculpture to create an architectural whole—made his accomplishments difficult to preserve. Schinkel deliberately rejected what he regarded as superficial architectural embellishments, such as free-standing decorative colonnades, and roundly denounced the "sham façades" that impart such an impressive unity to large-scale urban project's like Regent's Park and Bath. Instead, he relied on nature for his unifying elements. Trees and promenades, punctuated by sculpture and fountains, were used to create visual and spatial organization among loosely-linked groups of buildings. As a result, of course, his accomplishments as a great urban planner were vulnerable to the deterioration of time and to the vagaries of taste in succeeding generations.

But it is not my intent to lament the transience of Schinkel's creative use of nature. What is of interest to those of us committed to the ideals of Classical America is that in Schinkel we find a man of vision, someone who saw the city *en beau* and sought to create within that city a harmonic order that espoused the beautiful. Though he identified restraint as a key to true elegance, he also realized the central importance of ornamentation and monumental scale in setting the tone of urban life. Civic pride, to him, expressed itself most forcefully in plazas, buildings, and monuments whose appeal lay not in abstract intellectualism but in a clear statement of immediately perceptible grace and beauty. In his architecture, as in his city planning, he unflaggingly sought to realize these ideals. In this effort, he must be identified as a spiritual progenitor of the American Renaissance, and his works should be studied today as a source of inspiration for the City Beautiful.

The Prospect Park Boathouse

by

DONALD E. SIMON

IN the very early 1900s Brooklynites were still getting used to the idea that their community was no longer an independent city but was merely a borough of Greater New York. Since the consolidation took effect on New Year's Day, 1898, many of Brooklyn's residents felt that their worst fears had been realized. The merger was not a marriage. At best, they thought, Brooklyn was seen by New Yorkers and the rest of the nation as an attendant marching far behind the lovely bride—Manhattan. In response to this sense of dismay, many Brooklynites returned to the competitive posture they had held when the two cities were vying for fame, population, and riches.

The history of Brooklyn cannot be considered in a vacuum. Its growth, character, institutions, and even residents were often as they were because of events or personalities in New York. Although leaders of both cities saw the East River as a barrier separating them, in reality, the waterway bound them together with ever-increasing maritime trade. Long before the act of consolidation was approved, the two cities had experienced combined government administration in the "metropolitan" commissions which the state had established in the 1850s and 1860s to regulate police and health administration for the port region. State commissions were responsible for the creation of the region's, and perhaps the nation's most influential parks: Central in New York and Prospect in Brooklyn. No metropolitan park board had been created in this case mostly because it did not appear that Brooklyn was yet ready to establish a system of public parks. Once Central Park began to draw praise and attention, however, Brooklynites were quick to act. By 1860, only four years after the creation of the Central Park Commission, Brooklyn, too, had a park plan and an organization to carry out the work. Although the outbreak of the Civil War prevented the project from going ahead, during the years of inactivity the board made one fundamental decision: to retain Frederick Law Olmsted and Calvert Vaux—now famous for their New York park—to design Prospect Park.

Both Central and Prospect parks were designed as pastoral retreats where man-made structures would be limited to those absolutely necessary. These would be as inconspicuous as possible. This philosophy prevailed despite various attempts to ornament the grounds in a formal tradition. Richard Morris Hunt's proposals for the southern gateways to Central Park were in part rejected because they represented an intrusion of power, class, and privilege in what was perceived as a democratic playground. Elaborate additions to both parks had to await the popularizing of the classical motif which was accomplished with the 1893 World's Columbian Exposition in Chicago. Prior to the fair a number of ornate additions were made to each park. But, following it, public enthusiasm stimulated an outpouring of plans for classical structures, monuments, and buildings.

Thus, it is not surprising that when in 1905 the Brooklyn Park Commission planned to replace Prospect Park's rustic boathouse and skating pavilion, it opted for a magnificent structure in the classical manner.

The commission was given to the Brooklyn firm of Frank J. Helmle and Ulrich J. Huberty who based their design on Sansovino's Library of St. Mark's Cathedral in Venice. The two-story boathouse was sited so the setting sun would shine on its white terra cotta façade. The building was designed to accommodate those seeking simple refreshments at the ground floor counter. More elaborate meals were served on the upper level. Especially popular was a late afternoon supper on the upper level terrace where the activity below could be watched in the soft light of the setting sun.

Helmle and Huberty surrounded their structure with an elaborate granite landing terrace which was detailed with handsome dolphin-motif lamp standards—standards almost identical to those in the small park which is at the western tip of the Ile de la Cité in Paris. The boathouse floor and the terrace were paved with yellow brick between granite slabs. The first floor ceiling is green Guastavino tile. The red tile roof was the most striking feature of the building and immediately drew one's attention. The lower floor of the boathouse was originally open on the western side.

Rustic boathouse and skating pavilion built ca. *1871. Photo; courtesy of Long Island Historical Society, Brooklyn.*

The new boathouse in 1909. Photo: courtesy of Long Island Historical Society, Brooklyn.

The western façade and terrace showing advanced stages of deterioration, 1968. Photo: courtesy of New York City Parks Administration.

A detail of the western façade which shows the archway enclosures behind the terra cotta wall, 1968. Photo: courtesy of New York City Parks Administration.

Winter winds, however, soon chilled enough patrons to prompt the park commission to install a series of sliding wood and glass doors.

The Prospect Park boathouse suffered from neglect for most of its life. The elaborate terra cotta blocks were not able to withstand the severe winters and soon began to crack and spall. The Lullwater, a serpentine body of water that leads from the boathouse to the Lake filled with silt. By the early 1960s boating was all but impossible and with the opening of an artificial ice rink, the focus of activity moved to another part of the park. In 1964 the Park Department decided to replace the boathouse with a simple dock and ticket booth near the ice rink. Everyone seemed to have forgotten the glory and beauty that had existed. A *New York Times* article described the plans under the headline, "Gaslight Relic Sails into Oblivion."

But, unlike so many similar stories, this one has a happy ending which also marks the beginning of the restoration of New York's historic landscape parks. A public outcry forced a change of heart. The then Park Commissioner, Newbold Morris, remarked that he was elated to find people who care about Prospect Park. In quick succession the planned demolition was canceled, the boathouse was awarded designation as

Southeastern corner of the boathouse. Note the plant growth in the gutters and the sag in the cornice at the left, 1968. Photo: courtesy of New York City Parks Administration.

Ceremonies on August 24, 1972, marked the completion of the exterior restoration. Photo: courtesy of New York City Parks Administration.

The restored western façade, 1973. Photo: courtesy of New York City Parks Administration.

Detail of the western façade, 1973. Photo: courtesy of New York City Parks Administration.

Northwestern corner, 1973. Photo: courtesy of New York City Parks Administration.

an official Landmark by the newly created Landmarks Preservation Commission, and plans for the restoration were begun.

The victory was less than total. A consultant architect was retained. But the plans for the re-use of the building constituted far less than a restoration. They incorporated public restrooms, permitting the demolition of one of the park's earliest extant structures, and contained design details out of harmony with the building's spirit. Again public protest swayed officials and the plans were abandoned. The Park Department's own engineers and architects then modified the consultant's product to produce an authentic restoration. All this took time, but finally in the spring of 1971 the work got underway. The dredging of the Lullwater was also begun. The project required the removal of all exterior terra cotta and roofing tile. New terra cotta, roof tile, doors and windows were fabricated. When completed in August of 1972 the exterior was an exact replica of the original. Since then construction has been underway on the terrace (including renewal of the dolphin lamp standards). The old restroom building will soon be restored, completing the entire complex.

The cost of the boathouse, restrooms, and dredging will be nearly $1.5 million. The cost for a replace-ment facility capable of providing the necessary functions would be but a tenth of that sum. But far more was at stake with the boathouse. Here the City of New York made its commitment to historic preservation. Here the City recognized its responsibility for preserving its architectural heritage. No longer would preservationists be viewed as obstructionists. From the boathouse battle came a number of organizations, including the Friends of Central and Prospect Parks, dedicated to educating the public and government to the needs of the City's historic parks. The decade since the boathouse crusade began has seen a change in the climate of opinion which has led to the planning of massive park restoration projects. High among the priorities are programs to protect and refurbish the best of New York's classical heritage.

Credits for the Boathouse project are: *Design:* PRCA Design Division, Victor Losco, Architect-in-Charge; *General Contractor:* A. Belanger & Sons, Inc., Cambridge, Massachusetts; *Terra Cotta:* Interpace Corporation, Sacramento, California; *Construction Supervision:* Brown, Lawford & Forbes, New York, New York; Edwin Forbes, Architect-in-Charge; *Project Supervisor:* Donald E. Simon.

The author was formerly Director of the Department of Parks and Recreation, New York City.

Daniel Burnham: A Consistent Classicist

by

THOMAS R. ELLIOTT

THE standard view of Daniel Burnham holds that his career was sharply divided by the 1893 World's Columbian Exposition. Prior to the Fair, according to this interpretation, Burnham was just another Chicago School architect, although notable, perhaps, for an impressive administrative talent. But with the choice of Burnham and his partner John Wellborn Root as consulting architects for the Fair, a turning point was reached in Burnham's career, and when Root's death in 1891 left Burnham as presiding architect, he embarked on a new course, marked by large-scale plans and the use of the classical style. His chief interest was now city planning, rather than the design of individual buildings.

Louis Sullivan, emphasizing the conversion to the classical style, saw the Fair as a disaster not only for Burnham's artistic soul but for American architecture in general. According to Sullivan, Burnham abjectly capitulated to the Eastern architects he had helped choose, and in so doing accepted the servile, academic sterility which the Fair helped foist off on America. He had turned his back on his earlier, honest work.

A recent and far kinder scholar of Burnham—Thomas Hines—has emphasized the importance of Root's death in the effect of the Fair on Burnham. Root, he says in his exhaustive dissertation on Burnham (University of Wisconsin, 1971), had served as Burnham's "esthetic gyroscope," providing him with the security of a sounder artistic judgment than Burnham felt himself to possess: "His failure after Root's death to find the same kind of *human* authority forced him gradually into a dependence upon 'the book,' upon the abstract academic authority of the 'classics.' " Without Root to tell the good from the bad, then, the Fair was potent in influencing Burnham to choose the authority of academic classicism. Hines also relates this attitude toward the academic to Burnham's failure to be admitted to either Harvard or Yale, which apparently was a trauma for him and his family. If he had experienced academic life, the argument runs, he would have been less in awe of academic authority when it presented itself in as attractive and plausible a form as the Court of Honor.

Hines also notes what Charles Moore, Burnham's biographer, emphasizes in his work; namely, the influence the Fair had in turning Burnham toward large-scale city planning. The Fair was, in effect, a city, with all the urban problems in miniature: transportation, congestion, sanitation, etc. As Chief of Construction, the solution of these problems was Burnham's province, along with the task of creating an esthetically pleasing over-all design; Burnham was *ipso facto* a city planner.

Moreover, the experience of the Fair brought to full fruition the organizational side of Burnham's talents. He was already known as the business half of Burnham and Root, and the Fair simply exercised and broadened his organizational talents. In fact, one of the most notable features of the Fair was the speed with which it was constructed, despite communication problems with distant architects, labor difficulties, bad weather, and a host of other problems. After the Fair Burnham's successor firms—D.H. Burnham, D.H. Burnham and Company, and Graham, Burnham, and Company—were marked by an efficiency of organization which made them models for the modern large firm.

There is, therefore, a good argument to be made that the Fair was the major turning point in Burnham's career. This can be overemphasized, however; the danger is that such a view implies a much more malleable Burnham than seems to have existed. I propose a counter-argument: although the Fair was an important influence, Burnham's career showed a continuity of concerns, many of which were given prominence in the Fair but which can also be seen in his work prior to the Fair. This continuity can perhaps best be thought of as the persistence of a classical attitude.

"Classical attitude" is not meant to refer to what is known as the classical style, a specific architectural idiom with historical roots in ancient Greece and Rome. Rather, it is what Kenyon Cox refers to as "the classical spirit" in *The Classical Point of View* (1911): "the disinterested search for perfection; it is the love of clearness and reasonableness and self-control; it is, above all, the love of permanence and of continuity."

In other words, it is classicism considered as a philosophical attitude rather than a historical phenomenon.

Classicism, in this sense, is best thought of not as a single specific doctrine which a given artist accepts or rejects *in toto,* but a body of ideas with a logical coherence and a history of association. This paper will discuss some of these ideas in an attempt to discover an architectural meaning for this concept of classicism and will try to show that at all stages of his career Burnham expressed classical ideals in his work.

A concern for man and his work is the attitude perhaps most readily identified as classical. The classicist says with the traveling Dr. Johnson—though perhaps not always so gruffly—"A blade of grass is always a blade of grass, whether in one country or another. . . . Men and women are my subject of inquiry; let us see how these differ from those we have left behind." The classical artist is not necessarily indifferent to nature, but it does not contain for him, as it does for the romantic, the immediate wellspring of his art. Cox, speaking of the classic spirit in painting, notes that:

It can make room—always has made room—for the study of nature. It recognizes that painting is essentially an imitative art, and that its raw material is the aspect of the external world. It can use any amount of knowledge of this aspect, and it has no toleration of ignorance or indolence; but it also recognizes that painting is an art, not a science, and that knowledge unassimilated and unsubdued to the ruling purpose of art is useless and obstructive.

If painting is finally governed by a "ruling purpose"—that is, by intellectualized human concerns—how much more true of architecture. For although the materials of building are the materials of nature, it is not "essentially an imitative art," in Cox's sense; most romantics would be quick to say that buildings are *not* objects of the natural world. Insofar as classical architecture is imitative, its models are not nature but other buildings—objects from the human world, not the natural.

This leads logically to the second major classical concern, a strong sense of human history, which is simply the concern for the works of man considered over time. To the classicist the world of man exists not simply in the present, but has a real existence in the past and future as well. T.S. Eliot, speaking of the provincialism "which confounds the contingent with the essential, the ephemeral with the permanent," complains that "It is a provincialism, not of space, but of time; one for which history is merely the chronicle of human devices which have served their turn and been scrapped, one for which the world is the property solely of the living, a property in which the dead hold no shares." The function of the classics, Eliot argues, is to combat this temporal provincialism.

The relevance to architecture of this attitude towards history is apparent. In answer to the objection that building in historical styles is false architecture, the classicist replies that there is not—or ought not to be—any such separation between past and present as the objection implies. Past buildings exist in present consciousness and what we build today cannot be separated from what we built yesterday. This is actually nothing more radical than a restatement of the "form follows function" theory, with the concept of function broadened to include the way a building works in a historical context. The function of a courthouse, for example, is not simply to house a certain number of legal and administrative operations, but also to stand for the whole history of human society under law and, by providing an example for the future, to keep this history unbroken. Therefore, one of the functional dictates of form is that the courthouse ought to look like what people have associated with courthouses.

It follows, then, that not only is the classicist not afraid of being charged with imitation, imitation is his ideal. One must understand by "imitation," however, not a slavish copying of detail for detail, but an imitation of spirit and, only incidentally if at all, of form. The *bête noir* of classicism is originality, a concept with such heavily positive connotations now that an effort must be made to understand exactly what it means to the classicist. It might be helpful to think of it as synonymous with "idiosyncratic," since the sense it has is of arbitrary or willful choice. The original in architecture is by definition not connected to the past and, by so disconnecting itself, it loses contact with the general nature of building and becomes merely local or specific. The original is therefore provincial in Eliot's sense of the word.

The social concerns of the classicist and the sense he has of his obligations to the past and the future, as well as the present, tend to make his art didactic. His goal is not self-expression but effective communication. He is interested in expressing general truths as clearly as possible and in changing social behavior. The romantic, on the other hand, owes his highest allegiance to the specific truth—often, the truth about himself—and only incidently to its effective communication. In architecture, then, we can see that structural functionalism is a romantic doctrine, since it involves the expression of a specific truth—the truth of the construction system of the building. The architectural classicist is much more likely to think of buildings in terms of their social effects: the attitudes and forms of behavior inspired or discouraged by the courthouse, for example.

The kinds of effects sought by the classicist, the ideal forms of behavior, tend to be restrained and

The Sherman House, Chicago.

orderly, and so, too, his art is ruled by the concept of decorum. This word is clear enough in its suggestions, but does not readily admit of a definition; Irving Babbitt is perhaps the most clear—though still far from pellucid—when he calls true decorum "only the pulling back and disciplining of impulse to the proportionateness that has been perceived with the aid of what one may term the ethical or generalizing imagination." We see again the pattern of social considerations acting as a check on imaginative impulses. The decorous building would therefore be grand rather than merely big, impressive rather than astonishing.

Finally, and it is a point of great importance, the classical spirit values the completeness of the whole, the subordination of parts to the over-all design. As Walter Jackson Bate says, "It is the inherent order and proportion of the whole which comprises, in Pope's words, 'the naked nature, and the living grace.'" Speaking specifically of the efforts of classical sculpture and painting to imitate the ideal, not the particular, he goes on to point out:

Such a purpose is ethical in the very broadest sense of the word; for the classical attempt to embody, in plot, design, rhythm, or visual proportion, an "imitation" of the fundamental order and decorum of the universal is not to be viewed as "abstraction" but rather as

"integration" and completion; it aspires to present an ideal end and a finished totality which the distinctive "expression" of the model, as a particular, cannot give.

The application of this to architecture is obvious. What is so unclassical about Sullivan's Transportation Building is not that it does not have Doric colonnades but that what one remembers about it is the doorway; the part surpasses the whole in importance. Similarly, the classical building observes proportion not only within itself, but also within the larger whole represented by its surroundings. Just as the classical spirit is concerned with man in the context of society and assumes that the ideal is a harmonious relationship between the two, so it tends to see buildings not in isolation but in relation to their surroundings.

Burnham and Root's earliest commissions, most of them residences, show a strong civic sense, echoing the growing civic self-awareness of Chicago, which Burnham, looking back, attributed to the devastating fire of 1871. According to Moore, Burnham felt the fire:

marked the beginning of civic consciousness, of cooperation among the people for the city's advancement, of willingness and even desire and determination to accomplish the seemingly impossible. Then and there the Spirit of Chicago, to which he so confidently and successfully appealed in later years, had its birth.

The Glessner House, Chicago.

The Sherman House, built in 1874 for Burnham's soon-to-be father-in-law, is a good example of the civic sense in the firm's early work. The house is marked by an unclassical profusion of imperfectly related details, as though the young architects were afraid they might never have a chance to use all their ideas for gables, balustrades, and chimneys. Nevertheless, in the relationship which the house develops with the street we can see the classical concern with architectural context and with the establishment of a harmonious relation of the individual to society. The front stairway, by its gentle rise and slightly opening curve, makes a gracious invitation to the street which is neither expansive nor forbidding. This sense of a decorous relationship between house and passer-by is contained by the low stone and wrought-iron fence, which quietly marks the boundary in a way which is definite, but which does not give rise to any feelings of exclusion; visually, the space of the front yard is continuous with the space of the street. A private enclosure is made unobtrusively to the rear of the house.

To get a better idea of what is meant here by the "civic sense" of the house, compare it to Richardson's Glessner House of 1885-87. The relative plainness of Richardson's large wall surfaces might make this house seem highly classical, placed against the fussiness of the Sherman House, but its relation to the street is, in contrast, one almost of hostility. This, in fact, is the house of which Montgomery Schuyler said that, considered as a dwelling, "the structure ceases to be defensible, except, indeed, in a military sense."

One might turn from the Glessner House to Burnham and Root's Goudy House of 1889-90 and note that not only is it plain in surface but by virtue of its many windows and the broad-arched porch only a few steps from the sidewalk it has the Sherman House's classic sense of closeness to the street.

Probably the two greatest works of Burnham and Root are the Rookery, 1885-88, and the Monadnock Building, 1889-92, and it is interesting to note that they represent two extremes of ornamentation. Nevertheless, each is in its own way an example of the rigorous subordination of parts to the whole.

The Rookery boasts an extremely large and varied program of ornamentation—it is reported that Root was worried that there was too much. It is controlled, however, to an extent that the ornamentation of the Sherman House is not. The strong horizontal divisions work to contain the detail in bands and therefore to

The Goudy House, Chicago.

minimize its over-all impact while permitting it still to enliven the surface. Furthermore, the ordinary view of the building, the view one gets when walking by the building or even from the other side of LaSalle Street, unless one is making a conscious effort, is really only of the first two stories, and their effect is one of extreme regularity and sobriety. They are kept from monotony not by ornament but by the contrast between the rough stone of the walls and the polished granite columns, and between both of those and the large window areas.

The Monadnock runs quite a different risk, that of being too stark. Its lack of adornment together with its great size might easily make it nonhuman in scale and appearance. After all, because they are weight-bearing, the walls of this sixteen-story building are enormously thick at the base, and there is an unavoidable sense of great mass. Burnham and Root seem to have realized fully the risk they ran of creating an immense dead cliff of brick and used such subtle features of design as the curve of the base of the wall and of the bottoms of the bays, not to make it any less impressive a building but to make it more alive, more clearly related to the shaping human intelligence.

One obviously does not have to argue that the

1893 Fair was classical, either in terms of architectural idiom or of spirit. The live question for our purposes is to what extent did the classicism reflect Burnham's choice. Sullivan, in depicting Burnham as subservient to the Eastern architects, suggests that he either had classicism forced on him or embraced it out of a combination of expediency and lack of imagination. Neither seems to have been the case.

Titus M. Karlowicz, responding to the charge that Burnham "sold out" the Chicago architects, points out that not only had he less of a free hand than is often supposed, but once it was determined that the Fair was to be national, not merely local, the choice of architects with a national reputation was inevitable; inevitable not only to the Fair organization, but to Burnham as well. If he was "railroaded" at all in the choice of architects it was not by personalities but by the logical consequences of a decision which he had helped to make. And this decision, the decision to be nonparochial, certainly represents the classical impulse to present the general, rather than the specific truth.

Furthermore, the Fair was classical in conception as soon as it was decided by Burnham, Root, Henry Codman, and Frederick Law Olmstead in the fall of

The Rookery Building, Chicago.

The Monadnock Building, Chicago.

1890 that "the buildings around the basin of the central court should be formal, impressive, and generally of the same stylistic mode." Here, even before the choice of "stylistic mode," we see expressed the classical ideas of unity and decorum. As further indication of Burnham's early commitment to classicism at the Fair, Moore points out that "the idea of a unified composition is contained in the letter of invitation to the Eastern architects, which was written by Mr. Burnham and gives ample evidence of his passion for orderly arrangement."

It seems clear, then, that whether or not Burnham had to be convinced of the desirability of the classical idiom, he was already firmly committed to the classical spirit in the planning of the Fair. The choice of the classical idiom, to which Sullivan and others have objected, is really secondary in importance to the decision to build for a unified effect with universal appeal. And this decision was made before Burnham had any extensive contact with McKim, Hunt, or any of the other demons of Sullivan's cosmology.

Obviously, the most important influence of the Fair on Burnham's career is the interest it sparked in city planning. When he went on to develop plans for Chicago, Washington, San Francisco, Cleveland, Manila, and Baguio it was with the vision of the White

City firmly in mind. This is particularly true in the case of the Cleveland Group Plan of 1903. This design for the grouping of public buildings in the civic center of Cleveland—regrettably, only partially executed— clearly echoes the arrangement of the Court of Honor, with the railroad station occupying a position analogous to that of the Administration Building. Many of the details of the plan are also reminiscent of the Fair.

City planning, by its very nature, is a classical activity. It implies an interest in the life of man in societies rather than in nature: man as the product of his own past. Moreover, it sees the city as a whole, an entity capable of treatment in a unified, rational way. The city may in reality be fragmented, but the city planner—at least, the planner who can see beyond the solution of merely engineering problems—operates with unification as an ideal which he must believe can be realized.

Burnham brought to the activity of planning a typically classical combination of an ideal vision married to a thoroughly practical awareness of the motivations of men. "With things as they should be," he and Edward Bennett wrote in the *Plan of Chicago*, "every business man in Chicago would make more money than he does now." Making money is not the goal— "things as they should be" is an independent ideal—

The Cleveland Group Plan, detail, south end of the Mall.

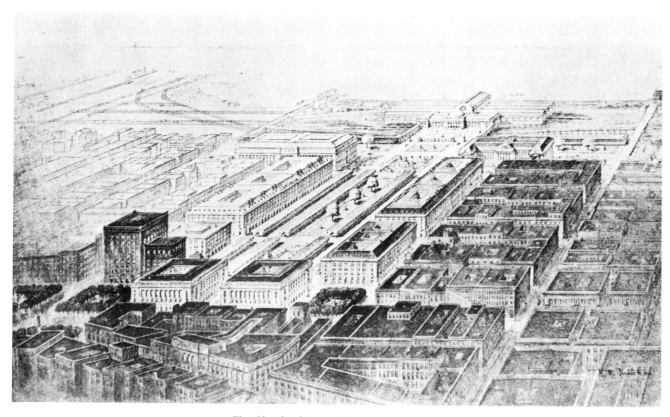

The Cleveland Group Plan, looking north.

but it is reasonable to expect that all things will be improved by the realization of the ideal. Indeed, one cannot really separate the two impulses towards the practical and the ideal: ''What is logical is also beautiful.''

Burnham was also aware of the didactic value of good city planning; ideals of order expressed physically can inspire the minds and conduct of the citizens. Pleasant and well-built schools and school grounds, for example, should create ''ties of remembrance that are restraining influences throughout life.''

Burnham's individual buildings after the Fair begin to use the classical idiom freely and effectively. A number of banks show such use, and Union Station in Washington is an excellent example on a larger scale. What is most classical about Union Station, however, is the way in which it is conceived with a specific relation to the whole city and to the space immediately around it. Moreover, functioning as the gateway to the city, as the Administration Building did at the Fair, it served a didactic purpose, symbolizing the ideal nature of the city to which the traveler had just arrived. As A.N. Rebori said of most of Burnham's monumental buildings, it ''placed before the public familiar and beautiful classic forms which could be readily comprehended without any extraordinary individual imaginary effort.'' Union Station, then, is a

Union Trust Company, Pittsburgh.

Illinois Trust Company, Chicago.

Union Station, Washington, D.C.

Union Station, Washington, D.C., project sketch.

Railway Exchange Building, Chicago.

lesson, an act of communication, as well as a utilitarian structure.

Those of Burnham's later buildngs which are not as directly inspired by classical forms still tend to show an awareness of classical ideals. The Railway Exchange Building is one such. Its arrangement of vertical piers and bulls-eye windows is reminiscent of Sullivan's treatment of the Wainwright Building, but here the expression of verticality is not the goal; the vertical divisions of the Railway Exchange have instead the effect of a colonnade, and the building, rather than emphasizing its own height, reminds us that it is, after all, a resident of Michigan Avenue, with relations to the street and to its neighbors.

We have seen, in the urban awareness of buildings as dissimilar as the early Chicago residences and the Railway Exchange, in the wholeness of the Rookery and the Monadnock, the unity and decorum of the Court of Honor, in the ethical sense of the human community expressed in the city plans, and in the didacticism of the monumental later buildings, that Daniel Burnham truly showed a consistent devotion to classical ideals. That he may not have been articulately aware of these ideas prior to the Fair and his acquaintance with the Eastern classicists does not prove that they were not operating subconsciously. Indeed, it is a large tribute to the compelling power of the classical spirit if it found expression in the work of one whose formal architectural education was as slight as Burnham's.

Residence of H. L. Dulin, Esq., Knoxville, Tennessee

by

WILLIAM ROSS McNABB

THE architecture of the so-called "eclectic" architects of the early twentieth century has long been despised by critics trained in the climate of opinion which prevailed following the dissemination of Bauhaus ideas in the 1930s. In this view such firms as McKim, Mead and White and their followers were backward-looking, imitative, and guilty of ignoring the new building technology developed during the nineteenth century. After thirty years of the austerity of Gropius, Mies van der Rohe, and their many followers, it is now easier to admire the richness and grace of many of the buildings designed by Beaux Arts trained architects during the first three decades of this century. An excellent example of such a building is the house which John Russell Pope designed for H. L. Dulin of Knoxville, Tennessee, in 1915.

Pope was born in New York City in 1874, studied architecture at Columbia, and then won the McKim scholarship to study at the American Academy in Rome. After several years in Rome, he went on to Paris, where he enrolled in the Ecole des Beaux Arts, where so many of the previous generation of American architects had studied. After completing the course, he returned to New York, setting up his own office in 1900. He was an immediate success and in the course of his career designed many of the finest buildings of his time, of which the National Gallery of Art in Washington was the culminating example. It was not completed until several years after Pope's death in 1937. In addition to his many grand and imposing public buildings, Pope did many houses. He worked in a variety of styles from Tudor to Louis XV, always with a scholarly attention to accuracy of detail. These houses were built in such places as Long Island and Newport by rich business men who sought a setting worthy of their station in life.

The entrance front with its diagonal wings and twin porches faces northwest. The front door is of wrought iron and plate glass. The delicate, low relief ornament in the lunettes over the French windows and in the circular placques between the upper windows is of cast concrete.

The narrow entrance pavilion avoids seeming pinched between the wings because of its projection and the greater relief of its major elements, the columns and doorway.

The centerpiece of the south side is this handsome façade facing the river. The Adam style composite columns repeat those of the entrance and are flanked by large Adamesque urns placed in arched openings. The space behind this façade was originally planned as an open porch but was enclosed with glass when the house was built. The placing of urns in front of a window is an idea Pope used also in the Ogden Mills house on Long Island and at Meridian House in Washington.

It was in Newport that the Dulins saw and admired the house which Pope had designed for Dr. Henry Barton Jacobs, and they commissioned Pope to design a similar one for them in Knoxville. The blueprint plans were dispatched to them in September 1915, and, after a few modifications were made, construction was begun. When the house was finished and curious Knoxvillians had an opportunity to see it, it was referred to, perhaps with a hint of jealous malice, as the "exposition palace."

What Pope had given the Dulins was considerably more than this term would imply. Inspired by spreading baroque plans, with diagonal wings such as that of the palace of Stupinigi near Turin, Pope devised an ingenious geometrical arrangement of rooms aligned on vistas which converge on an oval hall in the center of the house. If the plan owes something to baroque precedent, the elevations, in their cool elegance, owe a great debt to neoclassical architects of the late eighteenth century in England and France, particularly to Robert Adam. The style might be described as neo-neoclassicism, or neoclassical revival, and is very similar to that of Pope's nearly contemporary Ogden Mills house in Woodbury, Long Island. In both, the

detailing is based closely on Adam precedent, using Adam's composite capital for the columns, medallions, urns, paterae, and swag motifs. In the lunettes over the French windows the urn and swag motifs in low relief appear to be exactly alike. The spreading, symmetrical plans with twin porches are similar, and in both designs the handling of classical motifs and proportions is absolutely self-assured. In neither case is there an exact prototype. French and English neoclassical forms are combined carefully in an original design controlled by the strict discipline of classical order.

The plan of the Dulin house combines a number of handsomely proportioned and decorated rooms on the ground floor in a relationship ideal for entertaining. The front door leads to an elegant oval hall, marble floored, with the walls decorated with Ionic pilasters and a marble fountain in a niche. From this large room a curving stairway leads to the bedrooms above. Through large doorways on either side the main reception rooms are reached. Most of these rooms are designed in the chaste neoclassical style of the exterior, but the library is paneled in seventeenth-century style. The quality of the wood and plaster work throughout is

The oval entrance hall has a marble floor and a curving stairway. The entrance door is to the left of the photograph and the sunroom to the right. Ionic pilasters and entablature frame the doors, and there is a fine white marble wall fountain in the niche between the drawing room and library doors. The photograph was taken from the dining room doorway.

The dining room is fully paneled, the walls articulated by fluted pilasters with acanthus capitals. The entablature is of plaster as are the paterae above the pilasters. The mantel, of wood, is pure Adam. The furniture shown here, as in all the photographs, is that used by the Dulin Family—all chosen to carry out the Adam theme.

The drawing room is the same size and shape as the dining room across the hall. Here, however, the walls are of painted plaster with applied wooden molding. The mantel is of wood in the Adam style. The sconces are inlayed with Wedgewood placques. The furniture, as in the dining room, was selected to be in accord with the late eighteenth-century neoclassical style of the house. Elsewhere, however, Jacobean style furniture was used.

superb. At the rear of the house, behind the oval hall, is a large portico. Originally planned as an open porch, the plans were changed almost immediately to provide glass enclosure to form a sunroom. At either end of the house is a single-story porch with Tuscan columns. The first plan called for the one to the north, where the ground drops away, to have a wall fountain and pool on the outside wall. This delightful detail was omitted from the final plans and was never built.

The house was constructed with wood frame walls covered with two inches of stucco on the exterior. The exterior woodwork is of cypress, the columns and pilasters being of built-up, lock-joint construction of the same material. The capitals are of composition made from models approved by the architect. Other exterior ornament is of cast concrete and was made in New York under the direction of the architect. The roof was orignally to have been of green tile, as at the Jacobs house, but red tile was substituted.

The site is a commanding one on a bluff with a view of a bend in the Tennessee River. Little effort, however, was made to take advantage of the situation. The main rooms face north toward the street and away from the view, and only the sunroom faces south. Pope's was very much an architecture of ''good taste,'' a term which unfortunately has come to be derided. His designs were very good-mannered refinements of the great achievements of the past, pro-

duced for clients who were interested in social status, not in the risks of experimentation. Pope was able to provide sensitive and elegant, as well as impressive, designs for such people. He was not an innovator and he tended to be a bit cold, but his strengths as a designer should not be ignored—particularly in a time when new buildings of a comparable richness and elegance are very hard to find indeed. It is interesting to note the near coincidence in date of the publication of Geoffrey Scott's *Architecture of Humanism* in 1914 and Pope's design for the Dulin house a year later. This is not to suggest that Pope was directly influenced by Scott's book, but rather to point out that Scott's view of architecture as ideal form and his championship of the Renaissance in reaction to Ruskin is a verbal expression of Pope's approach to design. It was in the climate of opinion reflected in Scott's book that architects like Pope were educated and could flourish.

Mr. Dulin died in 1941, and Mrs. Dulin continued to live in the house until her death in 1961. At that time her daughter, Mrs. John Clifford Folger of Washington and Mrs. Folger's two sons founded the Dulin Gallery of Art, which has occupied the house since 1962. When the new gallery building now being planned for the lot next door is completed, the Dulin house will be restored as a house museum to show the present generation what an elegant setting a prosperous businessman of 1915 could provide for himself and his family.

All photographs are by James E. Thompson, c. 1920, and are now in the McClung Historical Collection, Lawson McGhee Library, Knoxville, Tennessee.

A Vernacular Classical Bank in the South

by

L. Y. DEAN, III

*T*HE *Eufaula Bank and Trust Company, of Eufaula, Alabama, illustrates the continuing tradition of vernacular classical architecture in the South. The following statement, written by the President of the bank, offers an interesting account of the reasoning which underlay the choice of style for the bank's new building. Other businessmen who silently acquiesce in bizarre and more costly modern building schemes* *might profitably ponder the good manners, good neighborliness, good sense, and good taste of this institution. The story is a modest but timely companion piece to this issue's cover article on the work of Atlanta architect Philip Trammell Shutze.*

THE EDITOR

*E*UFAULA is a beautiful, pleasant little town of about 12,000 people located in Southeast Alabama on lovely Lake Eufaula, which is the boundary between Alabama and Georgia. It was founded one hundred and fifty-three years ago and has many fine old antebellum homes—some with cupolas on top. Its streets are wide, with tree-lined parks down the middle. We have a pilgrimage of homes each spring,

and for all of the above reasons our town is filled with tradition.

"T," my wife, and I both have lived in Eufaula all of our lives and we love every nook and cranny of it. It really is a part of us.

At least twenty years ago we began to dream of a new building for our bank. There were two things we were quite sure of. We did not want a modern building,

Eufala Bank and Trust Company, Eufala, Alabama.

Lamps at the main entrance, Eufala Bank and Trust Company.

and we wanted our building to fit into and complement the architecture and tradition of Eufaula.

We did not want a modern building because we had found out over the years that most modern architecture does not last. During my years at the bank we have been to the openings of many new bank buildings. Practically all of these buildings have been modern in design. As a rule we were tremendously impressed at first. But over the years, as we saw these buildings time and time again, the beauty seemed to wear off and nothing much was left. They simply didn't last. We didn't want our building to be like this. We wanted it to last and to continue to add beauty and inspiration for the people of Eufaula.

It seems to us that most modern and traditional architecture can be compared to popular and classical music. They all make a hit at first, but modern architecture and popular music, as a rule, do not stand the test of time.

We love our building and we are sure that it will stand the test of time. As I have said, we dreamed about it for many years and we were sure of the general appearance of the building we wanted. Our architect, Mr. James J.W. Biggers, Sr., of Biggers, Neal and Clark of Columbus, Georgia, translated our dream

Bank side elevation, Eufala Bank and Trust Company.

Main staircase in the banking hall, Eufala Bank and Trust Company.

Board Room, Eufala Bank and Trust Company.

into an architectural design for us. Although we were sure of the general design of the building, Mr. Biggers is solely responsible for the lovely detail work on both the inside and outside of the building. Mr. Wade Lott of Mobile, Alabama, worked with "T" on the interior decorations and we are deeply indebted to him for the added touch which is typical of Wade.

The cost of the building was a little more than the cost of a modern building would have been, but it has been well worth its additional cost. We have visitors practically every day and they come from all over the United States and from many foreign countries. Almost every visitor who comes to Eufaula is guided to our bank by the Chamber of Commerce, the Heritage Association, or by some individual.

We were lucky to have a good general contractor, Pound Construction Company of Columbus, Georgia, and we had practically no problems in the construction of our building.

All in all, I might say that our building is a dream come true. We are very proud of it. It has been worth much more to the bank than its cost, and if we had it to do over again I don't believe we would change a thing.

In addition to this, the whole community is proud of our building and we are proud to be a part of the community and to add to its beauty.

Size of building—

    Inside—upstairs and down . .11,630 square feet
    Outside porches . . . . .640 square feet

    Cost of building $490,353.10
    Cost of furnishings 37,924.80

The bank is furnished largely with antiques and for this reason our furniture and fixtures appreciate instead of depreciating in value each year.

All photos are courtesy of the author.

A design for a flagpole at Valley Forge for the Sons of the Revolution. Architect Alan Greenberg, a professor at the University of Pennsylvania's School of Architecture, is a new member of the Board of Directors of Classical America.

Book Reviews

John Physick, *The Wellington Monument*, 176 pp., Her Majesty's Stationery Office.

Richard V. West, *The Walker Art Building Murals*, 36 pp., Bowdoin College Museum of Art.

We have before us two accounts of efforts in the way of public embellishment, one sculptural, the other mural, that illustrate some inherent difficulties that attend such undertakings. In the case of the monument to the Duke of Wellington erected in St. Paul's Cathedral, fifty years were consumed in wrangling and complaints, with all the original parties long in their graves before the work was completed. The lunettes for the Walker Art Building of Bowdoin College were commissioned and installed well within a decade (including trips abroad for inspiration). But the acrimoniously protracted struggle toward completion of the Wellington Monument culminated in a civic memorial that was the chief glory of nineteenth-century British art, matched in Europe only by Rude's *Le Départ* while the genteel discussion and unimpeded execution that characterized the conception and businesslike progress of the Bowdoin decoration resulted in a bland and mildly disagreeable lesson in the utter mishandling of architectural painting.

The conclusions reached in the histories of these projects in the book put out by Her Majesty's Stationery Office and in Bowdoin's Occasional Paper No. 1 are less drastic than those of the summary here. But the College is justifiably proud of having had bestowed on it a major mural decoration, and all interested Englishmen take for granted that the Wellington Monument is a product of supreme native genius, a fact in need of no emphasis.

John Physick's story does not touch on the development of Alfred Stevens's magnificent idea for the monument, fully conceived outside the events described, which commence with the circumstances leading up to the 1856 Memorial Competition. The first version of his design shown us, the Competition Model, differs not at all in fundamentals (and little in detail) from the majestic work now in the Cathedral. What Mr. Physick has tracked down for us are the details of the heart-breaking half-century-long course of construction. This is an absorbing and exasperating chronicle, but it has to do with administration and psychology, not art. The difficulties were posed by bureaucracy, misunderstanding, economy, rival commitments, primness, and perhaps most of all, the headstrong nature of the artist himself, a trial even to his supporters.

The Wellington Monument, by Alfred Stevens

Rome, *Elihu Vedder's lunette in the Sculpture Court of the Bowdoin College Museum of Art. Photo: courtesy of Bowdoin College Museum of Art.*

But these things are the familiar history of the world. What is to be remarked on is the acceptance almost from the start (once the error of awarding Stevens other than the First Prize was corrected) of every detail of his design. Much of the final anguish, in fact, was over making certain that his successors were faithful to Stevens's initial intentions. What this early and general recognition of the superiority of Stevens's scheme demonstrates is the advantage of a homogeneous artistic outlook. It was not the kind of design Stevens submitted, but its manifest excellence within its class, that won attention. It is worth noting that Tenniel's parodies of the Competition entries, shown in a page from *Punch* reproduced by Mr. Physick, are themselves both very beautiful and in keeping with the prevailing style. The lesson is that it is only in the absence of any question of style that judgment can be concentrated on merit.

As to Stevens himself, his strength derived from his talent and an early immersion in the art of the Italian Renaissance, which constituted his chief school. But the peculiar fitness of the monument to its purpose and location had another, deeper, explanation. The motto that identified his Competition entry, "I know of but one art," expressed his all-embracing view of his calling. Stevens was at once painter,

sculptor, architect. He could design a medal or a floor, a stove as readily as a newel post or caryatid; he could plot the outline of, as well as paint, a vase, lay out a pendentive and cupola plan for the Dome of St. Paul's, or paint a tondo or a portrait. In short, every artistic task fell within his scope, and he saw in each its full context. This largeness of approach was even more to the purpose than his command of Renaissance form.

The pity is that Victorian England was not so much unsympathetic to Stevens as unprepared for the vastness of his gifts. What we can be thankful for is that this maladjustment between age and artist failed to prevent the ultimate coming-into-being of the great Monument, though there were times when its fate was touch and go.

There were, for practical purposes, no obstacles to the rapid completion of the Walker Art Building decorations. The physical feebleness of John La Farge, the boasted incapacity for architectural work itself on the part of Abbott Thayer, were problems overcome, or at any rate they did not slow things up much. The funds were earmarked, with the donors generous and diffident, the architects were enthusiastic at all stages, and the painters pretty much kept their noses to the grindstone. Richard West has a relatively smooth tale to tell. All that is wrong is that these

Athens, *John La Farge's lunette in the Sculpture Court of the Bowdoin College Museum of Art. Photo: courtesy of Bowdoin College Museum of Art.*

easy-going people, given a wonderful opportunity to produce a veritable jewel box, came up with a very ill-painted hall.

McKim, Mead and White were a great force in incorporating painted decoration into American architectural practice, but its special nature somehow eluded them. At the beginning of the Nineties they had invited Elihu Vedder to undertake a panel for them in the Boston Public Library. Vedder declined, because they could not grasp the necessity of providing any information about the site, and, worse, panels alongside his were to be assigned to other artists, yet to be selected. Now, a year or two later, Vedder was approached by the firm to paint the main lunette, that facing the entrance, of the Walker Art Building Rotunda, then under construction, the other three lunettes to be left blank. Left free to choose a subject, "The Art Idea" (a title Vedder himself laughted at), he accepted, and the work was well along when he learned that the rest of the spaces were, after all, to be filled by other painters, and that subjects had been assigned, his being "Rome." This was the first great error: the elementary rule that harmony required a single painter for a room was lost on the architects.

Vedder hit the ceiling, but recovered, and complied only to the extent of changing his title from "The Art Idea" to "Rome." No nursing wolves, or pairs of fasces, or so much as a bust of Julius Caesar, were added to the scheme in progress. In the event, this proved perfectly satisfactory, but so did everything

else in this project. The record shows happy approval on the part of McKim, Mead and White and the Misses Walker, the donors, of every step taken by all four artists.

Vedder had been selected because of his reputation as the leading American pictorial designer, and the result was either the outright best of American mural panels or the best except for the later examples also painted by Vedder. Splendid in effect, his lunette was rich in color, imaginative and intricate in its arrangement, and expressive both of his strong personal style and the Italian tradition to which he had devoted himself. But this very triumph told against the success of the project as a whole, because no such claim can be advanced on behalf of its companions. These three are, with Kenyon Cox's "Venice" a slight exception, woefully bare in inspiration and design. Each consists of a dominant figure flanked by subordinate ones, but John La Farge's "Athens" lounges to one side of her lunette, while her satellites stand in disregard of, rather than deference to, her, the lesser of these being the actual central figure, though the absence of formality in La Farge's scheme deprives this of any significance. Design was not La Farge's strong point, which was talking.

Mr. West points out the shaky relation of Abbott Thayer's figures (representing "Florence") to each other and to the area they occupy, but Thayer made no secret of the fact that he was out of his element. More pains were gone to by Cox over "Venice," but there was a general listlessness in all three panels. None of the three painters had the gift of imparting life to his figures, with Cox the weakest in this regard. His male figure, "Commerce," is not only given an excessively languid pose, but a clumsy one, with this gracelessness shared by his girl-friend, "Painting." In this connection, Mr. West's inquiries reveal an air of sleepiness present throughout the actual enterprise. Thayer accepted the commission with the announcement that he would need six weeks rest before starting. La Farge, finding summer in the city difficult, had to have his canvas shipped to a vacation spot. And both he and Cox felt so slight a sense of urgency that they interrupted their labors for excursions to Italy.

Fundamentally at fault were the architects; they had no business dividing their rotunda among four painters to begin with. Having elected to do so, it became their responsibility to exercise every care in choosing their artists. Almost no decorative skill being in evidence, a competition would seem to have been in order, both as a test of competence and to put the candidates on their mettle. But one great man was settled for, and three of the firm's cronies. And although weakness was apparent from the start, not the least effort was made to buck up the artists. McKim, Mead and White had within their grasp the achievement of a perfect interior. Circumstances dictated a single course, that all four lunettes be entrusted to Vedder; but the obviousness of this escaped them.

The calamity of the Wellington Monument experience was that its creator's time and energy were wasted, time and energy that could have gone into other undertakings on the scale of the monument. But it is to the credit of the English that an artist of Stevens's stature was engaged in the monument to begin with. It is a cliché of criticism to patronize the Victorians for their failure to appreciate Stevens. But his name is known today only to a rare dilettante, and in his own day he was a famous man. Moreover, it is impossible to imagine any serious use in our times of his peculiar powers, yet the Victorians kept him constantly busy.

The sad story of chances missed at Bowdoin is one of ignorance and carelessness masquerading as enthusiasm. The final irony is that the architects need have taken even less trouble than they actually did (which was little enough). For only a few miles down the Maine coast was to be found the greatest composer and draftsman of the country, possessed of a largeness of style, seriousness of purpose, and vigor of handling which was ideally adapted to monumental painting—Winslow Homer. If the architects were unable to see this, La Farge and Cox were among the most ardent of Homer's admirers, and La Farge in particular had called attention to Homer's special fit-

ness for the mural task. Could he have been persuaded to fill its four panels (and convincing him might not have proven so difficult) the Art Building would have been made dramatic and magnificent, and where it is now a curiosity worth a visit by the specialist, Bowdoin would have been a place of pilgrimage for all lovers of painting.

—PIERCE RICE

Philipp Fehl, *The Classical Monument: Reflections on the Connection between Morality and Art in Greek and Roman Sculpture*, 115 pp. New York University Press, 1972. $15.

This will not be a proper book review at all, but rather a collection of fragments selected by me from Mr. Fehl's text which I hope will serve our purpose better. The words will be Mr. Fehl's. Mr. Fehl's text is so central to our understanding of classicism that I have presumed upon this method rather than attempting a condensation.

—JOHN B. BAYLEY

Among the tasks which a sculptor may be asked to perform, that of erecting a public monument must be ranked one of the highest and most committing. Here the work of the artist and the service of the public good are most intimately joined; and the artist called upon to celebrate the memory of merit, noble achievement, and great and affecting events, may become, by his work, a preceptor of mankind.

All monuments of antiquity, the Greek excepted, are . . . concerned with . . . the glorification of the power of a ruler and its continuation beyond the limits of death.

The Greek monument . . . life-sized or somewhat larger . . . nude or lightly draped . . . radiates gladness and resignation . . . erected in praise of the beauty which is poured over the sensitive and good . . . at a moment of great happiness, which they know . . . to be passing from the joyful present into the lonely realm of memory and death:

Short is the space of time in which the happiness of mortal men groweth up, and even so doth it fall to the ground, when stricken down by adverse doom. Creatures of a day, what is one? What is he not? Man is but a dream of a shadow; but, when a gleam of sunshine cometh as a gift of heaven, a radiant light resteth on men, aye and a gentle life.

—PINDAR

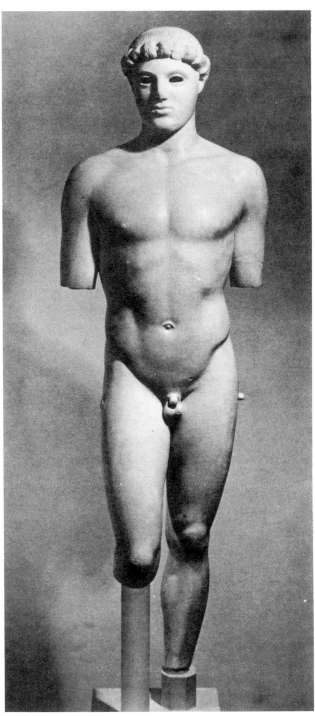

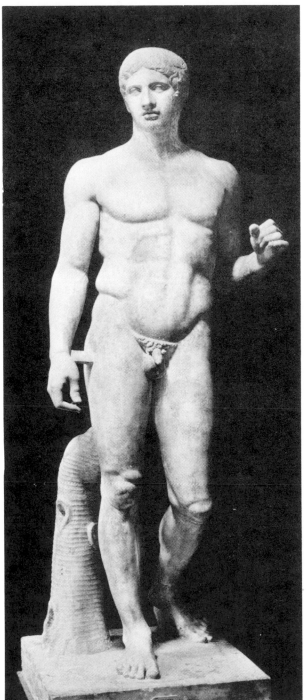

The Kritios Boy: Acropolis Museum, Athens·

The Doryphoros: Naples Museum

Statues of Greek athletes . . . depict the passing of time. Archaic . . . now so popular because of the abundant vigor they display, are still triumphantly unconcerned with this melancholy aspect of human existence . . . they still remain a kind of robot made by Daedalus.

From 480 B.C. . . . statues represent beings whose existence has a beginning and an end. The *Kritios Boy* . . . is one of the first statues to stand in a musing pose. Though he does not move, his inaction is the very opposite of the immobility of the stone of which he is made. There is a subtle motion—the sense of life—which runs through his body and makes him pause. The Greeks renounced the character of powerful lastingness (as in Egypt). . . . their reward was the greater gift of pathos.

The gentle humanity and the moderation of the classical victor statues remained for seven hundred years a model of perfection for the majority of monumental tasks. The feeling for the heroic pathos of humanity confined by death which made this possible, lived on, I think, as long as Homer was read:

Like Leaves on Trees the Race of Man is found,
Now green in Youth, now with'ring on the Ground,
Another Race the following Spring supplies:
They fall successive, and successive rise;
So generations in their course decay,

—*Iliad*, Trans., POPE

All academic tradition in the visual arts descends from the so-called Doryphoros (Spear-bearer) of Polykleitos.

So he made also a manly boy, the Doryphoros, whom artists call *canon,* inasmuch as they seek the outlines of the art as if from a kind of law and he is the only man who is thought to have made art itself a work of art.

—PLINY

The Spear-bearer . . . is a monument, the statue of an athletic victor. . . . As a monument the perfection of the harmonious pose and proportions all serve one major purpose: to bestow upon the work a noble and lyrical beauty in keeping with the praise of victory, youth, and beauty.

Socrates . . . showed . . . that there are two kinds of imitation in art: "a representation of things seen," and one which reproduces the character of the soul:

If deceiving the eye were the only business of the art . . . the minute painter would be more apt to succeed; but it is not the eye, it is the mind, which the painter of genius desires to address; nor will he waste a moment upon those smaller objects, which only serve to catch the sense, to divide the attention and to counteract his great design of speaking to the heart.

—REYNOLDS

The following headings list some of the most elementary aspects of the Doryphoros. . . . I can do no more than attempt to show that Polykleitos' management of these elements builds a bridge between the arena of identifiable effects and the realm of character, dignity, and love.

NATURALNESS: . . . an avoidance of detail and a tendency to generalize . . . particularly . . . in the treatment of the hair.

Elements of the body concerned with motion and life are specially emphasized: the eye, the expression of the mouth, the joints (note the folds of skin under the knees), the muscles. . . . We forget how easy it would have been to indicate certain aspects of spirituality and the mood of the figure with the help of stylization, exaggeration, and symbolism. (Persians and Egyptians). . . . The Greek artists clearly imitated nature because . . . they found a superior charm in works of art which looked natural.

NUDITY: . . . Natural in the case of an athletic victor . . . has a certain timelessness and truth about it which gives a universal significance. . . . Victor statues and tombstones are rarely likenesses; they are instead, as Isocrates says, "a memorial to the virtues rather than bodily appearance." They may indeed be called "ideal," but this only means that they become more true—not less real.

YOUTH AND BEAUTY: Youth possesses . . . a kind of completeness coupled with innocence, and a certain natural grace only revealed when the young naïvely become aware of their charm and realize that it must pass. The Doryphoros has a particular kind of beauty—"quadratus," (four-square) as Pliny calls it:

In that, Pittacus, you are mistaken; the difficulty is not to be good, but on the one hand to become good, four-square in hands and feet and mind, without a flaw—that is hard truly.

—PLATO

SOULFULNESS: When Polykleitos was asked what he considered the most difficult part of his art, he said that it was the moment when it became necessary to work the clay with the fingernail. . . . The quick touch has to be given to the finish of the statue (especially the eyes and mouth) if it is to have the appearance of naturalness and freedom, and if the mood and fleeting breath of the soul is to be expressed. In the eighteenth century such a quickness of manner was called *touche facile.*

CONTRAPPOSTO: The weight of the standing figure rests almost completely on one leg . . . the pose suggests that the figure has just now completed a full step forward. . . . We do not ever imagine that the figure . . . might . . . take the next step and perchance move off the pedestal. The contrapposto is so subtly contrived that the figure appears to be in perfect equilibrium.

PROPORTIONS: Is the beauty of the Doryphoros a matter of absolute proportion, or is it based on an apt relation of the proportions of the figure to its character? Is the Doryphoros beautiful "as such" or is it the perfect spear-bearer? The question reflects two views of the meaning of Greek art—one abstract and formal, the other functional and moral. . . . An influential number of our contemporary historians of art would agree with the abstract. If we accept the other view . . . that the harmony of the work is based on a fitting correspondence of the proportions and the character, or ethos, of the figure, then . . . as Pliny describes them, figures of the gods, or of heroes and of women, would all differ in proportion, and for that reason each would be in harmony, not absolute or pure, but just and decorous. . . . The moralizing view of the perfectability of forms has survived most explicitly in the work of Vitruvius . . . (in *decor*, the fifth in his six elements of architecture). *Decor* . . . is observed when the Doric order is used in temples to Minerva, Mars and Hercules; for these gods, because of their might, buildings ought to be erected without embellishments. Temples designed in the Corinthian style will seem to have details suited to Venus, Flora, Proserpine . . . . According to Vitruvius, therefore, beauty depends on propriety . . . [*see* Edith Wharton's "suitability" in *The Decoration of Houses*].

TYPES OF MONUMENTS IN GREECE AND ROME: In the early sixth century A.D., Cassiodorus could still speak with wistful pride of the nation of statues and the abundant herds of bronze horses that filled the city of Rome. Pliny tells us that in Rhodes alone there were . . . seventy-three thousand statues . . . and at least that number in Athens, Olympia, and Delphi. Of all this wealth there survives . . . but a small fraction . . . . Until comparatively recent times, these were the models for the great majority of all monumental efforts.

In one way or another the comprehension of the uniqueness of a human life is, perhaps, the source of all gentler feelings for our fellow men . . . . In the contemplation of antique statues this comprehension is heightened and ennobled; . . . the Attic funerary *stelai* of the fifth and fourth centuries B.C. possess this lyrical excellence at its most radiant. The dead are identified in inscriptions only. Portraiture was not attempted . . . . The image on the *stelai* . . . celebrates the beauty of a simple action characteristic of the estate or age of the deceased. . . .

To represent great men convincingly it is necessary to stress their individuality. *Pericles* by Kresilas, which survives in a number of good copies . . . invites us to see in the face the likeness of a great individual. In great men . . . it is the face that matters . . . the majority of them are known to us in the form of busts. Such faces show at once the private character of an individual and his respect for the obligations of his civic status.

[The prince's] splendor obscures . . . his character as an individual. When the prince is exalted to the rank of a divinity, his image must wear the aspect of immortality; . . . the work will now inspire awe, but it can no longer move. The function of the ruler's image transcends that of the ordinary monument; . . . it takes the place of the absent prince and rules in his stead.

Such a presence on even the busiest market square causes a certain noble silence to fall upon the noises of the day.

The image of the prince *par excellence* is that of Alexander the Great. Hellenistic rulers naturally wished to see in themselves a new Alexander.

Roman imperial portraits . . . display a stateliness of a sterner sort. Caesar looks as if all order were taking its foundation in him . . . the giver of the law—a law to which he himself is as much committed in his capacity as ruler as all others are as subjects. If the name of Alexander is capable of inspiring enthusiasm . . . Caesar can command loyalty.

The air of authority conveyed by mastery over the horse and the obvious splendor of equestrian action lend themselves readily to the representation of the magnificence and order of supreme government, or indeed of all forms of leadership. . . . The Athenians . . . considered the erection of an equestrian statue too great an honor for any man. . . .

The supreme monument (the Marcus Aurelius on the Capitol in Rome) shows the prince . . . mounted on a quiet horse and reflects the majesty of his mere being. The statue now stands as the proper keystone of a majestic system of buildings and, to the lover of antiquity, as the very heart of the civilized world:

The sculptor of this statue knew what a king should be," observed Kenyon, "and knew, likewise the heart of mankind and how it craves a true ruler, under whatever title, as a child its father.
—HAWTHORNE

Here is the impression that the sculptors of the last three hundred years have been laboriously trying to reproduce; but contrasted with this mild old monarch their prancing horsemen suggest a succession of riding-masters taking out our young ladies' schools. . . . and one may call it singular that in the capital of Christendom the portrait most suggestive of Christian conscience is that of a pagan emperor.
—H. JAMES

VICTORY MONUMENTS: The principal Greek victory monument is the trophy . . . that is, a wooden pole and crossbar with armour upon it, to mark the site of the victory; a monument which by a rule of honor the conqueror must never repair and the conquered never pull down.

The triumphal arch appears to be a Roman invention . . . no arches have survived complete with the sculpture which was originally placed on top of them:

The purpose of placing statues of men on columns was to elevate them above all other mortals; this is also the meaning conveyed by the new invention of arches.
—PLINY

The honor of a triumphal arch was reserved for the very highest military achievement; . . . as a rule the victor was shown riding in a triumphal chariot . . . accompanied by a Victory or the goddess Roma.

MONUMENTS AND MORALITY: . . . monuments erected in praise of individuals. . . ; for religion they are a source of idolatry and for philosophy, ultimately, folly. The Bible . . . forbids the making of images of any kind . . . in the second commandment:

And the multitude, allured by reasons of the grace of his handiwork, Now accounted as an object of devotion him that a little before was honored as a man.
—*The Wisdom of Solomon*

First let me gain a name, then I shall have monuments in abundance.
—PLATO

. . . he [Diogenes] left behind him . . . the remembrance that he lived the life of a man: and this monument . . . Mausolus . . . is loftier and rests on a more solid base than thine!
—LUCIAN

CONCESSIONS OF THE MORALISTS: Plutarch . . . describes approvingly how Caesar, in his thirty-third year, burst into tears at the sight of a statue of Alexander, because he himself had not yet done anything great at the age when Alexander had completed his work. Thus . . . art spurred Caesar on to glory. The monument may therefore be used as an instrument of statecraft; the perpetuation of the memory of illustrious men will inspire others to emulate their actions.

THE RENAISSANCE APOLOGY: Leone Battista Alberti, the *fons et origo* of all modern literary study of art . . . began his discussion of the monument with a moral manifesto based on a story culled from ancient authors:

On the tomb of Sardanapalus, King of the Assyrians, was a statue which seemed to clap its Hands together by way of applause, with an Epitaph to this effect: "In one single Day I built Tarsus and Archileum; but you, Friend, eat, drink and be merry; for there is nothing else among Men that is worthy of this Applause." Such were the Inscriptions and Symbols used in those Nations. But our Romans recorded the Exploits of their great Men, by carving their story in marble. This gave rise to Columns, Triumphal arches, Porticos enriched with memorable Events, preserved both in Painting and Sculpture. But no Monument of this Nature should be made, except for Actions that truly deserve to be perpetuated.
—ALBERTI

We see that Alberti took it for granted that the subject of a Roman—or, may we say, a classical—monument could never be materialistic, as was that of the tomb of Sardanapalus. The classical monument by definition is committed to the celebration of truly noble and virtuous qualities.

THE VOCABULARY OF CRITICISM: Was the monumental art of classical antiquity really moral . . .

or is this merely a romantic prejudice of the Renaissance? In order to present my argument it is necessary to use the vocabulary of the academic tradition; for no other vocabulary exists . . . when the discussion of a work of art concerns its value, and not, as is usually the case in contemporary studies, its date, relative rarity, and place in a developmental scheme.

Polygnotos . . . was praised for the moral greatness of his work. At the height of the classical age it is echoed in Pericles' praise of the Athenians:

For we are lovers of beauty without extravagance and lovers of wisdom yet without weakness.
—THUCYDIDES

Plutarch likewise teacheth us that malice and revenge cannot settle their seats in such hearts as doe delight in these delicate elegancies.
—F. JUNIUS, 1635

Therefore, when we look at the images of the gods, let us not indeed think they are stones or wood, but neither let us think they are the gods themselves. . . . He who loves the gods delights to gaze on the images of the gods, and their likenesses, and he feels reverence and shudders with awe of the gods who look at him from the unseen world.
—JULIAN, Emperor of Rome, 361-3

On the surface there appears to be a keen conflict between the practice of the Christian faith and the love of statues of the Greek and Roman gods. The theoreticians of the Renaissance, however, took it for granted that these statues were to be seen not as true gods, but as representations in suitable form of universally valid truths.

THE FALSIFICATION OF HISTORY: Were it not for what one must call the blessings of hypocrisy in civil affairs, the history of the monument would be a sorry affair. Hypocrisy, or plain self-flattery, compels the mean and indifferent to desire a monument which will represent him as magnanimous and glorify his cause. Such a state of affairs is only possible . . . in societies where the example of magnanimity is known and publicly acclaimed. . . . Societies where the image of ruthlessness and vulgar ambition is a matter of pride are naturally excluded from . . . a truly monumental art; but as long as hypocrisy is still with us (and, unfortunately it has been losing ground of late against the "honesty" of shamelessness), there is hope for the monument. . . . In order to have monuments at all, we must allow them to praise what is truly worthy and beautiful, regardless of the deserts of the person whose name they bear, and regardless of his actual appearance:

. . . of Tragedies doth Gorgias also say very properly, that they are a kind of deceit, by which the deceiver is more just than he that doth not use such deceit; and the deceived likewise is wiser than he that is not deceived.

—DIO CHRYSOSTOM

THE MONUMENT IN LATE ANTIQUITY: The first and most immediately demonstrable new characteristic of the majority of monuments produced in this period (Third Century) is a lamentable lack of skill. Bernard Berenson . . . said of the four Roman emperors in porphyry (Fourth Century, Vatican Library), that they looked "like yokels being photographed at a country fair." Berenson could denounce these figures only by pretending that they were true likenesses. . . . His interpretation is probably no more correct than the now more fashionable view (justly despised by Berenson) which sees in the wide open eyes . . . the "agony and loneliness" of "man in late antiquity"; in their embrace, an awareness of futility; in the stiffness of the pose, firmness or a return to "sculptural form"; and so on.

ART HISTORICAL PERSPECTIVES: The somewhat confused peace between radical relativism and positive art criticism rests on the agreement that the value judgements are made "for our generation," that one is writing a history of art which must be acceptable to "twentieth century man," and that . . . each generation has the right (if not the obligation) to rewrite the history of art in accordance with the dictates of its own will to form (Riegl's *Kunstwollen*). One . . . judges with gusto, but with the proviso that the validity of the judgement is known to be an illusion.

The classical monument often fares badly at the hands of these critics. They disapprove of its moral sentiment and look upon its imitation of nature and its association with literature as corruption and impurity. In consequence, the arrival of late antique art is to them a welcome event, a purging of art, as if it had been a precedent in antiquity of the modern revolution against the tradition of the academies. Partisans of modern abstract art . . . hail the changes in late antique art as a liberation of form and simple mass from the tyranny of illusion, and those who favor expressionism salute it as an age of anguish and a glorious release of the passions from the yoke of moderation:

Though they differ from each other, these coins still contrast with their prototype in two important ways: first they do not represent a decadent stage of art, that is, an enfeebled imitation of a much superior original. Instead they are *adaptations,* semi-abstract for the most part, and done according to the degree to which each Gallic artist ruthlessly dismembered the Greek images and then recreated the pieces according to his own image of man. Secondly, these have in common a basic attitude of strong, and some even violent emotionalism directed toward their prototype, which permits us to assign these coin images to that special kind of art that is called "expressionistic."

—T.P. HOWE, "Expressionistic Fragments of Pre Roman Gaul," (1961)

Miss Howe sees in the act of destruction a refreshing demonstration of savage power. Her premise that the Gallic "image of man" is as valid or intelligent as any other is derived from Riegl's will to form, and need concern us no longer. But her endorsement of ruthlessness is a demonstration of a taste that must be challenged, if we are not to have it that the study of art, far from refining us, is preparing the way for our barbarization:

Thus originates art among the exotic nations who are still close to the mainsprings of their existence. Neither intellect nor calculation are involved in this genesis. Only lust is the bridge between maker and object. . . . Lust turned into art—that is creative power. Questions of style or other nonsense originating in the speculative zones of a mankind grown impotent do not arise. . . . Their art is illiterate, and that is good.

—W. HAUSENSTEIN, *Barbaren und Klassiker,* 1923

James Grady, *Architecture of Neel Reid in Georgia,* 204 pp., illus., University of Georgia Press, Athens (for the Peachtree-Cherokee Trust). $29.75.

Richard Pratt, *David Adler,* 227 pp., illus., M. Evans & Co., New York. $20.

Theo B. White, *Paul Philippe Cret, Architect and Teacher,* 160 pp., illus., The Art Alliance Press, Philadelphia. $10.

It is now a commonplace that American classical architecture of this century is having a comeback. The term "eclectic" lingers, but it is losing its pejorative sting, and it is no longer possible to dismiss the better classical architects of this century out of hand. One sign of this new or emerging sensibility is the quickening critical reputation of these men, as is indicated by the book-length treatment the three under discussion in this article have received in recent years. Two of them—Neel Reid of Atlanta and David Adler of Chicago—were primarily house architects, which once was a profitable type of practice, and the books devoted to them deal almost entirely with the houses they built. But the third, Paul Philippe Cret, had very important institutional commissions, such as the Pan American Union (now called Organization of American States) and the Detroit Institute of Arts and did but a few houses; it is partly because of that fact that Cret is remembered as one of the major figures of the architectural phase of Classical America.

Neel Reid's Massee Apartments, Macon, Georgia (1924), showing manneristic door arch, broken main pediment, and gabled second pediment. Photo: Kenneth Kay.

Georgian Doorway of Henry Tompkins House, Atlanta (1922), by Neel Reid. Photo: Kenneth Kay.

Neel Reid has long had a prestigious local reputation in Georgia and this first book on him by Professor James Grady of the Georgia Institute of Technology may give his work much more general recognition than it has had so far. The book almost certainly establishes that Reid was one of the most accomplished architectural talents of his day, which was the first quarter of this century.

Reid's practice was primarily, although not entirely, in Georgia and mostly Atlanta at that. He was associated with the firm of Hentz, Reid, and Adler and with another major Atlanta architect—Philip Trammell Shutze, whose work is discussed at length elsewhere in this issue. There was a great proliferation of work crowded into his career (much of it in the last years of his life), before he died at the age of 41. It has been pointed out before that Atlanta is one of the most classical of American cities—in the design of its buildings if not in the character of its city plan—and Grady attributes this to a reaction to the rigors of the Civil War and Reconstruction periods and a strong nostalgia

for a more distant past. At any rate, he writes that at about 1910, "Atlanta was ready for the eclecticism of Neel Reid. It was ready for the many and lavish buildings in several versions of the classical that Reid was to create." (That is to say, *mostly* classical, for Reid sometimes worked in the Tudor style too.)

Reid's Atlanta was the "old" Atlanta of West Paces Ferry Road and Ansley Park, the C&S Bank, the PDC (Piedmont Driving Club), the august Peachtree and Cherokee Garden clubs (which have jointly sponsored this book), the barons of Coca Cola money, and such prominent Atlanta families as the Dorseys and Calhouns. All quite removed from the bustling and troubled modern city of today that would be the Chicago of the South. Certainly its taste was finer and richer than the cottage, Colonial Williamsburg, Inc. manner of so much of recent suburban building in Atlanta. A more or less serious classical was the taste of old Atlanta, and Neel Reid and Philip Shutze were its favorite architects.

Reid's career was in some ways quite representa-

Façade of Dr. Will Campbell House (1914), by Neel Reid. Photo: Kenneth Kay.

tive of the American architects of his time who enjoyed his sort of practice. There were the early, *ca.* 1910, houses that smack of Greene and Greene and the cottage phase of Aymar Embury's career (and there is even an oddly designed early villa—the Schinholzer house of Macon, Georgia—that might have been some forgotten semiclassical work of Frank Lloyd Wright or Purcell and Elmslie at the turn-of-the-century). As the teens progress into the twenties, there are larger houses that tend more and more to an archaeologically correct brand of classical and, at that, to Georgian and colonial-federal styles, rather than to any of the continental modes (although here and there all through his career there are projects with an Italian or even a colonial Latin American cast). Finally, towards the end of his life, there are more and more large commissions for buildings other than houses—apartments, offices, railway stations.

In detail and in the finer points of his work, however, Reid's career was not at all representative, and from first to last in his practice he was capable of innovation and he repeatedly sold it to his (surely for the most part conservative) clients. One great value of publishing so many heretofore unavailable views of Reid's work, as Grady has done in *Architecture of*

Neel Reid in Georgia, is that they reveal anew a persistent strain in his work—his passion for extending classical and postclassical or baroque-rococo forms into new or idiosyncratic directions. As much as any other American architect of his time, Reid is comparable to such "eccentrics" as the great Italian mannerist masters or to Hawksmoor or Lutyens. As the unusually well-informed book jacket copy has it, "A baroque chimney piece may appear in a quiet living room. Oversized columns add importance to the porch. A window may be unexpectedly assertive."

And consider in *Neel Reid:* the enormous, overscaled overmantel in the drawing room of the Andrew Calhoun house—which elsewhere in this issue Henry Hope Reed attributes to Shutze—with its overpowering cartouche and carved draperies (no longer, alas, enclosing the Allyn Cox mural as it at first did). Or the top-heavy pediment with its vast *oeil-de-boeuf* window in the Massee Apartments, Macon, or the vast doorway to the same building, which is a full three-stories high and studded with details that seem to burst out of the classical and scrape up against art nouveau, or even the ornament of Gaudi, and must seem as unexpected on a Macon street as a domed rococo church does in a Mexican hamlet. Or the early (1910)

Mantelpiece, pilasters, and cornice, for Neel Reid's Jesse Draper House, Atlanta, Georgia (1922). Photo: Von Micklos.

Joseph Neel house of Macon, with its odd mantel enclosed in manneristic brackets. Even in his unusually restrained Anglo-Saxon interiors there can be classical serendipity, such as the crabby, triangular pediment topping the overmantel in the drawing room of the Henry Tompkins house in Atlanta.

Reid was capable of structural innovation that works satisfyingly too, and this was often true of his small story-and-a-half villas. One of my favorites is the Will Campbell house of Atlanta, a Federal row dwelling stretched out to six bays—a two-story porch making up one end of the house and an entrance hall the other—(Reid did several houses with eccentrically placed doorways). Another is the widely admired and elegantly sited Cam Dorsey house, with its octagonal porch, wings, and temple-like dependencies.

Grady rightly gives attention to the remarkable project in urbanism that developed in suburban Atlanta after about 1900 and in which buildings by Hentz, Reid and Adler and Philip Shutze played such a large role. Atlanta did not have the first, or even the largest, of the great leafy American suburbs, with each dwelling in its own large park, but it may well have the culmination of the movement and its best example, and one of the most satisfying to tour. The Buckhead section is, in Grady's words, "miles of carefully main-tained landscape framing houses that, with the landscape, have been professionally done." And then the author sadly adds: "Additions done since 1945 in the same area are strikingly inferior generally to the earlier work."

One thing Grady's book makes immediately apparent is the loving care Reid's buildings have so often been given. For the most part they are neatly maintained some forty to sixty years after their construction. Some have suburban gardens still nicely kept up. The interiors are mostly lush and sumptuous and, as one would expect in suburban Atlanta, most are decorated conservatively. Mrs. Parrish and Otto Zenke can have been here (and may have been literally), but it would be a great surprise to see a David Hicks interior in a Reid house.

Grady establishes anew what has "surfaced" as links between the Atlanta school—Reid and Shutze—and major Eastern architects and muralists of their day. Reid served a short stint at Murphy and Dana in New York at the beginning of his career and, according to Grady, admired Charles Platt exceedingly. Shutze and Allyn Cox were friends and their friendship led to a commission for Cox to do murals in an important Reid–Shutze building—the Andrew Calhoun house of 1923.

Neel Reid is far from being an exhaustive monograph; it is an introductory essay and a picture portfolio with extended captions, together with a number of documentary appendices. Grady's curious editorial device of limiting his coverage only to those buildings of Reid's now standing is bothersome for the reader who would like illustrations and commentary on such important but demolished Reid structures as the Howard Theatre (a section of which survives as part of a private house) and the Willis B. Jones house (which is reportedly being re-erected on a new site). The writer considers both of them, but particularly the Jones house, as having been among the most important and artistic accomplishments of the Atlanta school of classical architecture. And the role of Shutze versus Reid in the making of the Calhoun house is, again, bothersome; in his commentary Grady reports (as does Henry Reed in this issue) that much of the design is Shutze's. Why then is it featured in this book?

But, for what he has surveyed, Professor Grady's commentary is in every way useful and informative (with the exception of the "problem" of the Calhoun house), and gracefully written besides. The author is abundantly knowledgeable about the history of architecture in general, about American architecture and Reid's particular place in it, and about the architectural and social climate of Atlanta in a day when it was building lavishly and when its tastes went almost entirely to classical design.

The interested reader is left with a taste for much more. It would be interesting to know about Reid's library, if such an inventory exists. An article on his firm and the details of its practice would be very interesting. And so would detailed material on his gardens and whatever furniture he may have designed. And finally—and it would take a great effort—coverage of the surprising number of commissions by Hentz, Reid and Adler that were outside of the State of Georgia.

David Adler by Richard Pratt is an enthusiastic essay by an observer who has perhaps less technical knowledge than Professor Grady (even though Pratt has written often on traditional American houses), but who nevertheless brings considerable insight to his book. Adler's work seems of a somewhat more polished order than Reid's, if rarely as original, and was, for most projects, of grander aspect. Adler was certainly a figure of the first rank among those architects who built great houses in the classical styles during the 1910-45 period. It may not, however, be entirely accurate, as Pratt does, to call Adler the last of the great eclectic architects, for he had some very good contemporaries; in addition to Reid and Shutze, one need only name Arthur Brown, Jr., William Lawrence Bottomley, John Russell Pope, and Mott B. Schmidt.

Adler's work was notable on a good handful of accounts. It can serve to show that, despite the vast publicity the Sullivan–Wright school has received, Chicago in this century produced a good deal of important classical building, including many fine houses. There was surely a certain amount of architectural segregation, as it were, in the greater Chicago area, for so many of the Sullivan–Wright houses were in Chicago proper or in the River Forest–Oak Park suburbs to the west, while those of Adler were almost entirely in the great North Shore towns—notably Winnetka, Glencoe and, of course, Lake Forest.

For the writer of this review, the unforgettable thing about Adler's production was his remarkable sensitivity to the English Stuart and Georgian schools of building; in this he was on a par with Bottomley or such a New York partisan of English classical as the Embury of the twenties. Adler's masterpiece has been called the Richard T. Crane house, "Castle Hill," at Ipswich, Massachusetts (which is now a public park). It is of red brick with stone trim, close to the style of Honington Hall or Ham House—and all of it seems terribly, awesomely realistic. So much so that pictures of it from a distance in *David Adler* make it seem as if it might be a plate from Kip's *Views*. Here is the Queen Anne lunette door hood, the restoration period stairway, the curious small dome and lantern of the larger English house of this period, the octagonal wing projections, quoins, the dormer with ped-

iments in an aedicular motif—the whole late Stuart architectural *zeitgeist*. It is a curiosity of the house that it was built on the rusticated basement of what was apparently an earlier building in French or Italian classical styles. John Barrington Bayley, who has known the house since the days of the Crane family's tenure there, recalls what an extraordinary site it enjoys—a low hill overlooking the Massachusetts coast.

And a final thing to note was that Adler, who is credited with planning the furnishings and accessories for many of his buildings, had an almost perfect sense for good, well-scaled, pleasing interiors. This was true through a whole gamut of styles, from the extremely refined and polished French classical staircase and great rooms of the Charles Ryerson house to the cottagy, Colonial Deerfield bolection moldings and rustic keystones of the pine-paneled entrance hall at "Shorecrest," Lake Bluff, Illinois. Here and there there is an eccentricity such as the mirrored, Cole Porterish powder room at the Reid house in Lake Forest. Again, Adler seems to have found the English classical his most congenial style. The point is that, whatever sources he used, his eye for interiors was very nearly flawless. Every room pictured in *David Adler* seems to have a radiance and *mesure* both. A welcome contrast to so many of the more ambitious American interiors that others did in the same period—the heavy-handed, bombastic Louis XV and Italianate productions that fill so many of the pages of the big Lionel Williams volumes.

Pratt's treatment is admirable for what it attempts, but it leaves room for a scholarly and detailed monograph on Adler's work, with careful attention to sources and meticulous dating and attributions. The reader can only be grateful to Pratt for his material on Adler's work methods, the organization of his office, and the style in which he carried out his practice. (The architect clearly won his perfections by dint of much persistance and a certain amount of dragooning of his large staff of assistants.) There is also a very valuable inventory of the books in Adler's library.

Theo B. White's *Paul Philippe Cret* is little more than a brief essay on the architect's work, an anthology of Cret's writings and lectures, and a gallery of pictures of the architect's completed work and drawings. As a writer, Cret was hardly in the class with such American architect-thinkers as Henry Van Brunt and Montgomery Schuyler but he did deal sensibly with such problems as museum design, architectural education and, perhaps inevitably, classical-versus-modern styles—a conflict that, as we shall see, shows up clearly in his own work. As a designer, Cret was firmly classical in the first part of his career, with such projects as the Pan American Union (1907), which is now called the Organization of American States, and the little-known Washington

Recent view of the main façade of Paul Cret's Pan American Union (now Organization of American States). Photo: courtesy of Organization of American States.

Ballroom of Pan American Union (now Organization of American States). Photo: courtesy of Organization of American States.

Memorial Arch at Valley Forge (1912), which is most certainly one of our best commemorative arches. But there always seems to have been a thrust in his work towards the diluted classical that begins to edge into art deco or skyscraper modern. We see this most surely in his widely praised Indianapolis Public Library (1914), in his University of Texas Library (1930), and in the very pretty but severely bland Rodin Museum in Philadelphia (1928). Elements of ordinary entablature or column construction are subtly dropped here and there. Pilasters are devoid of entasis and become mere strips. In short, some of the normal vocabulary of the orders is deliberately left out. Indeed, Cret must have been something of a tastemaker in this sort of simplification.

By the late twenties, Cret has begun to abandon classical almost entirely in some of his buildings—for instance the exterior of the Folger Shakespeare Library, and the American Battle Monument at Château Thierry, France. In the thirties, he takes up the streamlined style in earnest and he becomes perhaps the most prolific of all designers of the streamlined train, having the Reading *Crusader*, the Burlington *Zephyr*, the Seaboard *Silver Meteor*, the *Empire State Express*, and the *Chessie* train all to his credit. It baffles the mind to think of the Hall of the Americas in the Pan American Union and the banquettes and chrome fixtures of the dining car of the *Zephyr* as having come from the same creator! To the classical enthusiast Cret thus gradually "finked out." But the classical phase of Cret's work, with its grand and important buildings, most certainly deserves a thorough monograph sooner or later.

As an interesting coda, *Paul Philippe Cret* offers reproductions of a few of Cret's charcoal drawings, which seem remarkably like those of the painter and Classical America Director, Pierce Rice.

—H. STAFFORD BRYANT

Coy Ludwig, *Maxfield Parrish*, 223 pp., Watson-Guptill. $25.

The Seventies aren't all bad. They have brought relief to all who have been plagued over the years by the course of taste. Everything is back in favor. This reversal of judgment has not taken quite the form hoped for, in that nothing has been dropped from favor. Insofar as the re-instated good has failed to replace the bad, vindication has been a little thin.

In that light, not too much significance can be attached to the appearance of Watson-Guptill's sumptuous volume on Maxfield Parrish. In a period when the publishers' lists contain catalogues of Coca-Cola bottles and a life of Tom Mix, one might wonder what kept them waiting so long. Parrish is on the order of these other phenomena, his life paralleling the span of the soft drink, and his reknown remarkably similar, in both date and extent, to that of the most famous of all the cowboy stars. The Model T, the crystal set, knickers, are artifacts of the Twenties neither more characteristic nor more widely distributed than the Parrish Print. John Held, Jr. is commonly put forward as the decade's representative artist. Measured against Parrish's saturation of the country, he disappears.

His admirers, of course, reject the idea of Parrish as a figure of consequence only, or primarily, as a period piece. Claims for consideration as a major painter are advanced on his behalf. But popular success is easily measured; artistic success is in the eye of the beholder. Parrish, as it happens, early in his career earned whatever there is in the way of certification as a fine artist. He was endorsed by the critics, elected an Academician, had Saint-Gaudens as a friend. But this professional esteem was presently balanced by his being held up as the very symbol of meretricious appeal in painting. His biographer, Coy Ludwig, credits this turn of opinion to the advent of modernism, but it was conventional practice that found, after a long attachment, that Parrish had become so distasteful.

It was Parrish's good fortune to enjoy, to almost the mid-point of his life, the best of two worlds. He was the darling of the publishers and the toast of his profession. Professor Ludwig mentions youthful essays in landscape painting, but no example is shown nor any evidence that real notice was taken of these. Parrish's name was made by his posters, as often as not covers or illustrations but conceived within the poster convention, with this sufficient for critical acceptance in an era that enshrined Chêret and Lautrec.

Nationwide fame came to Parrish for his *Collier's Magazine* covers but, far from in any way modifying the approval of his brother artists, this use of his pictures was regarded as akin to bringing Grand Opera and Shakespeare to the people. When, presently, great decorative commissions were offered him, not the least contradiction was seen. These murals, in particular those for the Curtis Building (Philadelphia's secret treasure, as inaccessible as the Barnes Foundation at its most ferocious), represent the high point of his professional reputation.

At that stage in his career, on the eve of the First War and still a comparatively young man, Parrish's rank as a serious artist was as firmly established as his position among the great popular favorites. He was alone, among artists, in achieving this. Then the bal-

Panels from the decoration of the Curtis Building, by Maxfield Parrish.

ance shifted, and a gap began to appear between the critical and popular successes that had hitherto kept pace with each other.

His work had been, after all, commercial art, of so elevated a character that it earned recognition as fine art, but commercial art nonetheless. But, roughly during the course of the War and probably not even by conscious intention, Parrish began to think of his pictures as fine art, distributed commercially. The *Collier's* prints had lent themselves, ideally, to framing. Now the inspiration struck of omitting the intervening

stage. It became Maxfield Parrish's business to provide pictures intended from the start for the buyer's wall. The formula worked like a charm, and his reproductions engulfed the country.

But the increase in wealth and fame that this brought was attended by a sour note. It not only eclipsed the very high degree of professional approval he had won for himself, but that chorus of adulation itself grew fainter. Presently it was hardly to be heard at all, and this silence was succeeded by attacks. While still a great name among the people, to the artists Parrish became a figure of fun. His work was singled out not merely for criticism but for ridicule. How much of a trial this outright scorn provided for its target we are not informed, but Parrish was not shielded indefinitely even by the comfort of his popularity. That began to recede with the advent of the Thirties, and he spent the final decades of his life in a not quite opaque obscurity; forgotten by the public, he remained to his calling the image of all that was deplorable in conception and execution.

The picture is over-simplified. If Parrish grieved over, or resented, the hostility expressed, he could do it in style, because enough of a market still existed for the single calendar he painted each year into the Sixties (and his own eighties) to command what may have been, and in any case was close to, the highest price paid in the world for a work by a living artist. And, however their numbers were depleted, he was never quite without serious admirers, whose championship of their hero was all the heartier for the strength of the opposition.

The story outlined here (and told with a somewhat different emphasis by Professor Ludwig) is dramatic in itself, independent of the work that is the substance of it. To a degree, the ups and downs of Parrish's reputation are accounted for by factors—social, historical, personal, themselves outside the work—which remained remarkably consistent, whether he was adored or abandoned by the public, or extolled or castigated by the critics. The development and enrichment of his ideas and methods (even their possible deterioration) are secondary to the unvarying central characteristics. Interesting as that story is, it is the work that concerns us. Not least because, after all, Parrish lived for close to a century, and it would have been more surprising for the response to his pictures to have remained the same than to have undergone changes.

Acceptance is of more consequence than rejection, when the latter is, as in this case, the product of the former, so it is to our purpose to inquire into the extent to which the elements that drew so many to Parrish's paintings were genuinely artistic. An immediate example of one that is not is the balminess and placidity of the undateable and strifeless world that was his principal subject. This vision of a land where the leaves never fall and cats don't scratch was strictly a literary concoction.

The U.S.A. at large, which for a long time could add to its enjoyment a satisfaction derived from an assurance that the pleasure taken was to its credit, supposed that what was doing it good was Parrish's painstakingly minute transcriptiveness. In fact, this delicate rendering (which resembled, but had little to do with, drawing of any power) was the sheerest entertainment. The least of Parrish's talents were for drawing and painting.

The incontestably artistic factor in Parrish's work, of which the public was perfectly oblivious, but to the effects of which it was not a whit less susceptible than Berenson or Walter Pater (to choose, not at all at random, a pair of celebrated sensibilities of the era), was design. For Parrish supplemented very modest attainments with whimsy, industriousness, and a great gift for arrangement. And this last, in an era that took a very off-hand view of pictorial form, was his chief artistic distinction. If it was apparently, or actually, the sweetness of the Elysium he offered the customers a glimpse of, and the particularity of his presentation of it, that won their affection, it was the order into which he cast this combination which makes it worthy of a later generation's attention.

It would be interesting to learn what bent the young artist's inclination in this direction, but Professor Ludwig does not speculate along these lines. Suffice to say that the earliest Parrish idea shown us is an extraordinarily elementary one. At the start of his career he depended almost exclusively on the baldest symmetry: single figures almost hieratically posed, centered on the page, or flanking pairs, as often as not mirror images of each other. This faithfulness to a fundamental notion of form imparted great, if stilted, strength to his schemes. Of more importance, the very obviousness of the device imposed on Parrish himself a permanent link with the convention. The positive assertion of, rather than mere deference to, symmetry constituted the heart of Parrish's system over the course of his career. He became, with the passage of time, an increasingly resourceful and subtle composer, but all his efforts were in keeping with this central requirement.

It is remarkable that from the very start he was imbued with the absolute imperativeness of adherence to the frontal plane. This was the mold that would bind his conceptions for sixty years and give the slightest of his efforts artistic character.

Parrish could have deduced this universal principle of form from what he saw in the museums, but so, at least in theory, could anyone. Yet none did. The mystery, on which Professor Ludwig does not touch, is Parrish's very inquisitiveness in this area, an attitude foreign to the prevailing atmosphere at home or abroad. A likely explanation would be the guidance of an inspired teacher, but no candidate offers himself.

Parrish's color, too, came from the museums, and also his application if it: the two part and parcel of each other. His dependence on tradition here was much more apparent, because ideas on color and technique, though not on form, were very much in the air. Again, his conclusions were contrary to existing doctrine, but he was indulged, at least for a long time, because of the beauty of his results. It was by his color that Parrish was commonly thought to be identified.

Poster for the Red Cross, 1918, by Maxfield Parrish.

The Venetian Lamp Lighter, calendar for the General Electric Company, by Maxfield Parrish.

Apart from the truth of this notion, it is worth noting that Parrish is the only American painter of any conspicuousness about whom this thought could be framed. His color itself was like the design it accompanied in that its origins were in the Renaissance, the distribution of it was the product of intense care, and a degree of over-emphasis was employed that made for strength at the same time that it sounded a note of excess.

Free and easy brush-work, with tones mixed on the pallette, has been the dominant method of painting in oil since the closing decades of the last century. Parrish's elaborate system of monochromatic underpainting and glazing enabled him to attain effects impossible in this customary technique. But again, for all the richness so realized, Parrish's peculiar earnestness resulted in a shade more evidence of the mechanical side of the matter than is wholly agreeable.

It might be said that in each of these areas the viewer is made all too conscious of Parrish's system. There hardly can be such a thing as too much design or color, or care in execution, yet we are left with an impression that this is the case. The odd circumstance about Parrish as a figure of controversy is that the grounds for both support and detraction are immediately apparent.

There are other considerations that enter into the balance. Parrish was a master ornamentalist, a magnificent inventor of cartouches and scrolls, borders and arabesques, an accomplishment he was not above making use of on so humble a level as the design of headings and tail-pieces. Oddly enough, his powers here were not brought into play in his outright architectural work, though he far excelled the leading mural painters in this their own province. But Parrish was so instinctive and natural a decorator that it could almost be said that he was unable to curb himself. Nothing was safe from him; he labored to make not only his house but every detail of it beautiful, and whatever left it as well. He took pains with the correspondence that went forth both inside and outside the envelope; the very stamps were often enclosed in borders, and the boxes that carried his pictures to the editors were themselves works of art. In that sense Parrish was all artist, an anomaly in an age whose god was nature.

There is a murkier side. His complicated technique, old masterish enough to be acclaimed or deplored on that ground, hovered perilously close to the realm of machine production. There was current for a long time an understanding that Parrish's pictures actually were photographs. The recent coming into circulation of his originals assures us that they really are, after all, paintings. And a chapter in the book before us spells out how the famous effects were achieved.

The painful circumstance becomes clear that the Parrish process made very modest use of the human hand. Free-hand work, proficiency in which one would think the first requirement in pictorial creation, played no part in it at all. Professor Ludwig's justification for Parrish's dependence, from the beginning of his career, on the camera was that draftsmanship having been mastered, its further demonstration was superfluous. But there is very little evidence, none whatever in examples in the book, of this accomplishment. And the great man himself is quoted in perfectly cheerful admission of an utter incapacity for original sketching.

The ethical issue here is obscure. We are not sure what exactly is wrong with computerized music or poetry. It was not always so. Forty years ago there was a Royal Academy scandal when it came out that a portrait on its walls had been painted from a photograph. A recent book on the subject, Van Deren Coke's *The Painter and the Photograph*, reveals that this practice was not quite common, but at least frequent, almost since the coming into existence of the camera; but it was done on the sly. Norman Rockwell, in his *Autobiography*, describes the scorn shown him once word was abroad that he was projecting photographs onto his canvas. So much for old times. It is a rare portrait today in which the color slide plays no part. Moreover, in New Realism there is not even a pretense that the camera is not the main instrument. In this light Parrish is in tune with the times, but *our* times; he was quiet enough about his methods in his own day. Still, professional acknowledgment of photography's paramountcy is the mere fact of the matter. We are still entitled, even at this late date, to reservations of our own.

If Parrish's devices are not fairly to be taken exception to on the grounds that they were no worse than anyone else's, the revelation of them, at best, adds no gloss to his reputation. Beyond that, however, this revelation explains some shortcomings. The immobility of any number of his figures, the posturing of those intended as comic, the lack throughout his whole body of work of any real grace of movement, all mark the intervention of the lens.

Professor Ludwig smiles at archaic objections to all this tracing, and has no room for the thought that the photographic outlook itself might be not so much wicked, as detrimental to artistic purpose. In Parrish's case what went hand in hand with his lofty conception of form was generalization, and the substitution for this of the sharp momentariness of the snapshot is an almost ruinous inconsistency. Furthermore, it deprived his work of that monumentality which would have established his right to consideration as a major American painter.

Of less artistic consequence, it has to be noted

1909 Cover for Collier's *magazine, by Maxfield Parrish.*

that Parrish's complicated devices did not always succeed. His habit, because perspective was not his strong point, was to attempt to realize depth by means of parallel receding planes, in the manner of stage scenery, but this did not prevent some extraordinarily unconvincing juxtapositions of figures and background.

Professor Ludwig has completed a great labor, for which an unknown number of never-say-die Parrish enthusiasts must be forever grateful. Much of the information collected was most likely laid hold of just in time. It would be unreasonable to expect a biographer's interests to be identical with one's own. In any case, at this stage some questions may defy answer. We wonder, for example, about Parrish's relations with his contemporaries. There were, after all, other immensely popular artists and artists who worked similar veins—rivals or friends. Parrish can (we hope) hardly have been so lordly as not to have expressed opinions on these; admiration, disdain, but something. A handsome tribute of Will Bradley's is quoted, but without Parrish's response, and Bradley was a peer, himself a great designer. John Sloan called on Parrish in 1951 and spoke of letting by-gones be by-gones after fifty years. What can that have been about? Our author tells us that in the *Century Magazine* poster competition Leyendecker was awarded first prize only because of Parrish's disqualification. But stories like that have the air of family tradition and need a little documentation. The circumstances that attended the painting of Kenyon Cox's portrait of him would be interesting to learn. Perhaps the record is dim on these matters, but we miss the fleshing out of Professor Ludwig's subject that more homely detail would provide.

Parrish lived through two great wars, and must at least have weighed (if adversely) participation in a third, that with Spain, but we are given no hint of his reaction to these (or any other) great events. The posters of the Second War were in a class with its songs, but the First produced some examples still famous, and popular artists were prominent in the propaganda campaign in general. There must be some explanation of Parrish's absence from this effort. His Quaker background would be a perfectly adequate excuse, but it is not advanced. This episode in history, which left no life untouched, is covered here by the appearance of his magnificent Red Cross poster, but not a line of text. From the want of the personal note, we are left, in the end, with a very filmy impression of the man himself.

It is the artist that counts, of course, but even here there is much that is not gone into. Parrish was a very strange article. He was typical of his times only because he imposed himself on them with such force and

needs accounting for far more than his less idiosyncratic brethren. But we are offered not even a hypothetical provenance for the exotic concoction that constituted the Parrish style. The two names put forward as having impressed Parrish in his teens, Zorn and Sargent, are of interest in that they represent the outlook completely rejected by him. We are given no hint of what steered him toward a channel of tradition noted only in passing by a generation whose heroes were Velasquez and Hals.

It was not only from the masters of the past that Parrish was ready to help himself. His *Young Gleaner* is a girlish version of Jules Breton's *Song of the Lark,* a picture too well known at the time for Parrish to have intended any deception. The same was the case with his *Alberich the Dwarf,* who blusters in the fastnesses of Arnold Böcklin's *Dragon's Lair,* but no comment is made on these little exercises in parody.

Reference is made in passing to Parrish's use of Dynamic Symmetry. But to a designer who anguished over the interaction of every square centimeter, the system on which he based the distribution of the elements of his pictures was of crucial importance, and the lay reader, in particular, is due at least a rough outline of what was involved.

The volume itself is exceptionally handsome. If there are items we miss, disappointment at their absence is balanced by pleasure at the discovery of examples hitherto unknown to at least one reader. The dust jacket is a wrap-around reproduction of *Daybreak,* a perfect choice for the purpose. But the distress any trifling with his laboriously calculated proportions occasioned Parrish is mentioned several times in the text, and *Daybreak* has been subjected to exactly that. Perhaps this could not have been avoided. What no alibi could cover is the strange letter chosen for the title, on both jacket and title page. Parrish concerned himself all his life with typography, and his unvarying reliance was on an alphabet derived from the column of Trajan, an alphabet which we learn from the text existed as a carved three dimensional studio property. What this circumstance ought to have dictated goes without saying, but some unaccountable process of thought led the designer, or the editors, to hunt up a letter to spell out *Maxfield Parrish* too remote from the Roman even to qualify as a caricature. To take note of what might be thought mere production matters, not, at that, even pertaining to the body of the book, might seem carping. But these instances are departures, in an undertaking given over to his honor, from the very spirit of Parrish. His peculiar strength was his sensitivity to the slightest nuance of form. In a note (itself a pleasure simply to gaze on) preserved in the *Archives of American Art* he worries about the damage done the tonal schemes of his pictures by the white pages on which they are printed! Frank Crowninshield told of a day spent in Parrish's studio, a day entirely taken up with the moving about on the canvas in search of the one right place for it of the cut-out silhouette of a single figure. In the degree of care taken over distinctions largely invisible to the world, which these items testify to, there is nothing comparable in the history of American painting. There is much in Parrish that one can be unsympathetic to, perhaps even repelled by, but in this fundamental artistic area, of the selection and distribution of pictorial factors, his judgment can only be deferred to.

—PIERCE RICE

Werner Hegemann and Elbert Peets, *The American Vitruvius, An Architect's Handbook of Civic Art.* Reissued 1972 by Benjamin Blom, Inc., New York.

This monumental work appeared in 1922. The publication of a facsimile edition exactly half a century later is an act of courage. Never was American opinion more averse to the ideals of the "City Beautiful" movement which this book presents more completely than does any other work. It is therefore most surprising to the contemporary reader that Hegemann and Peets said in the early twenties: "Indeed, the authors feel that the young profession of city planning is drifting too strongly in the directions of engineering and sociology."

It is even more surprising in view of the life and work of the authors. Werner Hegemann, a German architect and historian, was a consistent and courageous fighter for social justice. During his first stay in the United States at the beginning of the century he was to be found on the picket lines in San Francisco. After his return to Germany he organized the International City Planning Exhibition of 1910 in Berlin. His introduction to its catalogue is one of the seminal contributions to the understanding of the modern big city. Central is his concern about the appalling overcrowded housing conditions of the mass of the working population; his attacks against those responsible for these conditions led to brushes with the Kaiser's courts of justice. World War I found Hegemann in the United States where he established a practice together with Elbert Peets, an American landscape architect. After his return to Germany, the leading architectural and city planning journals which he edited provided the platform for the progressive developments of the Weimar Republic associated with the name of the Bauhaus. Hitler's rise to power brought him again to the United States; his premature death in 1936 interrupted his work on a book on city planning and housing. Elbert Peets continued for many years his work for improved housing initiated by the New Deal.

So it was certainly not lack of interest in or understanding of "engineering and sociology" which prompted these men to complain about planners' neglect of "Civic Art." It was a profound conviction of the overriding importance of the visual experience of the urban environment in which a growing majority of Americans spend most of their lives, coupled with the conviction that the art of shaping this environment was known and teachable. The Foreword says: "The objective has been the compilation of a thesaurus, a representative collection of creations in civic art . . . to show the universality of the principles in art."

The Introduction identifies these principles with the "ideals of Vitruvius . . . that the fundamental unit of design is not the separate building but the whole city." It states that the uncontrolled chaos of the contemporary urban environment is "detrimental to the advancement of the arts and it must be changed . . . so that by willing submission of the less to the greater there may be created a larger, more monumental unity; a unity comprising . . . finally even, it may be hoped, entire cities." This defines the first enemy in their three-front war: chaos, reliance on "happenings," refusal of the part to submit to the whole.

The second front is the fight against abstract, geometrical, two-dimensional paper planning. Chapter I, entitled "The Modern Revival of Civic Art" expounds the ideas of Camillo Sitte, the Viennese architect who in 1889 had revived the interest in the spatial beauty of squares, in the importance of continuity and enclosure, and in the interrelationship between outdoor space and the monuments of architecture and sculpture.

Sitte had illustrated his insights by many examples from the European Middle Ages, as well as from Antiquity and from the Renaissance and Baroque periods. Against the engineers' obsession with straightening and flattening out any irregularity he advocated adaptation to the terrain as well as to existing buildings and property lines. Some of his followers had developed this aspect of Sitte's teaching into a system of "informal" planning which, in search of the "picturesque," deliberately avoided any regularity.

Against these three enemies: unplanned chaos, abstract formalistic, and romantic informal planning the book sets the classical ideal: "in matters of plan and mass inspiration can be found wherever builders strove for order, symmetry, balance, and harmony . . . that deep rhythm structurally expressed"; and they identify it with "the spirit of traditional art in America, the spirit of Vitruvius, Palladio, Christopher Wren, the Adams, and Thomas Jefferson."

It is characteristic of the authors' total commitment to this tradition that all of the 1203 illustrations show "Western" examples—with two exceptions, both dealing with the environment not of the living, but of the dead. The discussion of cemeteries shows the Borobudur of Java and six small photos of burial and temple grounds in Tokyo. Certainly Hegemann and Peets were too cultured to identify the classical spirit simply with any specific "style." They repeatedly emphasize this and many of their illustrations show buidings in styles other than those derived from the hellenistic-roman heritage; but neither did they reject this heritage.

After Chapter II has presented "Plaza and Court Design in Europe," the subsequent five chapters deal primarily with American practice, with occasional reference to parallel efforts in Europe. Hegemann and Peets felt that America had taken the lead in civic design in the development of schools and university campuses, hospitals, and parks, but in particular of the World's Fairs in Chicago, St. Louis, San Francisco, and San Diego, and of the Civic Centers which followed in their wake.

As only a few isolated and deserted buildings of these great exhibitions remain, it is difficult to visualize the impression they made when they were filled by enthusiastic crowds. But the contemporary aversion to the attitude which they expressed may have deeper roots. Referring to their own contemporaries, Hegemann and Peets say: "This grouping of houses into units . . . unified façades . . . expresses the same civic pride which makes them willing to put on their best clothes, march in parades . . . ." But the generation of the 1970s prefers to put on jeans and to "do their own thing."

Neither parades nor the festive crowds of the World's Fairs enliven the Civic Centers presented in this book. They are either empty or filled with cars. It is also striking that the many illustrations drawn by the authors never show people—in contrast to the old illustrations which they reproduce. The authors quote Palladio's remark that a piazza should be proportioned to the number of people who use it, neither so small that it is cramped nor so large that it is empty. But they apply neither this observation nor the studies of Maer-

tens, to whom they refer, on the size of buildings in relation to the size of the human person to the problem of scale in the modern big city. Certainly Hegemann, who as far back as 1910 had noted that this new phenomenon had little more in common with the city as we know it from history than the name, was not unaware of this problem. He notes that "the enormous plazas which have been attempted in modern times often dwarf the surrounding buildings, making them appear like far-off villages"; and, discussing Burnham's Chicago plan: "it is doubtful whether areas of such magnitude and so loosely framed can be esthetically dominated by placing on one side a domed structure even if it should grow . . . to maximum size." Peets, who wrote the book's concluding chapter on "The Plan of Washington" warns: "Imperial grandiosity as an ideal . . . that is the great danger to Washington."

In the next to last chapter, "City Plans as Unified Designs," it is recognized that this is "so involved in an intricate maze of closely related problems . . . that it is almost too much to hope for . . . . So far the problem has not been solved and its solution may be the great ideal of civic art left for American genius to realize." It is most questionable whether any genius can solve it. By classical definition a work of art is an entity from which no part can be omitted and to which no part can be added. But in the everchanging city, parts constantly appear and disappear. This is not to say that there can be no elements of identity and continuity in urban development; but they cannot consist of a preconceived "Grand Design." They can only be subtle *leitmotifs,* guiding the adaptation of each new develoment to the previously created environment. But in every such step the principles of civic art retain their validity. Americans are fortunate that this splendid new edition gives them access to the words of two of the wisest thinkers on urban planning and to a thesaurus of instructive and fascinating illustrations.

—Hans Blumenfeld

Note.—Members will no doubt be interested in two fine books published by former directors of Classical America. *Lost Chicago* by David Lowe (Boston: Houghton Mifflin, 1975), and *The Twilight of Splendor* by James T. Maher (Boston: Little Brown, 1975). Both books bear upon the Society's concerns.

"Bloomfield," residence of George McFadden, Villanova, Pennsylvania, 1923; view of the Front Entrance, Horace Trumbauer, architect. From "Newport's Favorite Architects," an exhibition presented by Classical America and arranged by Alfred Branam, Jr. Photo: J. B. Bayley.

901 Fifth Avenue, Dr. A. H. Rice residence, New York, 1922; view of the main façade. Horace Trumbauer, architect. From "Newport's Favorite Architects," an exhibition presented by Classical America. Photo: S. Gottscho.